Practical
Financial
Management
New Techniques for
Local Government

Edited by
John Matzer, Jr.

PRACTICAL MANAGEMENT SERIES
Barbara H. Moore, Editor

Practical Financial Management
Capital Financing Strategies for Local Governments
Creative Personnel Practices
The Entrepreneur in Local Government
Human Services on a Limited Budget
Microcomputers in Local Government
Shaping the Local Economy
Telecommunications for Local Government

The Practical Management Series is devoted to the
presentation of information and ideas from diverse
sources. The views expressed in this book are those of
the contributors and are not necessarily those of the
International City Management Association.

Library of Congress Cataloging in Publication Data
Main entry under title:
Practical financial management.
  (Practical management series)
  Bibliography: p.
  1. Local finance—Addresses, essays, lectures.
I. Matzer, John, 1934-   II. Series
HJ 9105.P73   1984   352.1   84-21730
ISBN 0-87326-043-0

Printed in the United States of America.
90898887868584
54321

Foreword

Sound financial planning and management underlie everything else that local governments do—their programs, services, and other activities. Local administrators and elected officials know this, but they may not always know how to improve their financial management systems and ensure continued financial health.

Practical Financial Management provides information and ideas for better financial management, describing new techniques that have been developed in response to fiscal stress and showing how established techniques are being newly applied in local government. It focuses on improved methods for financial evaluation and policy making, revenue management and forecasting, infrastructure programming and financing, and creative purchasing. Cases, examples, and work sheets help practitioners apply the techniques in their own organizations.

This book is part of ICMA's continuing Practical Management Series, which is devoted to serving the needs of local officials and university professors for timely information on current issues and problems.

We are grateful to the organizations that granted ICMA permission to reprint their material and to John Matzer, Jr., City Administrator of San Bernardino, California, who organized and compiled the volume. Thanks also go to David S. Arnold, who was of great help in planning the entire Practical Management Series.

William H. Hansell, Jr.
Executive Director
International City
Management Association

352.1
P881m

Practical Financial Management: New Techniques for Local Government

The International City Management Association is the professional and educational organization for chief appointed management executives in local government. The purposes of ICMA are to strengthen the quality of local government through professional management and to develop and disseminate new approaches to management through training programs, information services, and publications.

Managers, carrying a wide range of titles, serve cities, towns, counties, and councils of governments in all parts of the United States and Canada. These managers serve at the direction of elected councils and governing boards. ICMA serves these managers and local governments through many programs that aim at improving the manager's professional competence and strengthening the quality of all local governments.

The International City Management Association was founded in 1914; adopted its City Management Code of Ethics in 1924; and established its Institute for Training in Municipal Administration in 1934. The Institute, now known as the ICMA Training Institute, provided the basis for the Municipal Management Series, generally termed the "ICMA Green Books."

ICMA's interests and activities include public management education, standards of ethics for members, the *Municipal Year Book* and other data services, urban research, newsletters, *Public Management* magazine, and other publications. ICMA's efforts for the improvement of local government management—as represented by this book—are offered for all local governments and educational institutions.

About the Editor

John Matzer, Jr., is City Administrator, San Bernardino, California. He was previously Distinguished Visiting Professor, California State University—Long Beach, where he now teaches graduate courses in financial management. Mr. Matzer has served as Deputy Assistant Director, U.S. Office of Personnel Management; City Manager, Beverly Hills, California; Village Manager, Skokie, Illinois; and City Administrator, Trenton, New Jersey. He received B.A. and M.A. degrees from Rutgers University, New Brunswick, New Jersey.

About the Authors

Following are the affiliations of the contributors to *Practical Financial Management* at the time of writing.

Robert W. Burchell, Center for Urban Policy Research, Rutgers University, New Brunswick, New Jersey

Ronald Chapman, Assistant Director, Department of Public Works, Dearborn, Michigan

David P. Dolter, Project Manager, Cadillac Fairview Homes West, Daly City, California

Robert A. Feger, Vice President–Construction, Arizona Contracting Division, Kitchell Contractors

W. Maureen Godsey, Assistant Project Director, International City Management Association

Harvey Goldman, Partner, Arthur Young & Company

Sanford M. Groves, Project Director, International City Management Association

Ross C. Kory, Principal, American Management Systems, Inc.

Harry Levine, Management Consultant, Philadelphia, Pennsylvania

David Listokin, Center for Urban Policy Research, Rutgers University, New Brunswick, New Jersey

G. Stephen Lloyd, Principal Associate, Public Administration Service, Chicago, Illinois

Roger Mansfield, Assistant City Manager, Redondo Beach, California

Sandra Mokuvos, Senior Consultant, Arthur Young & Company

T. Ashby Newby, Purchasing Agent, Virginia Department of Highways

Philip Rosenberg, Director of Marketing for Public Finance, American Management Systems, Inc.

Larry Schroeder, Syracuse University, Syracuse, New York

Richard B. Stern, Principal Associate, Barton–Aschman Associates, Inc., Evanston, Illinois

Darwin G. Stuart, Principal Associate, Barton–Aschman Associates, Inc., Evanston, Illinois

C. Torben Thomsen, Professor of Accountancy, California State University, Fresno, California

Contents

Introduction

During the last decade local governments have been subjected to fiscal stress resulting from declining revenues, a reduction in federal assistance, voter-initiated tax and expenditure limitations, and difficulty in marketing their bonds. One positive result of these financial problems has been an increased awareness of the importance of sound financial planning and management. Both elected and appointed public officials have become more cognizant of financial issues and the need to improve the quality of financial management. Public demand for greater financial accountability has provided another impetus for streamlining local government financial services.

There is major interest in the development and application of financial techniques aimed at reducing conditions that lead to fiscal strain and increasing the efficiency and effectiveness of finance administration. Governmental finance administration itself has become more complex. Local governments have been criticized for failure to follow generally accepted accounting standards and to achieve full disclosure in their financial reporting. Finance professionals are being asked to evaluate the performance of municipal activities and to better integrate budgeting and accounting. Greater emphasis is being placed on the need for cost accounting, cost analysis, and pricing techniques to assist in determining the true value of services. This information provides the basis for service charges and contracting out selected services. Because of the multitude of capital financing options, special knowledge and skill are required to make the best choice. Deteriorated infrastructure has led to the search for better methods of capital programming and budgeting. Procurement officials are expected to increase their productivity and employ techniques to reduce costs.

Numerous tools and techniques are available for improving local government financial management. The purpose of this book is to provide a basic introduction to a select group of financial techniques that are currently in use. These techniques merit attention because they offer considerable potential for improving the efficiency and effectiveness of local government financial management.

The articles here are not intended to provide an exhaustive and detailed examination of each technique. Rather, the objective is to offer an introduction to the terminology and basic elements of each one and to stimulate an interest in further exploring their application. Every effort has been made to include articles of practical value for public officials and others interested in sound financial management. An extensive bibliography directs the reader to sources of additional information.

Techniques for financial evaluation and policy making

Local government experience with fiscal crises and strain have resulted in the development of techniques to predict, prevent, and resolve financial problems. Special attention has been directed to the identification of financial practices that jeopardize sound financial management and techniques that can enhance the quality of financial information. Part 1 reviews techniques for evaluating financial condition, formulating financial policies, assessing financial practices, and evaluating municipal services.

During the 1970s several cities came close to fiscal collapse. Observers who studied the experiences of these cities and the factors that contributed to their financial problems came away with lessons for other local governments. In fact, a positive aspect of financial emergencies has been the development of financial trend monitoring systems that use fiscal indicators to evaluate the financial condition of a governmental jurisdiction. Social, economic, political, demographic, and financial indicators have been established to review and analyze the causes of fiscal strain, to monitor fiscal condition, and to predict future financial problems. A historical trend analysis of the indicators serves as an advance warning system of problems that may not be immediately visible. The monitoring systems do not pinpoint the causes of problems or propose solutions. In-depth analysis is required to accomplish these objectives.

Fiscal indicators are not foolproof; they are only as effective as the accuracy of the data collected, and few standards exist against which findings can be measured. Another limitation is that fiscal problems develop slowly and may not surface for some time. Other problems include the unavailability of data, poor financial practices, political manipulation, and unique community characteristics.

Despite their apparent limitations, fiscal indicators bring to light key fiscal strengths and weaknesses and allow time for corrective action. Policy makers and administrators are better able to understand the financial condition of their community and can use the knowledge to formulate financial policies to guide future decision making. An ongoing assessment of fiscal health will promote a better comprehension of the long-range fiscal impact of financial decisions. "An Introduction to Evaluating Financial Condition" defines financial condition and the obstacles to measuring it. The article identifies twelve factors that represent the primary forces influencing financial condition and thirty-six indicators that measure different aspects of the factors. It also provides formulas for quantifying each indicator.

A significant benefit of a financial trend monitoring system is the ability to use the data developed to formulate financial policies. Formally adopted financial policies facilitate short- and long-range financial planning, preserve credibility and fiscal integrity, aid in responding to financial emergencies, improve financial practices, increase credit worthiness, and help monitor financial management performance. Financial policies should be reduced to explicit, understandable, and flexible written statements. Well-defined policies are an integral part of a formal long-range financial planning process that consists of an analysis of financial condition and formulation and implementation of financial policies. "Establishing Financial Policies: What, Why, and How" defines financial policies, identifies their benefits, and tells how to establish them. Sample policy statements are included.

Performance, operational, or management auditing is another evaluative technique for establishing accountability and improving program economy and efficiency. Performance or operational auditing extends the traditional financial and compliance audit. It involves an objective review of the financial and operational performance of the organization and its programs and functions, but with an emphasis on operational efficiency and quality. It reveals opportunities for achieving greater economy, efficiency, effectiveness, and accountability and examines the appropriateness and achievement of goals and objectives. In "Operational Auditing: A Must for Local Government," Harry Levine comments on the need and cost of operational auditing. He presents an audit work plan, outlines the steps required in an audit survey, and discusses the qualifications of auditors. The article by G. Stephen Lloyd reviews the background of management auditing, providing tips for conducting a management audit and describing how such an audit can be performed in house.

An additional tool for improving the economy and efficiency of government operations is cost analysis or finding. Cost analysis utilizes existing financial data available in the budget and accounting system. Payroll records, invoices, and contracts are sources of information for cost analysis. Direct costs are emphasized, and short-cut formulas are used in allocating indirect costs. Cost analysis may be done on a periodic and sampling basis.

In conducting a cost analysis, it is necessary to identify the units or activities to be measured and the appropriate sources of information, to define the cost elements involved, to calculate and allocate indirect costs, and to analyze the results. "Costing Municipal Services" by Ross C. Kory and Philip Rosenberg discusses the procedure involved in cost finding, how to make cost data meaningful, and how to use the cost information.

Revenue management and forecasting techniques

Local governments face difficult choices as they consider increasing existing revenues, creating new revenues, or reducing services. Part 2 introduces techniques for conducting revenue surveys, improving revenue collections, forecasting revenues and expenditures, and analyzing the fiscal impact of development decisions.

Public officials are constantly seeking new sources of revenues and ways to maximize existing sources. Consequently, elaborate revenue surveys have been conducted by many jurisdictions in an effort to increase resources. Citizen committees are often appointed to evaluate alternative methods of raising revenues and to provide a base of support for any changes to the existing revenue system. Local government staffs continually review existing revenue sources to assure that they are current and equal the cost of services whenever possible. Service charges have become a primary method of financing many services. Productive and equitable revenue systems mandate that frequent and thorough revenue surveys be conducted. "Strategies for Conducting a Revenue Survey" discusses the benefits of revenue surveys and proposes a method for carrying out an exhaustive study, including the collection and use of comparable data from other local governments.

While substantial attention has been concentrated on identifying new sources of revenue and improving existing sources, little attention has been focused on maximizing the collection of established revenues. Improved municipal debt collection practices can dramatically increase revenues, but cities in general have not been as aggressive and creative as the private sector in their collection practices. Delinquencies and evasion can drastically reduce revenues received.

Techniques for improving revenue collection include aging of accounts receivable, interest and penalties for delinquencies, dunning letters and phone calls, installment payments, collection agencies, lawsuits, computer matching, audits, increased enforcement, service termination, prepayments, and more frequent billing cycles. Revenue collection information is valuable in revenue forecasting, cash management, budgeting, and community analysis.

Signs of poor revenue collection include high delinquency rates, large writeoffs of bad debts, excessive evasion, failure to pinpoint accountability for collection, inadequate collection and enforcement resources, payment waivers and deferrals, absence of penalties, and failure to age receivables. David P. Dolter and Roger Mansfield's article "The City as Debt Collector" describes the efforts of Redondo Beach, California, to improve its debt collection and suggests indicators that can be used to measure collection performance.

Economic uncertainty has aroused increasing interest in multi-year forecasting of local government revenues and expenditures. Forecasting is an essential ingredient in effective financial planning. Revenue and expenditure forecasts are necessary to help policy makers understand the implications of their financial decisions. Unfortunately, uncertain economic conditions have made it difficult to forecast beyond one year. Some public officials have no confidence in forecasting because they do not understand the various methods and question the political feasibility of multi-year predictions.

A number of forecasting techniques are worth examining. These include best guess, trend analysis, deterministic, and statistical-econometric forecasts. Public officials can benefit from an understanding of the benefits and limitations of each method. Properly applied forecasting techniques are useful in determining the spread between revenues and expenditures and the impact of external factors on financial condition. Forecasts can illustrate both the immediate and long-term fiscal implications of various financial policy scenarios.

Financial forecasting is not an exact science. Problems are created if data are unavailable, outdated, or inaccurate. Other limitations include cost; need for staff trained in economics, statistics, financial management, and computers; and the amount of time required to complete some of the forecasts. Subjective judgment affects any forecasting approach. Successful forecasting requires complete and accurate data, simple and understandable relationships, a clear delineation of underlying assumptions, and active involvement of staff. Forecasters must be able to communicate their findings in nontechnical language. Larry Schroeder discusses the purpose and uses of multi-year financial forecasting, the types of forecasting techniques, and the administrative framework under which forecasts are made.

Interest in the calculation of the fiscal impact of intergovernmental, private, and local development is growing. Forecasts of the revenues and expenditures are needed to estimate the long-term implications of development. Different types of development generate different revenue and expenditure patterns.

Fiscal impact analysis techniques assist in the prediction of the costs and revenues associated with residential and nonresidential growth in a community. Information derived from fiscal impact analysis is useful in budget planning, growth management, capital programming, and evaluating the consequences of alternative policy choices as they affect land use. Selections from *The Fiscal Impact Guidebook*, published by the U.S. Department of Housing and Urban Development, spell out practical methods for determining the costs and revenues of residential and nonresidential development. Six different fiscal impact methods are described along with the legal climate and computerized models. Next, Richard B. Stern and Darwin G. Stuart discuss pitfalls in the six techniques that can negate the purpose of such analysis.

Infrastructure programming and financing techniques

Numerous studies, such as *America in Ruins*, have documented the serious deterioration of public facilities and the massive amount of money needed to correct the problem. Local officials are confronted with the dilemma of deciding whether to repair, rehabilitate, or replace the capital facilities and how to finance the work. Part 3 examines capital programming, budgeting, and financing techniques.

The infrastructure problem has produced renewed interest in capital programming and budgeting. Even the federal government is contemplating a capital budget. Capital programming and budgeting provides a systematic approach to determining capital needs and selecting appropriate methods to meet and finance them. A successful capital improvement process provides for the collection of information on the condition of public facilities, the use of evaluative criteria to assess their condition, the preparation of a multiyear plan, consideration of short- and long-term costs and benefits, ranking of projects in order of priority, analysis of financing options, and monitoring of projects.

The capital programming and budgeting process is not foolproof; there are deficiencies. Techniques for assessing the condition of public facilities have not been perfected. Organizational and procedural approaches can be improved. Techniques for deciding whether to repair, rehabilitate, or replace have not been refined. Priority-setting methods remain highly subjective. Project implementation and monitoring techniques need to be improved in order to control costs. Finally, the process will continue to be influenced by political factors. "Capital Planning and Programming Techniques" describes the benefits of the process and the steps involved in preparing, reviewing, and monitoring capital programs and budgets. Special attention is focused on assessing condition, setting priorities, and financing techniques.

Too often, subjective judgment and political considerations are the major factors in evaluating capital projects and making capital investment decisions. Yet traditional business techniques are available to help local governments make these decisions. One concept is net present value, the present value of cash inflows less the present value of cash outflows. The concept addresses the amount of value added to the local government entity if the project is initiated. Another is the internal rate of return, which is calculated by dividing the net annual savings from the project by the average investment in the capital asset. The payback method evaluates the time required to recover the capital investment through annual cash flow savings. Discounting to present value computes the present value of money that will be spent or received in the future. By considering the present value of all dollars associated with different capital financing methods, it is possible to identify the least costly alternative. Users of this technique are cautioned to consider the overall rate of inflation, differing rates of inflation, and opportunity cost, which is the loss to the governmental entity of the benefits that would have resulted if the project had been initiated.

Ronald Chapman's article "Capital Financing: A New Look at an Old Idea" describes three business techniques for making capital investment decisions. They are payback period, rate of return on average investment, and discounted cash flow. C. Torben Thomsen points out some of the dangers in discounting to present value. He cautions that indiscriminate use of discounting can lead to long-term strategic errors in capital budgeting.

Financing is a critical component of the infrastructure issue. Traditional financing options have been supplemented by many new and innovative financing methods. Voter and legislative actions have a profound effect on financing public facilities. States set maximum interest rates and the amount of debt that cities can issue. The federal government has reduced the amount of federal grants available for capital purposes and is considering restrictive legislation on such financing devices as industrial development bonds. Voters in some states adopt constitutional amendments that limit the ability of local governments to use general obligation bonds.

Financing is further influenced by bond ratings and market conditions. Harvey Goldman and Sandra Mokuvos identify and describe a large number of capital financing alternatives.

Creative purchasing techniques

Governmental purchasing professionals are utilizing more sophisticated concepts and techniques to improve the cost-effectiveness of local government purchasing. Part 4 describes the techniques of life cycle costing, value management, and value engineering.

Performance specifications, materials management, increased inventory turnover, stockless systems, value analysis and engineering, and life cycle costing are purchasing techniques that ensure consistent quality and encourage good vendor relations. Performance specifications set forth the requirements a product is to meet in order for it to perform and last as required. Manufacturers are given latitude in the design and production of products that achieve desired results. Tests or other criteria are developed to measure a product's performance and durability. Examples of products for which performance specifications are prepared include tires, batteries, highway reflective materials, and air conditioners.

Life cycle costing is another effective purchasing technique; it considers the total costs of ownership as well as acquisition costs. Total cost bidding and guaranteed maintenance are variations of life cycle costing. Total cost bidding resembles life cycle costing minus the discounting process. Guaranteed maintenance is similar to total cost bidding minus the buy-back provision. All of the techniques recognize the importance of operating and maintenance costs.

Life cycle costing consists of acquisition cost less trade in, initial one-time, operating, maintenance, and overhaul costs and a buy-back offset. Some jurisdictions do not include maintenance or buy-back provisions in their specifications. Life cycle costing involves estimates of useful life, operating and maintenance costs, and salvage value. The salvage value is subtracted from the ownership cost, and the amount of costs due in the future is discounted to present value in order to compare all costs on an equal basis.

Users of life cycle costing need to be aware of some of the pitfalls. The process is time-consuming because it involves estimates of present and future costs, and all costs are discounted to a base period. Other limitations include detailed record keeping, legality of repurchase clauses and the use of multi-year contracts, need for clear contract language, increased initial costs, reduction in number of bidders, and opposition from unions and operating personnel. Life cycle costing is resisted by some elected officials because of political concerns. "Life Cycle Costing" defines the technique, describes when and how to use it, and shows how to prepare a bid using the technique. T. Ashby Newby discusses the concepts of life cycle cost, guaranteed maintenance, and total cost purchasing as compared to initial acquisition price. Examples are provided on the application of the techniques, and tips are given on how to conduct an analysis and on suggested requirements to be included in the contract.

Value management, analysis, or engineering is another technique directed at reducing costs, improving quality, encouraging creative suggestions, satisfying user needs, and stimulating vendor involvement. Value management is the thorough examination of services, systems, equipment, facilities, and supplies for the purpose of achieving the essential functions at the lowest cost. The technique is a creative approach to obtaining optimum performance, reliability, and value.

Value management consists of value studies, value engineering, and value incentive clauses. Value studies and engineering are carried out by a multidisciplinary team that works through the six phases of information gathering, analysis, creative problem solving, evaluation, presentation, and implementation. This approach can result in savings ranging from $10 to $35 for each dollar of value analysis effort. The U.S. Environmental Protection Agency requires and funds value engineering for all wastewater projects costing over $10 million. Value incentive clauses are inserted in contracts to reduce contract costs by eliminating any requirements found to be in excess of actual needs. Contractors submit proposals to reduce costs without sacrificing the basic function or quality and share in the savings resulting from a net reduction of the present contract price.

Successful value analysis requires top management support, a broad-based multidisciplinary team; careful selection of products, services, or projects; detailed and creative analysis; and value analysis oriented vendors. "Value Management: Applications in the Public Sector" defines value management, describes the steps involved in conducting the analysis, identifies several options for establishing a program, and illustrates a number of applications. Robert A. Feger, in "The Value in Value Engineering," describes value engineering, outlines the steps involved, gives examples of its application, and suggests ways to maximize its use.

Taken all together, the selections in this book provide information and ideas for local managers and elected officials. The cases and examples show how various financial management techniques have been applied throughout the country and give practical guidance for improving financial management and accountability in other governmental organizations.

PART 1

Techniques for Financial Evaluation and Policy Making

An Introduction to Evaluating Financial Condition

Sanford M. Groves

During the 1970s, governments at all levels began to experience an increasing number of financial problems. These problems were related to increased demand for services, unionization of public employees, structural changes in the economy, shifts in population, double-digit inflation, and significant changes in intergovernmental relationships. The financial crisis in New York City in 1975 and the inability of other cities to secure long-term financing brought these issues to national attention. California's Proposition 13 and similar revenue and expenditure limitations in other states called even greater attention to the financial health of local governments. As a result, officials at all levels have been forced to place a high priority on financial problems.

Most financial problems do not develop suddenly. Instead, they build over time. Generally speaking, they can be traced to one or more of the following situations:

1. A decline in revenues
2. An increase in expenditure pressures
3. Decreasing cash and budgetary surpluses
4. A growing debt burden
5. The accumulation of unfunded liabilities
6. The erosion of capital plant
7. A decline in tax base or an increase in the need for public services
8. The emergence of adverse external economic conditions, such as increasing inflation or unemployment

Reprinted with permission from *Evaluating Financial Condition*, handbook 1 in *Evaluating Local Government Financial Condition* (Washington, D.C.: International City Management Association, 1980).

9. An increase in intergovernmental constraints and mandates and an overdependence on intergovernmental funding
10. The occurrence of natural disasters and emergencies
11. The influence of local political pressures
12. The lack of effective legislative policies and/or management practices.

Some of these situations, such as a growing debt burden, fall within the control of a local government. Others, such as the emergence of adverse external circumstances, may not. Nevertheless, with enough time a city may be able to take actions to mitigate their effects. For example, in the short run, a city may not be able to turn around a decline in tax base, but it may be able to reduce its expenditure levels to adjust for reduced revenues.[1]

What is financial condition?

The term "financial condition" has many meanings. In a narrow accounting sense, it can refer to whether a government can generate enough cash or liquidity over thirty or sixty days to pay its bills. This is referred to here as "cash solvency." Financial condition can also refer to whether a city can generate enough revenues over its normal budgetary period to meet its expenditure obligations and not incur deficits. This is referred to here as "budgetary solvency."

In a broader sense, financial condition can refer to the *long-run* ability of a government to pay *all* the costs of doing business, including expenditure obligations that normally appear in each annual budget as well as those that show up only in the years in which they must be paid. Examples of these latter expenditure obligations are pension costs; payments for accrued employee leave; deferred maintenance; and replacement of capital assets such as streets, equipment, and buildings. Although these costs will eventually show up in a budget or will otherwise make themselves known, a short-run analysis of one to five years may not reveal them. Therefore, this long-run balance between revenues and costs warrants separate attention and is referred to here as "long-run solvency."

Finally, financial condition can refer to whether a government can provide the level and quality of services required for the general health and welfare of a community as desired by its citizens. For want of a better term and for the sake of consistency, this will be referred to here as "service level solvency." A lack of such solvency would be seen, for example, in the case of a government that in all other respects had sound financial condition but was not able to support an adequate level of police and fire services, and it would suffer from cash, budgetary, or long-run solvency problems if it did provide them.

Few local governments face such severe and immediate financial problems that they are likely to default on loans or fail to meet payrolls and other current obligations. Therefore, this article will adopt a broad definition of financial condition to encompass the four types of solvency described above. By using this broad definition, we hope to deal with the concerns of the many local governments that find themselves in one or more of the following situations:

1. They are under the strain of a few identifiable problems and are seeking a way to put these problems in a broader perspective.
2. They sense the emergence of problems but are having difficulty pinpointing them.
3. They are in good financial condition but are searching for a systematic way to monitor changes and anticipate future problems.

Therefore, financial condition is broadly defined as the ability of a city to pay its way on a continuing basis. Specifically, it refers to a city's ability to:

1. Maintain existing service levels
2. Withstand local and regional economic disruptions
3. Meet the demands of natural growth, decline, and change.

Ability to maintain existing service levels   Maintaining existing service levels means: Can the local government continue to afford to pay for the services it is currently providing? Aside from the basic services funded from local revenues, this topic would also include the ability to maintain programs in the future that are currently funded from external sources such as federal grants where the aid is scheduled or likely to diminish and where the service cannot practically be eliminated when the aid does disappear. It also includes the ability to maintain capital facilities, such as streets and buildings, in a manner that would protect the initial investment in them and keep them in usable condition. It also includes the ability to provide funds for future liabilities that may currently be unfunded, such as pension, employee leave, debt, and lease purchase commitments.

Ability to withstand economic disruption   Financial condition is the ability to withstand local and regional economic disruption, such as a major employer's decision to move a manufacturing plant out of town and take away many of the community's jobs and a large piece of tax base in the process. A surge of national inflation that affects expenditures more heavily than revenues and thus leaves local government with more dollars but less purchasing power is another example.

Ability to meet future demands of growth and decline Finally, financial condition is the ability of a community to meet the future demands of change. As time passes, cities grow, shrink, or stay the same size. Each condition has its own set of financial pressures. Growth can force a city to rapidly assume new debt to finance streets and utility lines, or it can cause a sudden increase in the operating budget to provide necessary services. Shrinkage, on the other hand, leaves a city with the same number of streets and utilities to maintain but with fewer people to pay for them. Even a city that remains stable in size can experience financial pressure. For example, if population remains stable but undergoes changes in composition, the government often must respond with new programs. This necessitates expensive start-up costs, not to mention the fact that the new programs themselves may be more expensive. This many occur, for example, if a population becomes poorer or older.

The basic questions, therefore, are: Can the city continue to pay for what it is currently doing? Are there reserves or other vehicles for financing economic and financial emergencies? Is there enough financial flexibility to allow the city to adjust to the normal process of change? If a city can meet these challenges, it is in good financial condition. If it cannot, it is probably experiencing problems or can anticipate them.

Obstacles to measuring financial condition

Is your city in good financial condition? To answer this we first need to be able to measure financial condition. If we had chosen a definition of financial condition that considered only cash and budgetary solvency, we would have narrowed the range of measurement issues we need to discuss. By including long-run and service level solvency, however, we encounter a host of problems. These problems are related to:

1. The nature of a public entity
2. The current state of the art in municipal financial analysis
3. The current character of municipal accounting practices.

The social nature of a public entity Private firms can easily determine whether they are financially sound. The basic test is dollar profit, which roughly translates into efficiency. For the public entity, profit is not a motive and efficiency is only one of many objectives. The primary objectives are "health and welfare," "political satisfaction," and other issues that can be measured only subjectively. Therefore, by including the concept of service level solvency within our definition of financial condition we have to settle for something less than precise measurement.

The state of the art   Until the last few years, practitioners and researchers in the field of public finance have concerned themselves primarily with the issues of cash and budgetary solvency and have not paid as much attention to the issues of long-run and service level solvency. The exception has been the investment community, but it has more specifically concerned itself with debt-carrying capacity. During the last few years, local governments as well as others have broadened their concerns, but no one has yet developed a comprehensive and practical way to evaluate the financial condition of an individual local government.[2]

This can be attributed to a number of factors. First, the growth-oriented environment of local government prior to the 1970s did not always demand close attention to the broad range of issues that affect financial condition. Second, data on economic and demographic events are difficult and sometimes impossible to obtain. Third, the data that are available cannot always be compared from one city to another because each city is unique in size, function, geography, revenue structure, and other significant characteristics. Fourth, there is no accepted theory to explain the links between economic base and city revenues. How and to what extent, for example, does a decline in employment or a shift from manufacturing to retail specifically affect the revenues of a city?[3] Last, the state of the art does not provide normative standards for what the financial characteristics of a city should be. What, for example, is a healthy per capita expenditure rate, level of reserves, or amount of debt? The credit rating industry has many benchmarks for evaluating cities, but these benchmarks have to be considered in combination with more subjective criteria, such as the diversity of the city's tax base or its proximity to regional markets.[4] Some attempts have been made to develop standards by averaging various cities or otherwise comparing one city to another, but, because of the uniqueness of each city and the lack of sufficient objective data, these inter-city comparisons have fallen short of gaining authoritative acceptance.

The state of municipal accounting systems   During the early 1900s, local government accounting systems grew with an emphasis on auditability and on providing high visibility to dollars passing through the government accounts. The accounting systems stressed legal compliance and tracking the path of each dollar in and out of the local treasury. Thus, the concepts of fund accounting and flow of funds—that is, segregating current revenues and expenditures into bite-sized, auditable pieces—were developed with little attention given to cost accounting and measuring long-run financial health.

The result is that most cities do produce budgets showing revenues and expenditures, and most states require cities to balance them in one fashion or another. In addition, most cities produce year-end financial statements including balance sheets and operating statements.

These reports show the flow of dollars in and out of the city during a particular year, but they do not provide all the information needed to evaluate long-run financial condition. They do not show in detail the costs of each service provided. They do not show on an annual basis all costs that are being postponed to future periods. They do not necessarily show the accumulation of unfunded pension liabilities or employee benefit liabilities. They do not show reductions in purchasing power caused by inflation. They do not show decreasing flexibility in the use of funds that results from increasing state and federal mandates. In addition, they do not show the erosion of streets, buildings, and other fixed assets that are not being maintained, nor do they relate changes in the economic and demographic conditions to changes in revenue and expenditure rates. Finally, they are prepared for only a one-year period and do not show in a multi-year perspective the emergence of favorable or unfavorable conditions.[5]

The financial trend monitoring system

As can be seen from the foregoing discussion, evaluating a jurisdiction's financial condition can be complex. It is a process of sorting through a large number of pieces. The pieces include the national economy, population level and composition, local business climate, actions of the state and local government, and the character of the internal finances of the city itself. Not only are there a large number of these factors to evaluate, but many of them are difficult to isolate and quantify.

In addition, no single piece tells the whole story. Some are more important than others, but usually you cannot tell which these are until you have finished assembling the pieces. For example, revenues may be higher than ever in absolute amounts and may be exceeding expenditure levels by a comfortable margin. However, if a city does not consider that a 5 percent annual inflation rate during the last ten years has cut its purchasing power by well over half, and that it has had to make the adjustment by deferring street maintenance, it may be lulled into thinking that its financial condition remains as healthy as ever.

In the face of this complexity, of the lack of complete accounting data, and of the lack of accepted theories and normative standards, the question can be asked: Is it possible to rationalize the process of evaluating financial condition?

The answer is yes. Regardless of the obstacles, a city can still collect a great deal of useful information, even if this information is only part of what there is to know. Medical science has learned little about the human body compared with what remains to be learned. This lack of total knowledge, however, does not prevent doctors from using what they do know to prevent diseases and from diagnosing problems before they become serious.

The Financial Trend Monitoring System (FTMS) is a system that identifies the factors that affect financial condition and arranges them in a rational order so that they can be more easily analyzed and, to the extent possible, measured. It is a management tool that pulls together the pertinent information from a city's budgetary and financial reports, mixes it with the appropriate economic and demographic data, and creates a series of local government financial indicators that, when plotted over a period of time, can be used to monitor changes in financial condition. The indicators deal with thirty-six separate issues such as cash liquidity, level of business activity, changes in fund balances, emergence of unfunded liabilities, and development of external revenue dependencies.

Use of the system does not provide specific answers to why a problem is occurring nor does it provide a single number or index to measure financial health. What it does provide are:

1. *Flags* for identifying problems
2. *Clues* to their causes
3. *Time* to take anticipatory action.

It also provides a convenient tool for describing the city's financial strengths and weaknesses to a city council, a credit rating firm, or others with a need to know. It can provide a rational means for organizing internal staff priorities or it can provide a vehicle a council can use to set long-run policy priorities. Finally, if used just before budget time, it can provide a logical way of introducing long-run considerations into the annual budget process.

How does it work?

The Financial Trend Monitoring System (FTMS) is built on twelve "factors" representing the primary forces that influence financial condition. These financial condition factors are then associated with thirty-six "indicators" that measure different aspects of seven of these factors. Once developed, these indicators can be used to monitor changes in the factors, or more generally, to monitor changes in financial condition. The twelve factors, together with the thirty-six indicators, make up FTMS. The factors will be discussed first, and then the indicators.

The financial condition factors The twelve financial condition factors are shown in the boxes in Figure 1. They are more fully described by the items shown in the brackets.

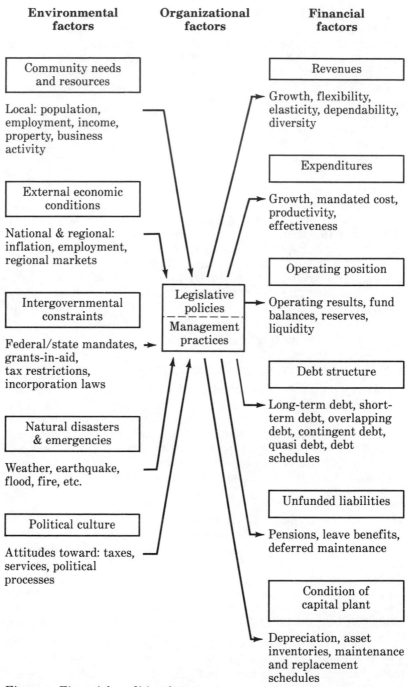

Figure 1. Financial condition factors.

Each factor is classified as an environmental factor, an organizational factor, or a financial factor. They are closely associated with and derived from the causes of financial problems listed earlier. Taken together, they represent an inventory of considerations and can be used as a guide to organize and assemble the varied and elusive issues that must be considered when financial condition is being evaluated.

The chart arranges the factors as if they were inputs to and outputs from each other. This type of relationship is not the only one that exists. For example, many factors at times feed back into themselves and other factors. In addition, the arrangement of the factors suggests that there is a clear cause-and-effect relationship between the environmental factors and financial factors, although this is not always true. The relationships shown here, however, are the primary ones and will be the focus for this system.

In short, the environmental factors representing the external influences on a city government are filtered through a set of organizational factors. The result is a series of financial factors which describe the internal financial structure of the governmental unit. The following discussion considers them in their broad context and discusses only the three factor categories.

The *environmental factors* affect a city in two ways. First, they create demands. For example, a population increase may force the city to add police, and the acceptance of a new grant may require new audit procedures.

Second, the environmental factors provide resources. For example, the increase in population that created the need for additional police services also increases community wealth and tax revenues. The new grant that required new audit procedures also provides funds to build a new city hall.

One way or another, the environmental factors may create demands, provide resources, establish limits, or do all of these. Underlying an analysis of the effect the environmental factors have on financial condition is the question: Do they provide enough resources to pay for the demands they make?

The *organizational factors* are the responses the government makes to changes in the environmental factors. We can assume in theory that any government can remain in good financial condition if it makes the proper organizational response to adverse conditions by reducing services, increasing efficiency, raising taxes, or taking some other appropriate action. This assumes that public officials have enough notice of the problem, understand its nature and magnitude, know what to do, and are willing to do it.

These are optimistic assumptions, especially in light of political constraints, the deficiencies in the state of the art, and the limitations in municipal accounting as discussed earlier. Underlying an analysis of the effects the organizational factors have on financial condition is the question: Do your legislative policies and management practices provide the opportunity to make the appropriate response to changes in the environment?

The *financial factors* reflect the condition of the government's internal finances. In some respects they are a result of the influence of the environmental and organizational factors. If the environment makes greater demands than resources provided and if the organization is not effective in making a balancing response, the financial factors would eventually show signs of cash, budgetary, or long-run insolvency. In this respect the financial factors are where untreated problems will eventually become visible if they are not responded to early enough. In analyzing the effect financial factors have on financial condition, the underlying question is: Is your governmental unit paying the full cost of operating without postponing costs to a future period when revenues may not be available to pay these costs?

The indicators   The indicators are the primary tools of the system. They represent a way to quantify changes in the factors discussed above. Figure 2 shows the thirty-six indicators along with the factors with which they are associated. Next to each indicator is an arrow pointing either up or down. These arrows should be read as "increasing" or "decreasing." If a city finds that an indicator is moving in the direction shown, it should be considered a potential problem requiring further analysis.

Indicators are shown for only seven of the twelve factors. This is for two reasons. First, not all the factors are quantifiable in a meaningful management sense, so some, such as Political Culture and Natural Disasters and Emergencies, show no indicators. Second, some indicators apply to more than one factor but are shown in only one place. For example, Percentage of Intergovernmental Revenues, shown under Revenues, could also be considered an indicator under Intergovernmental Constraints, insofar as it measures the dependence a city may be developing on grant revenues. Likewise, Operating Deficits, shown under Operating Position, could be considered an indicator under Legislative Policies and Management Practices. The indicators have been grouped under the factors into which they most logically or conveniently fit.

Formulas for quantifying each indicator are shown in Figure 3.

Conclusion

Many aspects of financial condition cannot be measured explicitly, but there is much that can be done. By quantifying the thirty-six indicators and plotting them over a period of at least five years, city officials can begin to monitor their government's financial performance. They can observe such things as increases in the city's un-

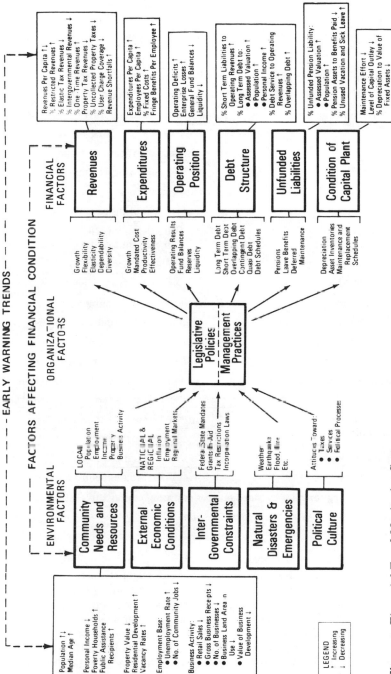

Figure 2. Financial Trend Monitoring System.

Indicator	Formula
Revenues per capita	$$\frac{\text{Net operating revenues in constant dollars}}{\text{Population}}$$
Restricted revenues	$$\frac{\text{Restricted operating revenues}}{\text{Net operating revenues}}$$
Intergovernmental revenues	$$\frac{\text{Intergovernmental operating revenues}}{\text{Gross operating revenues}}$$
Elastic tax revenues	$$\frac{\text{Elastic operating revenues}}{\text{Net operating revenues}}$$
One-time revenues	$$\frac{\text{One-time operating revenues}}{\text{Net operating revenues}}$$
Property tax revenues	Property tax revenues in constant dollars
Uncollected property taxes	$$\frac{\text{Uncollected property taxes}}{\text{Net property tax levy}}$$
User charge coverage	$$\frac{\text{Revenues from fees and user charges}}{\text{Expenditures for related services}}$$
Revenue shortfalls	$$\frac{\text{Revenue shortfalls}[1]}{\text{Net operating revenues}}$$
Expenditures per capita	$$\frac{\text{Net operating expenditures in constant dollars}}{\text{Population}}$$
Employees per capita	$$\frac{\text{Number of municipal employees}}{\text{Population}}$$
Fixed costs	$$\frac{\text{Fixed costs}}{\text{Net operating expenditures}}$$

[1] Net operating revenues budgeted less net operating revenues (actual).

Figure 3. Summary of indicator formulas.

funded liabilities, decreases in its business activity, and decreases in its property tax collection rates. They can carefully watch the city's liquidity position, calculate the effect of postponing capital facility maintenance, identify an increasing dependence on external revenues, or anticipate effects of previously hidden budget deficits.

The use of these indicators will not provide answers to why a problem is occurring or what the appropriate solution is, but it may provide the opportunity to make an informed management response.

Indicator	Formula
Fringe benefits	$$\frac{\text{Fringe benefit expenditures}}{\text{Salaries and wages}}$$
Operating deficits	$$\frac{\text{General fund operating deficit}}{\text{Net operating revenues}}$$
Enterprise losses	Enterprise profits or losses in constant dollars
General fund balances	$$\frac{\text{Unrestricted fund balance of general fund}}{\text{Net operating revenues}}$$
Liquidity	$$\frac{\text{Cash and short-term investments}}{\text{Current liabilities}}$$
Current liabilities	$$\frac{\text{Current liabilities}}{\text{Net operating revenues}}$$
Long-term debt	$$\frac{\text{Net direct long-term debt}}{\text{Assessed valuation}}$$
Debt service	$$\frac{\text{Net direct debt service}}{\text{Net operating revenues}}$$
Overlapping debt	$$\frac{\text{Overlapping long-term debt}}{\text{Assessed valuation}}$$
Unfunded pension liability	$$\frac{\text{Unfunded pension plan vested benefits}}{\text{Assessed valuation}}$$
Pension assets	$$\frac{\text{Pension plan assets}}{\text{Pension benefits paid}}$$
Accumulated employee leave liability	$$\frac{\text{Total days of unused vacation and sick leave}}{\text{Number of municipal employees}}$$

Figure 3. Continued.

1. For a discussion and case studies of cities that have had financial problems, see: Advisory Commission on Intergovernmental Relations. *City Financial Emergencies: The Intergovernmental Dimension.* Washington, D.C.: U.S. Government Printing Office, July 1973.
2. For a comprehensive review of work done to date on evaluating financial condition, see: (1) Aronson, J. Rich-ard. "Municipal Fiscal Indicators." An Information Bulletin of the Management, Finance and Personnel Task Force of the Urban Consortium. Washington, D.C.: U.S. Dept. of Housing and Urban Development, 1979. (2) Berne, Robert and Schramm, Richard. "The Financial Solvency of Local Governments: A Conceptual Approach." An unpublished report prepared for the Inter-

national City Management Association, March, 1978.

Individual works of particular interest include: (1) Municipal Finance Officers Association, *Is Your City Heading for Financial Difficulty: A Guidebook for Small Cities and Other Governmental Units.* Chicago: Municipal Finance Officers Association, 1979. (2) Dearborn, Philip M. *Elements of Municipal Financial Analysis.* Special report, Parts I–IV. Boston: The First Boston Corporation, 1977. (3) Peterson, George, et al. *Urban Fiscal Monitoring.* Washington, D.C.: The Urban Institute, August 1978. (4) Clark, Terry N.; Rubin, Irene S.; Pettler, Lynne C.; and Zimmerman, Erwin. *How Many New Yorks?* Chicago: The University of Chicago, April 22, 1976. (5) Aronson, Richard and Schwartz, Eli. "Determining Debt's Danger Signals," Management Information Service, Vol. 8, No. 12, International City Management Association, December 1976.

3. See, for example: Bahl, Roy W., Campbell, Alan K., and Greytak, David. *Taxes, Expenditures, and the Economic Base, Case Study of New York City.* New York: Praeger Publishers, Inc., 1974.

4. For a discussion on how credit rating firms rate local government bonds, see: (1) Smith, Wade S. *The Appraisal of Municipal Credit Risks.* New York: Moody's Investors Service, Inc., 1979. (2) Sherwood, Hugh. *How Corporate and Municipal Debt is Rated: An Inside Look at Standard and Poor's Rating System.* New York: John Wiley and Sons, 1976. (3) Moody's Investors Service, Inc. *Pitfalls in Issuing Municipal Bonds.* New York: Moody's Investors Service, Inc., April 1977. (4) Petersen, John E. *The Rating Game.* New York: The Twentieth Century Fund, 1974.

5. For a more in-depth discussion of some of the problems associated with current municipal accounting systems, see: (1) Mansfield, Roger. "The Financial Reporting Practices of Government: A Time for Reflection." *Public Administration Review,* March/April 1979. (2) Coopers & Lybrand. *Financial Disclosure Practices of the American Cities: Closing the Communications Gap.* Boston and New York: Coopers & Lybrand, 1978.

Establishing
Financial Policies:
What, Why, and How

W. Maureen Godsey

What are financial policies?

The financial performance of a city is difficult to assess. Unlike private entities, local governments have no "bottom line" profit figures by which they can measure their financial performance, nor are there any authoritative standards by which they can judge themselves. In recent years, many public organizations have adopted different types of management by objectives (MBO) systems as a means of measuring the performance of their programs and services. Under such systems, the governing board and management work together to set goals for the city as well as targets that allow officials to judge how well the goals are being met. Once these goals and targets are established, performance is evaluated by comparing actual results with the targets.

This article discusses how a local government can use long-range financial policies to establish similar types of goals and targets for the financial operations so that the manager, council, and community can monitor how well the city is performing and keep informed on its financial condition. The following pages contain a brief discussion of the uses of financial policies and suggestions on how to establish them.

Why set financial policies?

Establishing financial policies has many benefits. One of the most important is that it can help local officials view their present approach to financial management from an overall, long-range van-

Reprinted with permission from *Financial Performance Goals: A Guide for Setting Long-Range Policies*, handbook 4 in *Evaluating Local Government Financial Condition* (Washington, D.C.: International City Management Association, 1980).

tage point. In most communities, policies already exist in budgets, in capital improvement plans, in the general or comprehensive plan, in a charter, in grant applications, in council resolutions, and in administrative practices. When financial policies are scattered among these kinds of documents, are unwritten, or are developed on a case-by-case basis, it is likely that decisions will be made without consideration of other current policy decisions, past policy decisions, or future policy alternatives. This kind of policy making can lead to:

1. *Conflicting policies.* The governing board may be making decisions that are in conflict with each other.
2. *Inconsistent policies.* The governing board may be making certain decisions and following certain policies on one issue, then reversing themselves on a similar issue.
3. *Incomplete policies.* The governing board may not be making any policy or reaching any decision on some aspect of financial management.

Having a formal set of policies can help the chief executive and the governing board identify these conflicts, inconsistencies, and gaps in the present approach to financial policy. It can also help the manager and the council develop similar expectations regarding both managerial and legislative financial decision making.

There are other benefits to establishing financial policy. Some of these are:

1. Having publicly adopted policy statements contributes greatly to the credibility of and public confidence in the governmental organization. To the credit rating industry and prospective investors, such statements show a city's commitment to sound financial management and fiscal integrity.
2. Having established policy can save time and energy for both the manager and council. Once certain decisions are made at the policy level, the issues do not need to be discussed each time a decision has to be made.
3. The process of developing overall policy directs the attention of management and council members to the city's *total* financial condition rather than single issue areas. Moreover, this process requires management and council to think about linking long-run financial planning with day-to-day operations.
4. As overall policies are developed, the process of trying to tie issues together can bring new information to the surface and reveal further issues that need to be addressed.
5. Discussing financial policy can be an educational process for the council. It can help make the council more aware of the importance of their policy making role in maintaining good financial condition.

6. Discussing the financial issues and adopting a formal position will help prepare for a financial emergency and thereby avoid relying on short-run solutions that may be creating worse problems in the long run.
7. Setting policy can improve the city's fiscal stability. It can help city officials look down the road, set tax rates and plan expenditures for a two- to three-year period, and create a consistent planning approach.
8. Finally, having explicit policy contributes to a continuity in handling the city's financial affairs. The manager and membership of the council may change over time, but policies can still guide whoever holds these positions.

In summary, establishing explicit financial policy can in many ways help both management and elected officials make financial decisions. The extent to which these benefits can be enjoyed by a community will depend on how the policy is formulated and who participates in that process, what substantive issues the policies deal with, and what policy is actually adopted.

How to set financial policies

There is no single best way to set financial policy. In any particular community, successful policy setting will depend on such things as the relationship between the manager and the council, the kind of financial policies that already exist, the kinds of uses to be made of the policies, and the present and projected financial condition of the city. In some communities a comprehensive, systematic approach may work, where a variety of financial management policies are considered at one time. In other communities, a step-by-step approach may work better, where selected areas of financial policies are considered incrementally over a period of years.

Whatever the approach chosen, the steps involved are very similar. These are:

1. Determine who will be active in setting policy
2. Determine what areas of financial management will be addressed
3. Determine the content and format of the actual policy statements.

First, a policy study group should be selected that will consist of the persons who will identify and develop the policy issues to be dealt with. This group could include the manager, the finance director, administrative assistants, the department heads, the finance committee of the council, the council as a whole, citizen groups, or other persons as appropriate. Strong council involvement and leadership at this initial stage can be the key to the acceptability of the financial policies that are eventually established.

After this group has been selected, its first task is to choose the areas of financial management that it will study. One way to make this choice is to consider just the basic functional areas of financial management: budgeting, accounting, capital programming, debt management, and cash management. Another way to identify policy areas is to focus on current financial problems. Figures 1, 2, and 3 following this article show sample policy statements in the areas of debt, capital improvements, and revenues.

Once the areas of financial policy have been selected, the next step is to develop the actual statements of policies. For instance, if policy statements are to be formulated within the area of budgeting, a process needs to be developed to decide on the specific statements regarding policy. Here are some suggestions for that process:

1. *Pull together existing explicit and implicit policies.* Studying and pulling together existing policies can set the groundwork and indicate what further policy work is needed. Internal documents and manuals are probably the best starting place for this task. Local and state laws that apply to financial management need to be considered in setting policies.
2. *Use department heads.* Another way of developing policy items is to ask department heads to submit recommendations, both for setting new policy and for changing existing policy. The finance director especially should be active in this process.
3. *Focus on problems.* If a community undertakes a systematic evaluation of municipal financial condition, problem areas can be identified. The problem areas can then be used to pinpoint where policy statements need to be made.
4. *Use technical assistance materials and people.* There are many organizations and individuals who can be resources in the policy-setting process. Organizations such as public interest groups, state departments of community affairs, bond rating firms, consultants, and municipal leagues may be able to provide written materials, such as handbooks. Persons connected with these organizations may be able to help with their own personal expertise.
5. *Talk with other communities.* Another source of ideas for policy statements is to examine the policies of other communities. Figures 1, 2, and 3 are composites, taken for the most part from policy statements used in many cities.
6. *Get community input.* A sense of how citizens view the future is important and can be valuable in gaining community support. Key business organizations, such as the Chamber of Commerce or banks, and existing citizen groups, such as a

homeowners' association, can participate in the process of developing policy statements.

From these sources of information, a range of possible policy statements can be formulated, including those that set broad policy goals and those that set specific targets for meeting those goals.

Sample debt policies

The city will confine long-term borrowing to capital improvements or projects that cannot be financed from current revenues.

When the city finances capital projects by issuing bonds, it will pay back the bonds within a period not to exceed the expected useful life of the project.

The city will try to keep the average maturity of general obligation bonds at or below ____ years.

On all debt-financed projects, the city will make a down payment of at least ____ percent of total project cost from current revenues.

Total debt service for general obligation debt will not exceed ____ percent of total annual locally generated operating revenue.[1]

Total general-obligation debt will not exceed ____ percent of the assessed valuation of taxable property.[2]

Where possible, the city will use special assessment, revenue, or other self-supporting bonds instead of general obligation bonds.

The city will not use long-term debt for current operations.

The city will retire tax anticipation debt annually and will retire bond anticipation debt within six months after completion of the project.[3]

The city will maintain good communications with bond rating agencies about its financial condition. The city will follow a policy of full disclosure on every financial report and bond prospectus.[4]

Source: W. Maureen Godsey, *Financial Performance Goals: A Guide for Setting Long-Range Policies*, Handbook 4 in *Evaluating Local Government Financial Condition* (Washington, D.C.: International City Management Association, 1980).

1. Also see: Handbook 2, Indicator 20, "Debt Service."
2. Also see: Handbook 2, Indicator 19, "Long-Term Debt."
3. Also see: Handbook 2, Indicator 18, "Short-Term Liabilities." Tax anticipation and bond anticipation debt are two forms of short-term liabilities. Tax anticipation debt is issued in anticipation of the receipt of revenues, and helps to even out a city's cash flow. Bond anticipation notes are issued in anticipation of bond revenues.
4. Also see: Municipal Finance Officers Association. *Disclosure Guidelines for Offerings by State and Local Governments*, 1976.

Figure 1.

Sample capital improvement budget policies

The city will make all capital improvements in accordance with an adopted capital improvement program.[1]

The city will develop a multi-year plan for capital improvements and update it annually.

The city will enact an annual capital budget based on the multi-year capital improvement plan. Future capital expenditures necessitated by changes in population, changes in real estate development, or changes in economic base will be calculated and included in capital budget projections.[2]

The city will coordinate development of the capital improvement budget with development of the operating budget. Future operating costs associated with new capital improvement will be projected and included in operating budget forecasts.

The city will use intergovernmental assistance to finance only those capital improvements that are consistent with the capital improvement plan and city priorities, and whose operating and maintenance costs have been included in operating budget forecasts.

The city will maintain all its assets at a level adequate to protect the city's capital investment and to minimize future maintenance and replacement costs.[3]

The city will project its equipment replacement and maintenance needs for the next several years and will update this projection each year. From this projection a maintenance and replacement schedule will be developed and followed.

The city will identify the estimated costs and potential funding sources for each capital project proposal before it is submitted to council for approval.[4]

The city will determine the least costly financing method for all new projects.[5]

Source: W. Maureen Godsey, *Financial Performance Goals: A Guide for Setting Long-Range Policies*, Handbook 4 in *Evaluating Local Government Financial Condition* (Washington, D.C.: International City Management Association, 1980).

1. Also see: Municipal Finance Officers Association. *A Capital Improvement Programming Handbook for Small Cities and Other Governmental Units*, 1979.

2. Also see: Handbook 5, *Analyzing Financial Impacts.*

3. Also see: Handbook 2, Indicator 26, "Maintenance Effort."

4. Also see: Municipal Finance Officers Association. *A Capital Improvement Programming Handbook for Small Cities and Other Governmental Units*, Appendix A, 1979.

5. Also see: Handbook 5, *Discounting To Present Value.*

Figure 2.

Sample revenue policies

The city will try to maintain a diversified and stable revenue system to shelter it from short-run fluctuations in any one revenue source.

The city will estimate its annual revenues by an objective, analytical process.[1]

The city will project revenues for the next (three/five/other) years and will update this projection annually. Each existing and potential revenue source will be re-examined annually.[2]

The city will maintain sound appraisal procedures to keep property values current. Property will be assessed at _____ percent of full market value.

The year-to-year increase of actual revenue from the property tax will generally not exceed _____ percent. Reassessments will be made of all property at least every _____ years.

The city will follow an aggressive policy of collecting property tax revenues. The annual level of uncollected property taxes will generally not exceed _____ percent.[3]

The city will establish all user charges and fees at a level related to the cost of providing the services.[4]

Each year, the city will recalculate the full costs of activities supported by user fees to identify the impact of inflation and other cost increases.

The city will automatically revise user fees (with/without) review of the governing board to adjust for the effects of inflation.

The city will set fees and user charges for each enterprise fund such as water, sewer, or electricity at a level that *fully* supports the total direct and indirect cost of the activity. Indirect costs include the cost of annual depreciation of capital assets.

The city will set fees for other user activities, such as recreational services, at a level to support _____ percent of the direct and indirect cost of the activity.[5]

Source: W. Maureen Godsey, *Financial Performance Goals: A Guide for Setting Long-Range Policies*, Handbook 4 in *Evaluating Local Government Financial Condition* (Washington, D.C.: International City Management Association, 1980).

1. Also see: Municipal Finance Officers Association. *An Operating Budget Handbook for Small Cities and Other Governmental Units*, 1979.
2. Also see: Handbook 5, *Forecasting Revenues and Expenditures.*
3. Also see: Handbook 2, Indicator 7, "Uncollected Property Taxes."
4. Also see: Galambos, Eva C., and Arthur F. Schreiber. *Making Sense Out of Dollars: Economic Analysis for Local Government*, Chapter 7, "Pricing for Local Government: User Charges in Place of Taxes."
5. This may vary by activity. Also to be considered is the equity and ease of administration of the fee.

Figure 3.

Operational Auditing: A Must for Local Government

Operational auditing can improve financial management in American cities by providing information and methods that can be used by management to curtail the rapid escalation of local government costs and expenditures and to achieve balanced budgets. New York is not the only major city to face the threat of outright bankruptcy. Philadelphia, Cleveland, and several other major cities have experienced unprecedented financial problems that are leading them down the same path as New York. One of the most essential tools to eliminate the antiquated and inefficient systems and procedures and meet the needs of modern management is operational auditing. However, most major cities do not use this tool, and in Philadelphia the city controller had to enter suit in the Court of Common Pleas of Philadelphia County to establish his right to conduct operational audits at his discretion since neither the mayor nor the finance director wanted to perform these audits.

When performed properly, operational auditing will yield an insight into how best to go about curtailing the sharp increase in the costs of local government by improving financial management in American cities. Outside of the usual accounting and financial areas, audits can be done with operational auditing techniques in purchasing, inventory control, insurance, EDP, construction, traffic, management information system, advertising, production, and organizational control.

Background

Operational auditing is a term that was first used by progressive internal auditors some years ago to describe the work they were

Reprinted with permission from *The Government Accountants Journal*, spring 1980.

doing which had as a specific objective the improvement of the operations which were audited. Broadly speaking, operational auditing is characterized by problem seeking methods rather than eligibility of costs. One of the methods that I favor is work measurement for utilization of systems and equipment, and utilization of new equipment. The logic and the reality of the extension of the scope of internal auditing into operations was recognized when the statement of responsibilities of the internal auditor was revised in 1957. However, the concept was developed much earlier.

In the late 1940s, financial analysts and bankers showed a sharp rise in their desire for information suitable for management appraisal. Investors, governmental bodies, and many other groups had increasingly sought information by which the quality of management could be judged. As a result, the techniques of financial auditing were being applied more and more to the nonfinancial aspects of business operations and growing numbers of people became involved in this expanded scope of review and evaluation. In 1957, the Institute of Internal Auditors revised its statement of responsibilities to move internal auditing further towards operational auditing by lifting the restriction that internal audit deals primarily with accounting and financial matters.

Need filled by operational auditing

In most major American cities, traditional auditing techniques are employed. The historical audit approach does not require the accumulation of information which may lead to improving operations at a lower cost. As a matter of fact, the emphasis is primarily on whether cost has been properly spent in accordance with the appropriation.

In a large city, the mayor, finance director, and other top execu tives have too many responsibilities and too little time to act as information gatherers and problem finders. The various deputies, assistants, and others are normally used more for transmitting information than for generating and analyzing it. Since their terms of office and appointments may be relatively short, and some may have to run for reelection, their thinking may be motivated by political considerations.

These are the basic reasons why operational audits can be successful. Many functions in the cities have been relatively unchanged over a period of time, and there is no evidence of a thorough management review or any revision due to changing circumstances. These areas are most susceptible to the operational auditing technique. The heads of the departments many times do not have sufficient information about the various organizational elements of a city to make intelligent recommendations.

To illustrate, observation may show that a receiving department in the city is cramped for space. While the obvious correction might seem to the head of the department to be to enlarge the receiving area, this may not be the best solution for the city. The congestion in the receiving department may be only a symptom of lack of coordination, and the proper correction might be (1) better scheduling of incoming shipments by purchasing or traffic departments or (2) delivery of certain quantity shipments direct to storerooms or to using departments. Operational auditing appraises the entire problem as it relates to all of the organizational elements involved in this function, and does not limit itself to the department where the problem appears to exist.

Duration and cost of an operational audit

One of the better methods to determine duration and cost of an audit to be performed by an independent source is by obtaining a number of proposals from public accounting and management consulting firms to perform a survey to determine what areas would lend themselves to an operational audit. A firm should be selected to perform this survey. After results of the survey are completed, the firm would outline the results, and the controller would determine if there was a need for audit. If favorable, the controller, in consultation with the firm, would decide what areas will be covered, the length of time, and the cost.

Normally, no audit, in my opinion, should run much more than 120 person-days for any operational audit of a single department or function. The reason for a time limitation is that the objective of operational auditing is not to find all problems, but only those that are becoming or are likely to become economically significant.

The hourly rate should average between $30 and $40 an hour, and cost, say, between $10,000 and $12,000. This would result in a working budget of 500 to 600 hours for a single activity or department. When more than that time is spent, it is likely that a good deal more than the discovery and delineation of problems or opportunites has been undertaken.

Audit work plan

The recommended work plan by a firm for the audit of a function or department of a city includes the following activity phases:

1. Pre-performance preparation. This phase involves the general familiarization by the auditors with all the necessary background pertinent to the audit and includes:
   a. The development of essential information concerning the municipality, including working arrangements, responsibilities, operational and policy lines, approval levels and re-

porting requirements, and any other organizational and
functional aspects which may have a bearing on operations.

b. Reviewing all instructions, regulations, materials, and documents pertinent to all operational and audit areas, including all operating procedures, accounting and costing
policies, statistical accumulation, reports and work papers
of prior operational audits, and special reports to identify
pertinent operation practices, potential problems and/or
other items.

c. Evaluating the city's cost reports and related schedules
and work papers against the budget to identify those areas
and/or operations which necessitate special attention as
well as to tentatively determine the scope and extent of
audit coverage and testing.

2. Site orientation and survey. This phase involves the auditors'
orientation and survey of the city departments and its personnel, records, and facilities that will be involved in the audit and includes:

a. Holding an "entrance" conference with the city representatives and others to discuss the purpose, scope, timing, ac-
commodations, and modus operandi for the operational
audit.

b. Conducting an orientation session and physical tour of the
city's premises and operations to obtain familiarization
and identify vulnerable areas to facilitate performance of
the operational audit.

c. Performance of initial survey of the city's operations as
previously described.

d. Development of more detailed operational programs and
location time-phased plan based upon the results of the
surveys.

e. Establishing the permanent audit files based upon the information developed.

f. Preparing any special reports, recommendations or requests to the municipality regarding the survey findings
which necessitate action to facilitate continued audit.

3. Performance. This phase involves the actual performance of
the operational audit in those departments and functions
where it has been determined by both the controller and auditor that problems may exist as discussed above and includes:

a. General: (1) Developing approaches for accomplishing the
operational audit program, preparing related audit work
papers, and amassing supporting information and data; (2)
reviewing and analyzing designated records, documents,

files, taxes, etc.; (3) testing transactions, entries, and statistical data; (4) physical examination of certain equipment, inventories, and other resources; (5) determining
conformance and consistency of costs, allocations, distributions and data with city policies.

b. Specific: Carrying out aforementioned operational audit
programs pertaining to the following operations and departments providing survey disclosed potential problems:
(1) purchasing; (2) inventory control; (3) insurance; (4)
electronic data processing; (5) construction; (6) traffic; (7)
management information system; (8) advertising; (9) production; (10) organizational control; (11) accounting and financial areas.

4. Completion. This phase involves the conclusion activities of
each major operational audit area or location as well as for
the total audit, including the following:

a. Summarizing observations and recommendations, and formulating appropriate judgments and opinions for the report.

b. Preparing drafts of all required operational audit reports.

c. Reviewing, cross-referencing, and indexing the reports and
work papers.

d. Holding an "exit" conference with the representatives of
the city to advise them of the tentative result of the operational audit, and to obtain comments and/or agreement
with respect thereto.

e. Preparing and/or revising the required reports based on
the results of the operational audit and discussions with
those officials.

f. Final review and approval of the reports by a partner of
the CPA or management consulting firm for conformance
with professional standards before issuance of the final reports.

g. Issuance of the final reports.

5. Post operational audit. This phase relates to revising the
city's operational functions as may be requested by the city
controller.

Survey and quality of auditors

I can't stress sufficiently the imporance of a survey and qualified
auditors to perform a quality operational audit in a minimum of
time. At the risk of some repetition, this viewpoint will be clarified.

In performing the operational audits agreed to by the controller and the representative of the firm, the auditors should follow the
generally accepted approach by beginning with a survey of the city's
organization, accounting systems, and internal control mecha-

nisms. In this regard, they should analyze prior operational audit reports, tour the facilities, conduct interviews, make physical inspections, evaluate pertinent evidence and cross-reference the problems and issues for subsequent audit coverage.

The survey serves a vital purpose in creating the city's "permanent file" which should be updated with each subsequent operational audit. This takes on added significance as a source of important information and for saving audit time on subsequent operational audits of the same areas.

Generally the principal purposes of the survey will be to obtain a panoramic view of the city's operations and controls; develop background information, including the roles and identities of key personnel; identify additional actual and potential financial, managerial and operational problem areas; and determine whether and to what extent detailed audit tests may be required in each of the specific areas.

The audit survey charts the course for the operational audit. It sometimes can provide a clear enough view of operations to warrant immediate recommendations for action and the elimination of some tests traditionally considered essential. The time spent on the survey, therefore, is usually well repaid with a more economical audit and more informed personnel.

In the survey, the auditor gets to know the people, to understand the operations, and to focus on objectives, controls, and risks. The auditees' managers also benefit since they become acquainted with the direction and requirements for audit. Thus, an audit can be performed that is well planned, effective, and efficient—not just a haphazard traveling in unknown waters.

The success with surveys is derived from training and practice. This would enable the auditors to develop an understanding of what to look for, where to look for it, and how to document the results of their search. They are then able to draw a clear program to guide them toward their audit goals.

In performing this survey, the auditors should already understand the city's governing directives and other criteria to basically determine at each location and/or department involved:

1. What are its functions and activities?
2. Who does them?
3. Why are they done?
4. How are they done?
5. What are the financial, managerial and operational problem areas?

To develop survey information accurately, completely, and economically, certain qualities and abilities are required in the auditors:

1. They must be able to set a cooperative, participative tone for the survey during initial and final meetings with the auditees' staff.
2. They must have a clear understanding of the information they need, the sources for that information, and the various ways to obtain it. This especially includes pertinent survey material developed by others and basic operational and financial data.
3. They should be adept in the techniques of work measurement and flow charting so as to depict operation activities and control points to identify areas of survey and/or later operational audit concentration.
4. They must have an understanding of the auditees' program objectives (mission and purpose) and goals (measurable units to be achieved in meeting the objectives) and how to distinguish between the two.
5. They must understand the theory and applications of internal control, including both their false assurances and "overkill" possibilities.
6. They must know how to assess the capability, background, and training of people involved in department operations to recognize latent "people" causes of weakness in operations.
7. They must understand the principles of selective sampling and how and where to identify areas of greatest cost-benefit potential for detailed exploration.
8. They must appreciate the importance of an operational survey "permanent file" and how to develop and update it to serve the needs of future audits.
9. They must have the facility for anticipating the content of reports required by the city administration, which concisely but fully cover operational costs audited, suitable professional opinion cost adjustment, operational revisions, and identification of weakness.

Obtaining maximum benefits

In order for all local governments to benefit to the maximum degree from operational auditing, a mechanism should be used to convey the results of operational auditing in one city to other government entities. Keep looking for articles in publications of professional associations stressing some of the techniques and results of operational auditing. Another method that can be used to obtain maximum benefits is to have the audits performed by representatives of the federal, state, and local governments rather than an outside CPA or management consultant firm. For example, the "Get Set" audit in Philadelphia used this approach. I believe this was far more beneficial and done at considerably less cost by using the ad hoc government auditing team.

Cutting through the Fog of Management Auditing

G. Stephen Lloyd

In the past few years the terms "management audit" and "performance audit" have been appearing with increasing frequency in public administration literature. Like so many other concepts presented as panaceas for problems of state and local governments, management auditing is merely a repackaging of certain systematic actions that governmental officials should be using to improve services offered to the public. As this article will indicate, management auditing is what you want to make it. Consider the following definitions of management auditing:

1. A formal and systematic review by qualified individuals to determine the extent to which an organization, or a unit or function within it, is achieving the goals prescribed by management and to identify conditions in need of improvement. The forms that reviews take may include any or all of the following: analysis, evaluation, and description (American Institute of Certified Public Accountants).[1]
2. To assist agency management in attaining its goals by furnishing information, analysis, appraisals, and recommendations pertinent to management's duties and objectives (U.S. General Accounting Office).[2]

In essence, a management audit is a technique of systematically appraising an organization's effectiveness against appropriate standards and principles. Its objective is to assure those responsible for the organization that its aims are being carried out, and to iden-

Reprinted from *State and Local Government Review* 14 (January 1982): 20-24, by permission of Carl Vinson Institute of Government, University of Georgia, Athens, Georgia.

tify conditions for improvement. This definition leaves the whole concept open to whatever approach you want to use.

This article discusses some of the antecedents of management auditing, examines attempts in other fields that can be applied by local and state governments, reflects on the management auditing experiences of the author, and offers guidelines for local officials interested in developing their own management auditing program.

Some background

A review of information on management auditing provides some clues as to when the concept began to achieve its present status. William Leonard's 1962 book appears to be the first in which the term identifies the concept.[3] Leonard defines the management audit as "a comprehensive and constructive examination of an organizational structure of a . . . branch of government, or of any component thereof, such as a division or department, and its plans and objectives, its means of operation, and its use of human and physical facilities."[4]

The big push toward management auditing began in 1972 with the publication of GAO's *Standards for Audit of Governmental Organizations, Programs, Activities and Functions.*[5] The GAO *Standards* identified the three basic components of a comprehensive audit as follows: (1) the financial and compliance audit; (2) the economy and efficiency audit; and (3) the program results audit.

The first component is normally associated with the work of the financial auditor. The second component determines whether resources are being managed economically and efficiently and seeks to find the underlying causes of deficiencies. The focus here is on organizational structure, allocation and utilization of resources, and procedures. The third component focuses on program results—whether the organizational entity is achieving the expected results.

The GAO *Standards* contains guidelines for qualifying and maintaining the independence of the auditors, planning and conducting the audit, and reporting the results. As such, the guidelines are basic principles that leave the details of the audit programs up to the auditors and the entity being audited.

The publication of the *Standards* was followed by a flurry of activity in applying them to entire units of local government or to particular programs and activities. Beginning in 1973, the GAO and the International City Management Association (ICMA) organized a joint management audit project.[6] Thirteen government entities— 10 cities, 2 counties, and 1 council of governments—were selected to participate in the project. Each participating entity identified a program or activity it wanted audited. These programs ranged from the capital improvement process to a drug abuse program. The composition of the audit team varied from all local staff to a combination of local staff/GAO audit staff or local staff/outside consultant.

The auditing process also varied. One local jurisdiction emphasized gathering and analyzing statistical indicators of efficiency/economy and program results and commenting on deviations from self-imposed standards and objectives. Others took the standard analytical approach of reviewing existing operations and developing recommendations for improvement. For most, the project generated much ongoing interest, while others were not convinced that management auditing was the only way to go.

Although the GAO *Standards* project is perhaps the most recent attempt to apply certain management audit principles in the public sector, the roots of management auditing can be found in approaches outside local and state government circles. Two of the more well-known organizations attempting to upgrade programs through management auditing are the Joint Commission on Accreditation of Hospitals (JCAH) and several regional associations of colleges and schools. These organizations have done creditable jobs upgrading services and facilities of hospitals and educational institutions. Their importance to management auditing in local and state governments, however, lies in the approaches they use.

The JCAH approach is based on the use of certain published principles or standards.[7] An auditing team assesses the degree to which an institution meets these standards. Associations of schools and colleges use an approach consisting of three operations: (1) the self-study, during which the school evaluates itself; (2) the evaluation by an outside team, which lends objectivity to the process; and (3) the implementation stage, when the school implements those desirable modifications underlined by the evaluation.[8]

State and local governments would most certainly profit from the experience of the JCAH and the several associations of colleges and schools in conducting organizational evaluations. Both groups are consistent in their use of (1) principles or criteria to evaluate the institution, (2) the self-study approach, and (3) an outside evaluation team. But even without an outside team of experts, the self-study, using certain standards and criteria, would serve as an adequate incentive to spur the local or state unit to bring about organizational change.

Some recent experiences

Public Administration Service (PAS) has been requested to conduct management audits of the entire city governments of Farmington Hills, Michigan (population 56,000), and Garden City, Michigan (population 40,000).[9] In both cities, new home-rule charters were adopted with the following provisions:

Between the third and fourth year after the effective date of this Charter, the Council shall provide for a managerial audit of the functions of City government other than finance. Thereafter, periodically, but not less than once in each five years, the Council shall provide for a managerial audit of the functions of City government other than finances. Such audits shall be conducted by an independent consultant or consultants chosen by the Council. The Council shall determine the scope of the audit and the nature of the report to be presented to the Council.

Before going any further, it is important to note that those drafting the new charters had the foresight to include a provision for a regular managerial audit. It is presumed that the purpose of the provision is to ensure that the principles for which the new organization was established are still valid some years hence.

In both cities, the city councils determined the scope of the audits to include all city government programs and activities. In one city, the audit also included attitude surveys from employees and citizens. Thus, the city council obtained different perceptions of its city government—from auditors, employees, and citizens.

The role of the auditors   In planning for a management audit, several factors must be considered: (1) the composition of the audit team; (2) the scope of the audit and methods of conducting the audit; and (3) the reporting requirements.

Before beginning the audit, prepare a checklist—a series of questions to help determine whether or not your city's programs are being managed properly. If you don't have specific questions prepared, the audit will either lack uniformity or contain generalities. The accompanying checklist contains sample questions used in auditing the general organization and management function.

The audit team should consist of four members: (1) a team supervisor, who has expertise in general organization and management as well as some closely allied programs; (2) a finance specialist; (3) a public safety specialist; and (4) a public works specialist. If none of these people has skills in survey research, a fifth team member with these skills is needed to conduct the employee and citizen attitude surveys.

As stated in the GAO *Standards*, it is imperative that "the auditors assigned to perform the audit must collectively possess adequate professional proficiency for the tasks required."[10] An audit team should speak the language of those undergoing scrutiny, particularly if the team is conducting the initial management audit. If the audit team members do not have practical experience in the important program areas, the credibility of the audit suffers. The audit is perhaps one of the few opportunities for a department head to discuss accomplishments and problems with someone who has been in similar circumstances. This peer review process should not be taken lightly.

With respect to scope of the audit, the PAS commitment was to examine almost all facets of the operations. Although we were able to establish a basic understanding of all municipal operations, it was neither possible nor necessary to delve deeply into them.

Rather, the commitment, and the approach, was to compare operations with principles of municipal administration to determine the
more obvious strengths, weaknesses, and areas for improvement.
This approach is simply a way to get to the center of the organization's problems and to avoid trivialities. The site visits conducted by
the associations of schools and colleges last approximately three to
four days, leaving little time for detailed analysis of operating practices.

   Once the audit has been completed, reports should be made in
the following ways. The audit team should brief the administrator,
and perhaps a council audit committee, on the significant findings
uncovered during the week. A final written report should then follow.

**Sample of checklist questions used to audit a city's general
organization and management function**

1. Is the charter sufficiently broad to allow for internal organiza-
    tional changes without requiring a charter amendment?
2. Is the council forbidden by charter or ordinance from directing
    subordinate administrative officials other than through the
    chief administrator?
3. Is the span of control of the chief administrator sufficient to
    allow him/her to attend to external responsibilities (relations
    with the council, the community, other governmental officials,
    etc.) as well as to administer the day-to-day functions of city
    government?
4. Are the duties and responsibilities of all department heads and
    supervisory employees clearly defined and their relationships
    set forth in organizational charts and written instructions (by
    ordinance or administrative code)?
5. Have certain auxiliary functions been centralized, e.g., pur-
    chasing, automotive maintenance, building maintenance, print-
    ing and duplicating, and data processing?
6. Have you established in-service training for supervisors and
    other employees?
7. Do you hold regular staff meetings with department heads to
    communicate matters of interest and to coordinate their activi-
    ties?
8. Are department heads required to submit monthly or periodic
    reports to the chief administrator, and do these reports relate
    work accomplishments to annual objectives and budgeted pro-
    grams?
9. Are budget estimates prepared on the basis of annual objec-
    tives and work programs, and do they relate to measurable
    standards of performance where possible?
10. Have you established a performance evaluation system for de-
    partment managers which reflects their duties and responsibil-
    ities and performance objectives?

The report should be balanced. It should contain the most significant findings and recommendations for improvement. And it should point out programs and activities that are being conducted in accordance with high standards of municipal government. Detailed recommendations for operating practices, such as police beat design, fire ground procedures, street patching practices, and the like clearly would be inappropriate to the main thrust of the audit.

The attitude surveys After conducting more than 30 employee attitude surveys in conjunction with management audits and more detailed studies, we have found they give valuable insights into the operations of municipal government. This is particularly so when they are correlated with the auditors' findings brought out during the management audit. Our experience to date indicates that more than half the employees contacted are willing to respond. In some jurisdictions the figure approaches 100 percent.

The purpose of the employee attitude survey is to tap, in a relatively systematic way, the attitudes of employees about themselves, their jobs, working conditions, and the people of the community they serve. The employee attitude survey seeks to identify those problems perceived by employees that, if not resolved in the present, may lead to organizational problems in the future. The survey instrument should be constructed using three primary sources of information: (1) the experience of the management auditors in conducting similar surveys among other groups of municipal employees; (2) the audit team's initial observations during the field visit; and (3) the comments and suggestions of the government's administrators.

The survey instrument itself should be given to all permanent employees, with an introductory cover letter and stamped self-addressed envelope. Although the survey may request information about an employee's department, age, education, etc., the respondents do not give their names. All survey responses remain confidential.

If the management audit is to encompass the full range of topics, surveys of the attitudes of employees and citizens toward their municipal government should be included. Some municipal officials may feel that the majority of citizens have no idea what is going on and therefore could make no important contribution on ways to improve services. Other officials point to problems in conducting the survey that strike at its validity. Despite the usual reservations and problems surrounding citizen surveys, both the citizen attitude survey and the employee attitude survey are important components of a comprehensive management audit. Both can be conducted quickly and inexpensively using proven survey research techniques.

The third component of the management audit is the citizen

attitude survey. Gradually, the sample survey of municipality residents is becoming a tool widely used by municipal officials. Well-designed surveys conducted among randomly selected city residents can provide officials with citizens' evaluations of past or present municipal programs. The surveys can also indicate the directions the public would like to see pursued in the future.

The instrument used in a citizen survey should be developed in consultation with local officials, particularly members of the governing body. In our experience, the telephone interview is the most efficient method, with each interview lasting approximately 15 minutes. All interviewers in the cities where we have used this approach have been community residents hired, trained, and supervised by a member of the audit team.

The response to a citizen attitude survey has been noteworthy. In one community we audited, a random sample of 707 residents were telephoned during two evening sessions. Of those called, 442 (62.5 percent) completed surveys while 265 (37.5 percent) declined to be interviewed. This rate is comparable to rates encountered in other telephone survey projects.

Time requirements   The time involved in conducting the audit depends on the audit scope and the amount of staff resources you can devote to the audit. If the audit is intended to be a spot check of all functions, a massive commitment of staff resources is unnecessary. In a medium-sized city of 40,000, a period of 20 to 25 staff days is required to gather the necessary data to complete the checklists and obtain answers to the second level of questions. If you have an audit team of four, the elapsed time can be decreased appreciably. You should count on another 15 days for writing the audit report and presenting your findings.

A citizen survey yielding about 450 responses will require about five days for the actual survey and five to seven days for analysis and presentation of results. The time to analyze and present the results of the employee survey depends on the number of responses. A good figure to use is about seven days for a city with 300 employees.

To complete a management audit of all governmental departments in a city of 40,000 with 300 employees, including the use of an employee survey and a citizen survey, should require between 50 and 60 staff days.

How to proceed on your own

Although most of the management audit can be conducted with in-house staff, it may be advisable to use outside assistance on the employee and citizen surveys. The city council and staff should certainly indicate the topics they want the surveys to cover, but there is a difference between what should be asked and how the questions should be worded. Most cities are simply not equipped technically to conduct the surveys and analyze the results.

If you decide to do a management audit without outside assistance, you should assign someone in the organization to put together checklists for each of the functions, to develop the employee and citizen surveys, and to coordinate all aspects of the audit. This may be easier said than done unless you have someone within the organization you feel is qualified to do these things. After you have developed checklists, survey instruments, and approaches, you should tell the department heads what is going to take place. This simply means that you should review the checklists with each department head, solicit his or her suggestions and comments, and establish a timetable for completion. Since this will be a self-audit, the department head must be thoroughly briefed on items pertaining to his or her department.

The next step is to conduct the actual audit; that is, to complete the checklists, conduct the two surveys, and write the report. The results coming from the checklists will probably be mixed, but you should stress ahead of time that you are not looking for simple yes or no answers. You want explanations. For example, if your finance officer says he is making cash projections, make sure he indicates how he is doing it. The chief administrator may know what the finance officer does, but those outside management, e.g., the council members, may not.

The management audit coordinator should combine the results of the checklists and surveys and write a report to the chief administrator and the council. The chief administrator should establish some priorities for addressing the problems uncovered by the audit, and the department head should agree on these priorities.

Conclusion

Essentially a management audit is simply an attempt to determine if an organization is doing what it is supposed to and doing it properly. In conducting management audits at the local government level, we learned the following lessons:

1. A management audit is what the name implies. It is a brief and inexpensive way to assess the health of a local government.
2. Management audit concepts can be applied with or without outside assistance. Peer contact and review are as important as any other part of the management audit.
3. The audit should be structured and formalized. The development and use of checklists facilitates the audit process.
4. The audit should identify strengths as well as weaknesses, resulting in a balanced accounting of the organization.

5.   Employee and citizen attitude surveys are important components of a management audit. They assist the jurisdiction in obtaining the perceptions of employees and citizens about the local unit. And they can be conducted inexpensively using proven survey research techniques.

Management audits are no panacea—they rarely offer simple solutions. The problems uncovered cannot usually be resolved without considerable effort. Nevertheless, the management audit, if properly conducted, does provide local officials with a reliable means of assessing organizational performance in light of contemporary standards. It is another tool for the progressive community to use in upgrading its services.

1.   Eifler, Thomas. "Performing the Operations Audit," *Management Education Portfolio.* New York City: American Institute of Certified Public Accountants Professional Development Division, 1974.
2.   U.S. General Accounting Office. *Internal Auditing in Federal Agencies.* Washington, D.C.: U.S. General Accounting Office, 1974, p. 1.
3.   Leonard, William P. *The Management Audit: An Appraisal of Management Methods and Performance.* Englewood Cliffs, New Jersey: Prentice-Hall, 1962.
4.   Ibid., p. 35.
5.   Comptroller General of the United States. *Standards for Audit of Governmental Organizations, Programs, Activities and Functions.* Washington, D.C.: Government Printing Office, 1972.
6.   Management Information Service. *Performance Audits in Local Governments—Benefits, Problems, and Challenges.* Washington, D.C.: International City Management Association, April, 1976.
7.   Accreditation Council for Psychiatric Facilities. *Principles for Accreditation of Community Mental Health Services Programs.* Chicago: Joint Commission on Accreditation of Hospitals, 1976.
8.   Commission on Schools, North Central Association. *The NCA Guide for School Evaluation: A Workbook for the Self-Study and Team Visit.* Boulder: North Central Association of Colleges and Schools, 1976.
9.   Public Administration Service. *Organization and Management of the City of Farmington Hills, Michigan: A Managerial Audit.* Chicago: Public Administration Service, 1977; and *Organization and Management of the City of Garden City, Michigan: A Managerial Audit.* Chicago: Public Administration Service, 1979.
10.   Comptroller General of the United States, p. 13.

Other references

Institute of Government, University of Georgia. *Internal Control Checklist: Optimizing the Flow and Control of Revenues and Expenditures.* Athens: Institute of Government, 1978.

International City Managers' Association. *Checklist on How to Improve Municipal Services.* Chicago: International City Managers' Association, 1958.

Kimball, Warren Y. *How to Judge Your Fire Department: 500 Questions with Commentary.* Boston: National Fire Protection Association, 1972.

National Advisory Commission on Criminal Justice Standards and Goals. *Report on Police.* Washington, D.C.: U.S. Government Printing Office, January, 1973.

Costing Municipal Services

Ross C. Kory and Philip Rosenberg

Budget cuts, high interest costs, reductions in intergovernmental transfers. More and more, large and small governments face fiscal problems like these. In this environment, local officials seek to improve government output, develop alternative revenue sources and shrink the budget. Consider the possible approaches to coping with fiscal stress. Would you: Reduce services and personnel? Initiate or increase user fees and charges? Sell underutilized or worn-out equipment? Develop a productivity improvement plan? Contract with the private sector to perform certain services?

Unfortunately, these alternatives pose a difficult choice for policy-makers, finance officers and department heads. Clearly, a variety of elements must be considered before a decision is made. Cost, however, is an underlying factor in all these questions necessary for wise decision making:

1. How much does it cost to provide the service?
2. Is the cost of maintaining a piece of equipment more or less than replacing it?
3. Is it cheaper to have a private contractor perform the work?
4. Is the cost per unit of service output increasing or decreasing?
5. How much do we save by cutting a program?

Good cost information, essential to answering all these questions, accurately reflects the total financial resources necessary to provide government goods and services. This article develops a framework on which government officials can collect accurate, com-

Reprinted with permission from *Governmental Finance*, March 1982.

plete cost information and use those data to support sound management decisions.

Two basic components help determine the cost of government activities and services. First, there must be an accounting for the use as opposed to the purchase of resources. Second, to make cost figures meaningful, they must be related to some type of output measure.

Generally accepted accounting principles (GAAP) require the collection of financial information on an *expenditure* rather than *expense* basis for general fund activities. An expenditure is a charge incurred when goods and services are acquired. Our concern here, however, is not with the purchase of items. Rather, our focus is on the total *cost* incurred to carry out an activity or provide a service and its relationship to the cost per unit produced. So it is necessary to collect expense data that relate to the *use* of goods and services.

Historically, local governments gathered cost data for municipal enterprises such as water, sewer, power and light and hospitals because of the businesslike nature of these services. In these examples, financial information is recorded for revenues earned and expenses or costs incurred, and these costs are converted from a general responsibility area (e.g., hospital) to a direct service or category (outpatient clinic). Determining the cost for activities within the general fund is more difficult.

To determine the cost of government services, it becomes necessary to convert expenditures to expense data. This is a two-step process. First, translate expenditure data into expense data; and second, convert those data from the general responsibility area to the direct service or activity areas, as in business-type municipal enterprises.

The traditional method of converting expenditure data to expense data is cost accounting, "that method of accounting which provides for assembling and recording of all the elements of cost incurred to accomplish a purpose, to carry on an activity or operation, or to complete a unit of work or a specific job."[1]

Cost accounting—also called managerial accounting—is an ongoing process which collects, classifies, analyzes, records and summarizes cost data for the user within a formal cost accounting system. It may be job-related, as in the use of construction projects, or process-oriented, relating to services or activities.

It might seem that any attempt to collect cost data for municipal activities is too difficult to undertake. A less rigorous approach is cost finding, ". . . a less formal method of cost determination or estimation on an irregular basis. There may be no formal accounting entries during the year to record costs incurred in specific cost accounts. Instead, cost finding usually involves taking available fund financial accounting data and recasting and adjusting it to derive the cost data or estimate needed."[2]

In other words, cost finding is the process of utilizing available financial data, or finding costs from budget details, the budgetary accounting system, analysis of detailed transactions (such as payroll records, invoices, store requisitions and contracts) and interviews with staff. These data are collected, assembled on worksheets and analyzed to determine costs for units of service or projects.

All expenditures eventually become expenses, but sometimes there is a significant time lag between the incurrence of an expenditure and the associated expense. As a result, three different sorts of transactions are possible:

1. The expenditure and the expense occur simultaneously or near enough in time not to be usefully differentiated.
2. An expenditure of the current period will not become an expense until a future period. This is an expenditure that is not an expense.
3. An expenditure of a previous period becomes an expense during the current period. This is an expense that is not an expenditure.

For most transactions, including payroll and purchases for current consumption, the expense and the expenditure are equivalent. To illustrate how these different transactions relate to converting expenditure to expense, Exhibit 1 is a review of the FY 1981 snow removal program for Peoplesville, USA.

FY 1981 expenditures for the snow removal program equaled $95,000, which included labor, materials and supplies, agreements with private contractors to remove snow and vehicle purchase. Several calculations are needed to determine the expense or cost of operating the snow removal program in FY 1981.

First, identify items acquired in FY 1981 that will benefit future periods and deduct those expenditures from the FY 1981 total expenditure. In this case, the purchase of a new vehicle for $20,000 must be capitalized. Further, the public works director took advan-

Total FY 1981 expenditures	$95,000
Less: Purchase of new vehicles	(20,000)
Purchase of supplies at end of year for use in FY 1982	(2,000)
Purchase of salt and sand for use in FY 1982 and FY 1983	(10,000)
Plus: Depreciation on building and vehicles purchased	15,000
Materials purchased in FY 1980 used in FY 1981	2,000
Total FY 1981 costs	$80,000

Exhibit 1. Peoplesville snow removal program.

tage of an opportunity to save money by purchasing in bulk a three-year supply of salt and sand. The $10,000 portion of the bulk purchase not consumed in FY 1981 is deducted from the current period. In addition, an expenditure of $2,000 for supplies not used in FY 1981 must be deducted.

Second, we must include in the total cost for FY 1981 items purchased in previous periods and consumed in FY 1981. Depreciation on the portion of the public works garage applicable to the snow removal program and snow removal vehicles is $15,000. Further, materials purchased in FY 1980 but used in FY 1981 are valued at $2,000.

Based on this simplistic analysis, the cost of the snow removal program in FY 1981 is $80,000 compared to program expenditures of $95,000. Knowing the difference between expenditures and expenses is critical to the questions posed earlier. For example, if the full purchase price of the vehicles and the bulk purchase of salt and sand were included in the program cost for FY 1981, the view of program operations could be distorted.

Allocating personal services, materials and supplies must be approached with caution. Personal services constitute more than 70 percent of the total budget in most departments, so it is essential to be as accurate as possible when calculating the true dollar amount for personal services. Some factors that can cause distortion are:

1. A position is vacant for the first nine months of the fiscal year.
2. A long-term sickness causes the hiring of a temporary worker paid through a contract and not charged to the personal services account.
3. Pay increases often occur randomly through the fiscal year, yet have full-year cost implications for the next year.
4. A peak load demand requires an outside contractor to perform an activity normally undertaken by the municipal work force.
5. Payroll records may not show an employee temporarily on loan to another activity.

Governments often budget on the obligation basis. That is, budget limits are enforced on the basis of purchase orders and contracts issued (i.e., encumbrances). At the end of the fiscal year there may be a significant dollar value of open purchase orders and contracts outstanding. These amounts are neither expenditures nor costs to the government. So the actual or estimated amounts of open encumbrances should be eliminated from cost calculations. Often, however, these amounts do not vary greatly from year to year, and, if this is the case, eliminating open encumbrances might be more trouble than increased accuracy warrants.

So far this article has focused on the direct costs associated with service delivery. After determining the direct costs, the indirect cost must be allocated to the organization(s) providing the services being measured. Knowing the direct cost of snow removal does not indicate the full cost of the snow removal program. In Peoplesville indirect costs consist of significant items like fringe benefits and pensions as well as central support services like administration and finance. These elements can considerably increase service cost. Exhibit 2 depicts the flow of costs through the Peoplesville government to the sanitation division of the department of public works.

No rule specifies what is a direct or indirect cost. Depending on the operating environment, a cost might be considered either direct or indirect. For example, if all fringe benefits are budgeted and recorded in each operating division, fringes should be treated as direct costs of the division. If they are budgeted and recorded in a central expenditure account, they may be allocated as indirect costs.

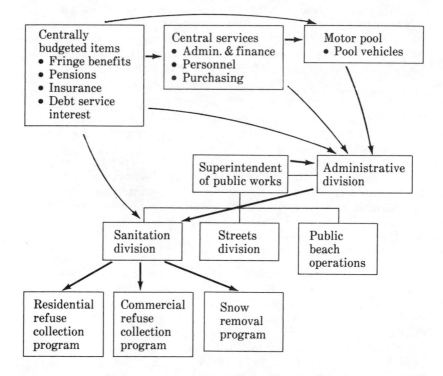

Exhibit 2. Cost flow through the Peoplesville government.

In Exhibit 2, note the relationships among the government's various indirect costs. The motor pool, which provides support to public works, receives support from other central support functions; these central services also provide direct support to public works. Step-down allocation, a technique for reflecting these relationships, is used to determine an indirect cost rate for various municipal programs.

Using Exhibit 2 as a guide, the following steps should be taken to determine the full cost of the snow removal program.

Step 1: Allocate the costs of items centrally budgeted and accounted for to each organizational unit involved in the study. For example, fringe benefits must be allocated to central services departments, the motor pool and each of the public works divisions. This will produce the full cost of central services and the motor pool.

Step 2: Next, allocate the full cost of central services and the motor pool to the public works department, in total. This will produce the city-wide overhead component of the department of public works overhead costs.

Step 3: Allocate the department overhead costs—consisting of the cost of the superintendent's office, the administrative division and city-wide overhead—to the operating division.

Step 4: Finally, allocate the full cost of the sanitation division obtained in Step 3 to the three services provided by the division.

The methods outlined above are appropriate for costing a wide variety of ongoing government services. In some special situations, however, it is impossible to simply develop historical cost data for a particular service. In such cases, consider performing a study to directly measure the cost of the activity in question.

For example, to determine the cost of issuing a building permit for a particular $500,000 office building:

1. Record the actual time building department staff spend on the project.
2. Record direct supplies, materials and other expenses (e.g., travel, if necessary).
3. Determine the full hourly cost of time spent by city personnel by developing a factor that reflects fringe benefits and the cost of actual hours worked versus hours paid.
4. Develop factors for the variable components of indirect cost, such as secretarial support, reproduction costs, etc.
5. Develop factors for other components of indirect cost to reflect utilities, depreciation and other city-wide overhead expenses.
6. Finally, calculate the cost of the project by applying these factors according to reasonable allocation bases.

This approach could also be used on more extensive job-type activities undertaken by the government—for instance, determining the cost of a specific street and sidewalk repair job estimated for completion in one month.

Making cost data meaningful

Earlier it was noted that to make cost information meaningful, financial resources must be related to output or work load. To know that trash collection cost $450,000 last year gives a limited view of what taxpayers are receiving in return for their tax dollars. Statements such as "residential refuse collection cost $40 per residence or $80 per ton last year" gives added meaning to how the sanitation department performs this function.

The formula for calculating unit costs may be stated as:

$$\frac{\text{Investment}}{\text{Output}} = \text{Unit cost}$$

Suppose that in Peoplesville, residential refuse collection cost the public works department $235,000. The amount includes direct costs such as salaries, depreciation of garbage trucks, supplies, etc., and indirect costs such as utilities, payroll, fringe benefits, etc.

Peoplesville has 5,910 residences. Dividing the total cost for 1981 (investment) by the number of residential households (output) yields an annual, per household cost of $39.76 (unit cost).

Cost-per-unit information takes on added meaning when compared to neighboring jurisdictions, national standards, prior years, existing fees and charges for the services and the private-sector cost for comparable service.

In determining the cost of service, it is essential to properly define what is to be measured. Failure to properly define the meaningful output for each activity to be measured produces misleading or useless information. For example, is there more interest in the cost per lawn mowed or the cost per acre mowed? To guide the selection of proper output measures, governmental activities may be defined as either *job order* or *process*.

Job order costing should be used when the activities performed are atypical or dissimilar within a cost center. Job costs relate to a well-defined, specific piece of work—a job. Construction and improvement projects, maintenance activities, vehicle repair and grant activities are typical job orders.

Process costs are uniform costs associated with a continuous operation. They refer to ongoing or routine municipal services. Typical examples include trash collection, water and sewer service, police protection, data processing and accounting.

The key distinction between job order and process costs is that the cost of job-type activities varies significantly from job to job, while the cost of process-type services basically remains constant. For example, the cost of a curb replacement program is a function of the length of the curb being replaced. Determining program cost on a cost-per-replacement basis would be misleading because it would not distinguish between a replacement job of 50 linear feet and 10 linear feet. In this example, a much more accurate measurement would be cost per linear foot or cost per cubic yard of concrete used.

It is important to select service measures where data are readily obtainable and meet management needs. In setting user charges for residential refuse collection, it would be more appropriate to collect cost data on a cost-per-residential-household basis rather than by cost per ton or cost per cubic yard of trash collected.

Contrasting cost per residential household and cost per ton illustrates how the unit of measure can affect the cost-finding exercise. The sanitation division might collect refuse from residences and commercial establishments. To determine the actual cost per residence, classify the costs of the refuse collection program into two categories, residential and commercial, to eliminate commercial collection costs from the total. This classification is unnecessary in determining cost per ton irrespective of whether refuse is from residences or businesses.

A middle position would be to calculate the cost per pickup, ignoring the perhaps significant differences between commercial and residential pickups. Such an approach might be appropriate in the smallest jurisdictions; but in general, the costs of commercial refuse collection are different enough to justify separate analysis. Also, localities will have an easier time charging residences and businesses full cost for refuse collection.

Using cost information
Sound cost information can be used in a variety of government decisions, including user fees and charges, privatization and budget.

User fees and charges   Increasingly, local governments are turning to user fees and charges in efforts to diversify their revenue bases. California has witnessed a tremendous increase in pricing local government goods and services. With the enactment of Proposition 2½, Massachusetts towns and cities are likewise considering increases in user fees and charges. Knowing the cost of providing a service provides one basis to establish a fee or charge. Although local officials might find that the true cost of providing a service is far beyond what they would consider charging the public—or beyond what state law would permit—accurate cost information provides the foundation to determine public policy issues such as rate setting, general tax levy support for the activity, user's ability to pay, cost by type of user and cost and method of collection.

Further, cost information permits public officials to present the citizenry a clear understanding of the diverse and perhaps substantial financial resources necessary to support service provision.

Privatization   A number of local governments ask the private sector to furnish goods and services traditionally provided by the public sector. Garbage collection and solid waste disposal, transit systems and police and fire protection offer examples of service areas generally available from the private sector.

A community must consider many factors when making the decision to contract out for services. Cost is a prime management consideration. Can the private sector provide the service at a lower cost than the public sector? Will it be cheaper for the city to buy the service than to provide it with city resources?

Cost finding can help answer these questions. If the XYZ Refuse Company can provide residential collection at an annual cost of $30 per household, and Peoplesville collection costs $40 per household, it *appears* that contracting with the XYZ Refuse Company can save the city $10 per household in the contract's first year.

For Peoplesville officials to determine the least costly option, cost analysis would indicate the fixed and variable costs in the refuse collection operation. If fixed costs (those costs that remain after the work has been contracted out) exceed $10 per household, it may be less expensive for Peoplesville to continue providing the service. Officials must project, however, what fixed costs will be for future years to understand the long-term cost impact of their decision.

A budgetary tool   Cost data gathered with data collected during the year provide a basis for developing next year's budget. Cost data used with conventional budgeting techniques allow local officials to structure budgets based on anticipated personnel and equipment needs, projected service levels and attendant support costs.

In some communities, departments are asked to spend no more than they did in the prior year. Clearly, some departments require more money than last year, and some might be able to perform their functions with less. Unit cost analysis, together with projections of service levels and anticipated revenues, offers a more rational approach to budget deliberations than the traditional incremental and across-the-board level funding approaches.

Cost data give local officials an excellent data base to analyze personnel, equipment and productivity as well as budgetary impacts of various management decisions.

For example, cost analysis might disclose whether one additional refuse collector increases or decreases the collection cost per unit. It might show an excessive cost for operating a particular truck, or point out that a new truck will be cheaper than the cost of repairing an existing truck. Or, it might show that modest increases in service delivery will result in dramatic increases in operating expenses.

In this era of federal aid reductions, cost-finding data will provide a basis to determine the full impact of funding cuts on service delivery. Further, if the jurisdiction wishes to continue the service, it will have a basis to determine the additional local investment necessary to sustain the service.

Understanding that certain departments share costs in service delivery might help guide the budget allocation process. For example, the recreation department and the public works department might jointly provide personnel and equipment for municipal tennis courts. If a budget cut in the public works budget diminishes the department's capacity to maintain and repair the tennis courts, the recreation department might be prevented from operating a tennis instruction program.

Comparing results to plan   Monitoring unit costs to internally set standards allows managers to compare current unit costs to those of prior years. Historical comparisons help determine how various programs perform over time. If costs are up and output is down, management must pinpoint trouble spots and take corrective action.

Once the cost of producing a unit of service is known, there is a basis to determine the efficiency of program or departmental operations. Efficiency measurements indicate how well an activity is being carried out. For example, if the cost per residential unit for trash collection was $41 in 1980 and $48 in 1981, management should know why this cost increase occurred before it is passed on to the user. Was there a general pay raise? Was major equipment purchased? Were employee benefits increased? Did inflation drive up general operating costs? Answers to these and similar questions give top management a basis to determine the efficiency of the refuse collection program.

Variance analysis—the determination of the amount, nature and cause of differences between planned and actual output—is used to compare planned output with actual output. It requires determining planned output for each cost element so management has a basis to compare *what is* with *what ought to be*. For example, here is a simple illustration of cost variance for a tree planting program:

Planned budget:	50 trees @ $80/tree	=	$4,000
Actual cost:	50 trees @ $90/tree	=	$4,500
Variance:			$ 500

This information can be further broken down (see accompanying box).

	Planned cost/unit	Actual cost	Variance
Materials	1 tree @ $60 = $60	1 tree @ $65 = $65	$5
Labor	1 hour @ $20 = $20	1¼ hrs. @ $20 = $25	$5
Total cost/unit	$80	$90	$10

The analysis shows the tree planting program was $500 over budget. This excess is attributed to the additional $10 to plant each tree. Further analysis indicates that cost per tree increased $5, and an additional one-quarter hour of labor was required to plant each tree. Once management has isolated where and why costs increased or decreased, corrective action can be taken. For example, management might concern itself with why additional time was required to plant each tree. Is the program operating less efficiently? This could be the case, but more detailed analysis is necessary.

A closing thought

Costing municipal services emphasizes unit costs. It focuses attention on production volume and efficiency, not quality. To achieve higher quality might require increased unit cost. This factor should not be forgotten in efforts to make government operations more cost effective.[3]

1. *Governmental Accounting, Auditing, and Financial Reporting*, Municipal Finance Officers Association of the United States and Canada (Chicago, IL: 1980), Appendix B, p. 59.
2. William W. Holder, Robert J. Freeman and Harold H. Hensold, Jr., "Cost Accounting and Analysis in State and Local Governments," *Cost and Managerial Accountants Hand-*book, Dow Jones-Irwin (New York, NY: 1979), p. 797.
3. The authors wish to thank the Executive Office of Communities and Development of the Commonwealth of Massachusetts for its support in the development of *Costing and Pricing Municipal Services*, the book on which this article was based.

PART 2

Revenue Management and Forecasting Techniques

Strategies for Conducting a Revenue Survey

John Matzer, Jr.

Periodic revenue surveys are a technique for maintaining an effective local government revenue system. A properly designed and administered revenue survey provides the mechanism for evaluating the adequacy of the existing revenue structure and identifying new sources of revenue. Constant reappraisal of revenue sources contributes to a diversified and current revenue system and is a major component of sound financial planning.

A primary objective of a revenue survey is improvement of the revenue system and a better understanding of the revenue structure. Revenue surveys produce the empirical information local officials need to choose among alternative methods for improving the revenue system, including increased rates, base modification, and more effective methods of revenue collection and administration.

Benefits of revenue surveys

A comprehensive revenue survey has several benefits. First, it gives visibility to local government's most needed resource. The survey will identify erratic revenue sources and will provide information on possible inequities due to high levels of evasion or use of regressive rates or revenue bases. Information gathered during the survey helps decrease arbitrariness and unfairness in the revenue system. The survey also focuses public attention on the importance of revenues and demonstrates local officials' commitment to financial planning and management. Multi-year trend analyses and jurisdictional comparisons produce valuable information on the performance and appropriateness of specific revenue sources.

A second benefit of a revenue survey is that it highlights weaknesses of the present revenue system. It provides information on the adequacy of rates, bases, yield, and administrative procedures and on the extent to which the system is diversified. It also exposes collection problems, excessive administrative costs, lack of adequate penalties, the extent of evasion and delinquencies, and inadequacies in revenue records and accounting. Survey results can be used to formulate recommendations to correct weaknesses and support necessary improvements in the system.

Survey administration

Several approaches are available for conducting a revenue survey. A city can use existing staff, a consultant, a citizens' committee, or administrative interns.

The staff approach offers the advantage of involving individuals who are familiar with the existing revenue system and sources. An individual staff member or a task force may be given the assignment. Weaknesses of the staff approach are competition for staff time from other important duties, bias toward the present system, and unavailability of skilled staff.

The retention of a consultant offers the benefit of professional specialization, experience, and objectivity. This approach may be the most effective but has the disadvantage of higher cost. If the existing revenue system is poorly constructed and adequate records are unavailable, the consultant will require a commitment of staff time, which will add to the cost. It is a good practice in any case to assign a staff member to provide assistance to the consultant, to monitor the survey work, and to learn the methodology in order to maintain the system that is developed. Another problem associated with the use of a consultant is the natural resistance to change from the staff.

A third approach, the use of a citizens' committee, offers an opportunity for citizen participation in an area of prime concern and provides the local government with expertise not available inside the organization. Citizens' committees offer the advantage of building community support for the recommendations. Disadvantages include the need to provide staff assistance and the potential political implications. Without proper staffing and guidelines, a citizens' committee may stray from the principal objective of the survey and become highly political.

A fourth approach is the use of administrative interns. Many public administration graduate programs require internships, and graduate students are eager to obtain practical experience. An advantage of this approach is that students are often trained in the use of research methods and know how to design questionnaires, select statistically accurate samples, and analyze survey findings. Interns also may have access to university computer facilities and academic experts. The local government is generally able to obtain talented staff at minimal expense. This approach is limited by the need for more than an average amount of direction and supervision. Some staff time will be required to orient, direct, and monitor the work of the interns.

These approaches also may be combined. Each governmental unit should select an approach that best meets local conditions. The basic objective is to conduct a survey that provides complete and accurate information.

Collection of data

The first step in conducting a revenue survey is the collection of data. Initially every effort should be made to search existing records for previous revenue studies. Discussions with staff involved in the revenue system, including revenue managers, cashiers, and accounting personnel, can produce valuable information on revenue performance and suggestions on where improvements may be needed. Operating personnel in the departments are often overlooked as a source of information on revenues. They are in an excellent position to evaluate existing revenue sources as well as to recommend new sources.

The next step is to examine the revenue classification system and the revenue records. A system that consolidates all types of a specific source of revenue such as licenses and permits makes it difficult to gather information on specific licenses and permits without undertaking the horrendous task of constructing historical data by examining receipts and card files. Data collection is greatly simplified if the revenue classification and accounting systems accumulate yield data for each specific source of revenue rather than broad classes of revenues such as fines or taxes.

Detailed revenue records, a revenue manual, and estimating files are critical to effective revenue management and analysis. A revenue manual simplifies data collection because it provides information on the legal basis, yield over a five- or ten-year period, rates, bases, administrative costs and procedures, extent of delinquencies, and unique problems such as extent of exemptions and waivers and the amount of penalties for each specific source of revenue. An estimating file includes historical information on revenue estimates and forecasting method, which facilitates a comparison of estimated and actual collections.

Depending on the availability of data, a decision must be made as to the revenues to be included in the survey. One approach is to select five or ten of the most productive revenues based on a five- or ten-year trend analysis. Another approach is to select a particular revenue category, such as business licenses, that has not been reviewed for several years. The amount of staff time needed and availability of information will directly influence the coverage of the survey.

Familiarization with state and local laws is an important part of the process because it provides data on the legality of revenue sources. State constitutional, charter, or other statutory action is generally required to authorize a revenue source. Identification of illegal revenues is often a side effect of a revenue survey along with the discovery of authorized sources not being levied.

Every effort should be made to thoroughly examine the revenues selected for the survey. This involves gathering information on the legal basis, yield over a ten-year period, extent to which rates and bases have been adjusted, amount of delinquencies or evasion, collection, and other administrative problems including cost.

Once detailed information is collected on existing revenues selected for the survey, a questionnaire should be designed to collect information from other governmental units. Information on what other cities are doing can also be obtained from state leagues of municipalities, state departments of local government, taxpayer associations, and revenue studies conducted by other cities and professional associations such as building official and finance associations. These sources, while valuable in identifying trends and new sources of revenues, are limited in their scope and timeliness. Very often information is not provided on the rates and bases of specific sources, or the data are outdated. Revenue studies conducted by other jurisdictions are helpful in providing information on formats, techniques, and advantages and disadvantages of specific revenue sources.

Because of the limitations of published revenue data, a questionnaire should be designed to collect comparable information. This requires a careful definition of each revenue item included on the questionnaire. Differences in terminology and revenue structure exist among municipalities. Construction permits, for example, may be based on linear or cubic feet. Plumbing fees may be based on the number of "opens" or "ends." Business licenses may be based on gross receipts, flat rates, or number of employees or seats in a theater or restaurant. Confusion can be limited by asking the respondents to describe the specific rates and bases they employ.

Reasonable length is essential to a good response. Therefore, it is not advisable to cover too broad a range of revenue sources on one questionnaire. Local officials receive a multitude of surveys and are more likely to ignore those that are excessively long or complex. Response can be encouraged by advising the participants that they will receive a copy of the results by a particular date.

Questionnaire distribution

Considerable care should be exercised in distributing the questionnaire. Attention should be focused on how the data collected will be used. Because the revenue survey is based on comparable data, it is important to isolate the different characteristics associated with the governmental units surveyed. Consideration should be given to socioeconomic, economic, and geographical factors. Elected officials are particularly interested in the practices of geographically contiguous communities, and questionnaires should be distributed to these communities. This is important because of the comparative perspective it provides for the area and the high contact rate among citizens.

A second method of comparison is by socioeconomic characteristics. Communities are selected on the basis of comparable socioeconomic factors such as percentage of college graduates, median years of school, median family income, and percentage of families earning more than $25,000 a year. Such data are beneficial in developing and selling recommendations.

A third category of comparative respondents is those with the same economic characteristics, such as median income level or economic base. This classification is less desirable than the socioeconomic one because significant differences may exist among communities with similar income levels.

A fourth comparative group is all the communities that respond to the survey questionnaire, limited only by the amount of available data and the degree of rate structure comparability. Census data and other information gathered by planning departments and regional planning agencies is available to aid in determining the appropriate groups to survey.

Analysis of data

After the questionnaires are distributed, work can begin on an analysis of the revenue sources being studied. A ten-year trend will present a good picture of the performance of a particular revenue source, because most factors that affect revenue collections will occur over a ten-year period. Other aspects of the analysis include identification of the factors that influence the yield of each source, the extent to which rates have been adjusted over the years, and the appropriateness of the base. Administrative costs and problems associated with the revenue source should also be reviewed. Information gathered during this stage will be useful in developing recommendations for improvements to the revenue system.

When the questionnaires are returned, the data are assembled according to the previously determined categories of respondents. Averages are computed for the different groups, including socioeconomic, geographical area, economic, and total. These averages are then compared with the city's revenues. Graphs are an effective device for comparing the data.

Several problems are associated with a comparative analysis of revenues. Various municipal rate structures may not be comparable.

A group average may apply to only a small number of respondents, which distorts the findings. The data may point to the need to change rates or bases, which may not be politically feasible. Unique local conditions may not be clearly identified in the returns. Considerable analysis and in some cases followup may be necessary to resolve questions generated by the review of the returns.

After organizing the revenue survey data, it is helpful to create summary charts, graphs, and a narrative explanation and interpretation of the findings. Group comparisons should be summarized according to the classification system used and all deviations explained. Nationwide, regional, or state studies of revenues may be used as a further check on the findings with the understanding that such information is limited by its timeliness and other factors.

Report preparation

Once the revenue data are analyzed, a final report is prepared. The report should briefly summarize the findings and recommendations, describe the methodology and the rationale for selecting the specific revenue sources, and discuss the findings in detail. Graphs and tables are excellent for illustrating how the community's revenues compare to those of other jurisdictions. Inadequacies of the existing revenue system should be identified and discussed. These may include poor financial records, the failure to periodically adjust rates and bases, poor collection practices, high delinquency rates, and other administrative problems, including the absence of adequate penalties.

Finally, the report should recommend ways to improve the present revenue sources and suggest new sources. Recommendations need to be fully substantiated by the data gathered during the survey. In developing the recommendations, attention should be focused on revenue diversity, the existence of adequate revenue administration machinery, the appropriateness of rates and bases, and methods of keeping the survey data current.

Conclusion

Well-designed and -administered revenue surveys are an essential component of an effective revenue planning and management system. They are not a panacea for local government revenue problems. Surveys must be supplemented by formalized revenue policy statements, state-of-the-art forecasting techniques, a revenue manual and detailed revenue classification system, an aggressive collection and enforcement program, and a system for costing and pricing services. Use of these techniques will help local officials provide equitable, efficient, and adequate revenues.

The City as Debt Collector

David P. Dolter and Roger Mansfield

Would your city like to increase city revenues without increasing city fees, charges, or taxes? If the answer to this question is yes, then you may want to seriously look at the merits of what we call municipal debt collection administration.

Municipal debt collection administration can simply be described as getting the money that is due and payable to your city. This is an often overlooked but very important area of municipal finance administration. Its importance has been underscored by the passage of Proposition 13, which in severely limiting the ability of California cities to modify existing tax rates, placed new emphasis on maximizing the return from existing sources.

Adding to the need to maximize the return from existing revenue sources has been the recent passage of Propositon 4, the spending limits initiative, which places a limit on the "proceeds of taxes" that city councils can appropriate in any given year. This will cause cities to impose more fees and charges to meet their revenue requirements, since the appropriation of the "nontax" proceeds are not limited, as long as they are used to finance the service they are charged for.

As cities make the shift and start billing for these services, there are always those individuals who, for one reason or another, won't pay their bills. It then becomes the responsibility of the governmental entity to collect these debts.

Collection survey

The city of Redondo Beach [California], in an effort to improve the effectiveness of its debt collection, sent a questionnaire to each of

Reprinted with permission from the August 1981 issue of *Western City*, the official publication of the League of California Cities.

the 426 incorporated cities in the state. The information provided by the 352 cities responding to the questionnaire reveals that many cities have not yet taken all the measures available to them to collect their bills.

Among the survey findings:

1. Eighty-seven percent of the respondents do not have an adopted accounts receivable or debt collection policy. Even more of the cities do not establish accounts receivable collection goals. It is, of course, difficult for a city to assess its own collection performance if it must be measured against an unstated collection policy.
2. Of those cities responding, 36 percent do not, as a matter of policy, pursue delinquent accounts in small claims court.
3. Another 53 percent of the cities do not use outside third party debt collection services.
4. Fifty-eight percent of the cities do not track the age of their accounts receivable, noting whether they are 30 days past due, 60 days past due, 90 days past due, or over 120 days past due. Such information is important because of the relationship between the length of time an account has been outstanding and the rate of collection and probable net loss from bad debts.
5. A significantly higher percentage (approximately 90 percent) of the cities do not perform periodic calculations of ratio percentages and other figures necessary to measure collection performance.
6. Only 10 percent of the cities have taken steps to ensure compliance with the state's Fair Debt Collection Practices Act (Section 1788 of the California Civil Code). While the Legislative Counsel's office has given an oral opinion that the act does not apply to cities, it would seem that the standards of fair play for debt collection that are required of the private sector should set a standard for government debt collectors, since government must be expected to set an example of fairness in all its dealings with the public. Consequently, cities may want to review with their city attorney their existing debt collection procedures and practices in light of what the state has prescribed for all other debt collectors.

Measuring collection performance

When cities make a decision to seriously pursue debt collection, they may wish to consider some of the techniques used in the private sector for measuring and managing outstanding debt. Several indices commonly used in the private sector that can be applied to the public sector are the collection index, the average collection period, and the past due index.

Collection index   The collection percentage, which is one of the most commonly used of the collection indices, is determined by dividing the total amounts collected during a period (such as a month) by the total receivables outstanding at the beginning of that period as shown in the formula:

$$\text{Collection index} = \frac{\text{Collections made during period}}{\text{Receivables outstanding at beginning of period}}$$

Average collection period   This index gives an estimation of the average length of time receivables are outstanding. If, for example, the net collection index is 50 percent, indicating that only one-half of the outstanding receivables were collected during the month, receivables would "on the average" be outstanding 60 days. This estimate is made by using the following formula:

$$\text{Average collection period} = \frac{\text{Net credit period}}{\text{Collection index}}$$

Past due index   This measure involves the determination of the proportion of all accounts, in amount or in number, that are past due. It is computed by dividing the total past due by the total outstanding as follows:

$$\text{Past due index} = \frac{\text{Total past due}}{\text{Total outstanding}}$$

The survey results seem to highlight the need for California cities to examine their municipal debt collection practices and procedures as a possible means of increasing city revenues. However, much of the revenue received by cities is intergovernmental in nature, so cities should also look at how effective other agencies of government are at collecting the city's money. This point was brought into focus for the city of Redondo Beach when it took over the collection of parking citation fines and forfeitures from the local municipal court district.

As a result of the *San Diego* vs. *the San Diego Municipal Court* decision, courts statewide began turning over the parking citation bail process to cities. Before the city of Redondo Beach took over the processing of parking citations, it received approximately $200,000 a year from the court. With the takeover, revenues have increased to an estimated $625,000 for FY 1980-81. While the city increased the parking citation bail from $5 to $10 during this time, the return per citation was also increased, primarily because the city reduced the length of time before the first and second penalty assessments were imposed. The court imposed the first penalty fee seven months or more after the issuance of the citation and second penalty two months later. The city imposed the first penalty 15 days after the issuance of the citation and the second penalty is now assessed approximately 45 days later. Since only about 35 percent of those receiving parking citations post bail within 15 days after the citation is issued, this change in penalty assessment procedure increased the city's return per citation.

This example illustrates the need to review how other agencies are collecting the city's money. If they are not doing what they can to maximize legitimate city revenues, then the responsible state, county, or other officials should be so advised to make the necessary changes.

The administration of municipal debt collection represents an opportunity for cities to maximize the returns from existing revenue sources. As its role expands, practitioners can make valuable contributions by sharing their respective successes and failures so that others may learn and benefit from their insights. In this way, cities can help each other minimize the economic constraints we all are facing.

Multi-Year Revenue and Expenditure Forecasting: Some Policy Issues

Events such as the fiscal crises of several major urban governments, the uncertain performance of the United States economy including both rampant inflation and the distinct possibility of recession, and the threat of tax revolts have stimulated interest by state and local governments in multi-year forecasting of revenues and expenditures as a part of their overall financial management strategy. The policy-makers and administrators who make the initial decision to enter into such forecasting ventures should recognize, however, that there are technical issues associated with such forecasting that have potential implications for the types of policy questions that these forecasting models can address. The intent of this article is to explain some of these more technical issues in a nontechnical manner emphasizing the policy-relevant choices that have to be made in conjunction with the decision to enter into multi-year forecasting.[1]

In order to provide some perspective on the role of fiscal forecasting in budgeting and financial management, the first section reviews the ways in which cities are currently using their forecasts. Since the technical issues that arise in conjunction with forecasting stem primarily from the fact that there are alternative methods that can be used to yield projections, the second section briefly discusses these alternative approaches. Sections three and four focus upon the technical problems that arise in econometric revenue and expenditure forecasting respectively, noting the potential policy implications of these issues.

Uses of forecasts

While relatively few local governments undertake systematic multi-year revenue and expenditure forecasts, there is an obvious

Reprinted with permission from *Urban Affairs Papers*, spring 1980.

interest in this subject.[2] Furthermore, a review of the cities currently undertaking such forecasts suggests that these cities find such projections of use in terms of both policy-making and general governmental administration.[3]

One of the principal uses of intermediate-term forecasts is the projection of fiscal "gaps" or revenue shortfalls. This is accomplished by projecting revenues and expenditures independently, under a set of consistent and well-defined assumptions. Then, if the projections suggest a major revenue shortfall, plans can immediately be made to ensure that the budget will balance without having to make "crisis" budget adjustments at the last minute.

It must be recognized that when the projection of a budget gap elicits policy changes which affect revenues or expenditures, the levels originally forecast will *not* be realized. These "errors" in the forecast do not negate the usefulness of the approach; indeed, that is exactly the rationale for undertaking the forecast. In other words, the forecasts are simply first steps in financial management; they are not prophecies.

Intermediate-term forecasts may also be used for analysis of policies with longer term implications. Among these are: analyzing the costs of wage negotiations involving multi-year contracts; analyzing the impacts on the budget of operating and maintenance costs associated with capital projects; contemplating the implications of nonrenewal of a state or federal grant during the forecast period. Likewise, at least some of the techniques described below allow for analysis of the impacts on the budget of alternative economic scenarios.

Finally, it should be noted that the *process* of forecasting may improve the overall administrative effectiveness of a city's operations. Compilation of multi-year forecasts forces policy-makers and administrators to consider implications of decisions beyond the traditional single year that is inherent in the usual budget process. While forecasting may not eliminate all myopic decisions in the public sector, it is an important step in the right direction.

Types of forecasting techniques

Once the decision to pursue multi-year forecasting has been made, the technique(s) to be used must be chosen. There are several approaches available for revenue and expenditure forecasting; each has its own particular advantages and disadvantages. The primary tradeoff among the methods concerns their costs and the amount of information they provide: in general, the more complex techniques require greater resources but provide far more information than the simple approaches.

Best guess or expert forecasts   By their nature, little can be said about "expert" forecasts since there is no specific method that is used in this approach. The key to successful forecasting in this highly personal approach is, of course, the "expert." In general, the successful expert forecasters are those who are most closely involved with particular revenues and expenditures. Likely candidates include the finance director, chief assessor, or a state and federal grants coordinator.

While this method is inexpensive and possibly accurate, especially in the short run, it suffers from its dependence upon the subjective "feeling" of the forecaster. Thus, it cannot easily be determined *why* next year's estimates will be higher or lower than last year's or why forecast errors have occurred. Furthermore, if the forecaster were to leave, the "model" would also leave. Finally, revenues and expenditures are likely to depend upon several factors operating simultaneously, which makes it difficult for an expert to take everything into consideration several years into the future.

Trend techniques For certain revenues and expenditures reasonably accurate and low cost predictions may be obtained by assuming that they depend solely upon time. The most common assumptions used in trend forecasting are those of constant percentage changes (a constant growth rate) or constant absolute changes (a linear time trend).

While this technique may be quite reasonable for projecting some revenues or expenditures, it totally ignores economic and demographic conditions.[4] It will never, therefore, predict a "turning point" unless the basic results of the trend analysis are altered by outside expert opinion. Furthermore, the approach is of no aid for analysis of the effects of future major economic or demographic changes that might occur in the city.

Deterministic forecasts Total revenues or expenditures of any sort are usually the product of a base times an appropriate rate. For example, annual garbage collection fees may be the product of the number of pickup sites times the annual charge per site. Similarly, total spending on gasoline is the product of the gallons of gas used times the price per gallon. Once values for these entries have been estimated or assumed, the resultant forecast can be derived "deterministically."

This technique, or variants thereof, is most often used for expenditure forecasting (described in more detail later). The technique may also provide reasonably accurate results for revenue sources for which projections of the base are easily made and that are unlikely to vary with business conditions, e.g., the number of households in a city using garbage collection services. The technique is less useful if the base of the revenue source is likely to vary as economic conditions change or if base variable data are difficult to obtain.

Econometric forecasting   Econometric forecasting combines principles drawn from both economic and statistical theory. While conceptually more complex than the methods cited above, econometric forecasting is likely to yield information more useful to the forecaster and policy-maker than any of the techniques described above. For example, econometric forecasting allows the investigator to consider the effects of simultaneous changes in several variables on a revenue or expenditure stream and it yields results that can be systematically analyzed using statistical techniques.

The most common approach in econometric forecasting is to forecast revenue or expenditure series independently using statistical regression techniques. The process involves specifying a functional relationship between the series of interest and appropriate independent or "causal" variables; collecting historical data for the series being analyzed and each of the independent variables; statistically estimating the hypothesized relationship using linear regression; and, finally, using projected values of the independent variables to yield forecasts of the revenue or expenditure series.

This approach has attributes not found in the previously described methods. Unlike expert or time trend techniques, an econometric model bases estimates on behavioral relationships that contain a theoretical foundation which can be evaluated by the user of the forecast. Also, the technique is capable of predicting turning points in revenues or expenditures.

Statistical methods also have advantages over their deterministic counterparts. Statistical inference can be used to test whether an observed relationship between variables is, in fact, statistically significant. Furthermore, unlike the simplest deterministic approaches, it permits several independent variables to be used simultaneously. This is an especially useful feature for policy analysis where, for example, it is felt that both inflation and local population changes will influence a revenue source.

The statistical approach is, however, likely to be more costly than the simpler models discussed above. It is likely to require the skills of someone trained in economics and statistics as well as the availability of a computer. Furthermore, each of the four steps listed above presents potential difficulties and possibilities of forecast error. These problems are discussed in more detail in the following section.

With alternative techniques available for intermediate term forecasting, it is not surprising to find that no two forecasting systems are identical. In general, cities currently projecting expenditures use some variant of the deterministic method, although the details of the approach differ in each. Thus, even when a single general method is used, decisions will have to be made as to the most appropriate approach within the context of the particular jurisdiction. (Details of expenditure forecasting methods are considered later.)

For revenue forecasts the choice of technique is usually tied most closely to the particular set of revenues applicable in a city, the administrative features associated with the revenue source and the cyclical stability of the local economic base. For example, trend and deterministic techniques are sufficiently accurate to project fees or taxes that generally do not vary greatly over a business cycle or intergovernmental grants that seem to be cyclically insensitive. Likewise, the administrative features of certain revenue sources, especially the property tax, may make it amenable only to expert opinion or time trend techniques.[5]

Nevertheless, there are numerous revenue sources that do show responsiveness to economic conditions. Examples include the local sales tax, hotel/motel taxes, local income taxes, and taxes tied to the revenues of local utilities. In these cases, it may be well worth the extra cost to undertake a full-fledged econometric forecasting approach for these revenues. Nevertheless, financial administrators and policy-makers must recognize that this approach, being technically more sophisticated, contains potential pitfalls that may have important implications when the results are used for policy making.

Problems in econometric revenue projections

Econometric forecasting techniques are being used with greater frequency by local as well as state governments, especially for revenue forecasting.[6] Expenditures for purposes that are sensitive to economic conditions, e.g., many health and welfare programs, are also amenable to such forecasting techniques.[7] However, these services are seldom the responsibility of city government; thus this discussion will focus on econometric revenue forecasting even though the same conceptual problems would arise when econometrically forecasting expenditures.

We consider the problems associated with each of the four steps of the econometric forecasting process cited above—specifying the model, collecting the data, estimating the relationships and deriving the forecasted amounts.

Model specification   While specification of an econometric forecasting model is the task of a technician, aspects of this task affect both the accuracy and usability of the final product. Specification of an econometric forecasting equation involves deciding what variable or variables are to be used as well as the functional form of the equation.

Since econometric forecasts are most often applicable to economically sensitive revenues, it is only natural that one trained in economics play a major role in this task. Yet, while economic theory can provide considerable insight into the underlying behavior that determines the size of a particular revenue base, it is seldom precise enough to yield a definitive statement as to exactly what variables should be included in an estimating equation. Furthermore, the peculiarities of a local situation are likely to mean that no single specification will necessarily work well in all jurisdictions.

For example, a common approach is to specify that annual sales tax receipts in a jurisdiction will depend upon the income of residents of the area.[8] But variables in addition to income might also be used, such as the local unemployment rate. This latter variable might be included under the assumption that while unemployment compensation constitutes income, those who are unemployed anticipate that their payments may cease and therefore will not make certain purchases, especially of consumer durables.

Likewise, since economic theory suggests that relative prices of goods and services affect the consumption choices of consumers, some measure of the relative rates of inflation of taxable and nontaxable items would appear to be reasonable additions to this equation.[9]

Just as there are numerous independent variables that can be used in revenue estimating equations, there are numerous functional forms that can be specified. Thus, while it is one thing to say that sales tax revenues depend upon income, there is also the question whether this relationship is purely linear (implying that a one dollar change in income has the same effect on sales tax receipts regardless of the per capita income level) or non-linear. Furthermore, if the analyst chooses a non-linear function he is then faced with the additional task of specifying the precise non-linear relationship between the causal (independent) variables and the revenue variable being estimated. (This is similar to the choice that has to be made in trend analysis between the assumptions of a constant absolute growth over time or a constant linear growth *rate*.) Importantly, the range of possible forecast results may be very wide depending on which alternative specification is used.

Other variables and functional forms may come to mind but the primary point is that a large number of specifications of revenue estimating equations exist with no one specification necessarily "best." Yet, a poorly specified equation is unlikely to predict accurately. While statistical theory can assist in the choice of which specification is preferable (which is why an analyst trained in statistics is also necessary in the econometric modeling approach), it must be recognized that model building is still as much "art" as "science" and that a certain amount of judgment will always be exercised by the forecaster. Such judgment may be aided by consultation between forecasters and policy-makers. At the same time it should be emphasized that the econometric approach, since it requires explicit specification of relationships and allows for *ex post* analysis of forecast errors, is still considerably more systematic than the pure expert judgment technique described above.

Finally, while the econometric technique is more amenable to analysis of likely effects of a change in an economic or demographic variable, such analysis can be conducted only if that variable is included in the estimating equation. Thus, for example, a policy-maker may wish to know the likely effects of a change in population on the size of sales tax receipts. But if population is not included in the specification of the sales tax equation, such a question cannot be answered directly. Thus, anticipation of possible policy questions of interest to policy-makers may alter the specification of a revenue estimating equation, again calling for consultation between model builders and those using its results.[10]

Data availability   While specification of estimating equations creates problems for econometric revenue forecasters, the lack of data is likely to create even more difficult problems. Indeed, final specification of estimating equations is often limited more by what data are available than by the lack of a well-defined economic theory. Problems associated with data can be most conveniently classified as being related to internal or external data; that is, data available from within or outside the organization. Before undertaking the econometric approach to revenue forecasting it must be recognized that the need to resolve data shortcomings is likely to add to the overall cost of producing such forecasts and, unless resolved, such shortcomings will constitute a major barrier to any systematic forecasting effort.

Internal data   Econometric forecasting requires collection of historical data on the projected revenue series. To obtain reasonable results, a series of from ten to fifteen years of observations is necessary. Therefore data-gathering often constitutes the major initial cost of the overall forecasting project since data are not always accessible in a form that is directly usable in the forecasts. Two aspects of the data collection problem include changes in definitions over the time period and changes in the rates and bases of revenue sources.

Although major revenue sources are usually reported on a consistent basis over time, this is not always the case for minor revenue sources. For example, during some previous periods, fees from all sources may have been aggregated into a single amount and reported as such in both the budget document and the annual financial report. In other periods the several components comprising these fees may have been reported separately. One must either combine the disaggregated amounts to form a single consistent time series or attempt to disaggregate the series in those periods when they were reported as a single entry. The first approach is simpler but loses information, while the second approach requires considerable effort to reconstruct the series from historical documents.

A more important problem, especially for the major tax revenue sources, is to account for all discretionary changes in the rate or base of the tax. For example, a particular tax may have yielded $1 million in revenues for two or three years and then suddenly brought in $1.5 million. A 50 percent increase suggests that either the rate had been increased or the base broadened. If one were to use these data directly in a regression equation without attempting to account for the variation due to legal alterations in the base or rate, no set of economic variables is likely to work well in explaining the observed variations in the revenue data. In this case it is necessary to "clean" the series of the purely administrative changes.

Different methods are available for this cleaning operation.[11] Essentially the techniques attempt to factor out the effects of discretionary changes in rates or base definitions by estimating what revenues *would have been* in the absence of discretionary changes. The techniques not only require substantial investigation of the legal bases and rates of revenue sources but also can involve considerable computational effort. Thus, many forecasters opt to clean only the major revenue series.

External data   External data are unlikely to require cleaning, but may involve other problems. Probably the most severe problem concerning external data relates to their availability. This holds for both historical data and future projections of these data series.

Historical data are seldom available in exactly the form the analyst would prefer. Federal government, a traditional source of much state and local government economic and financial data, does not provide large amounts of data on a timely basis for cities. Sometimes state agencies (e.g., the labor department or the revenue department) or a local Chamber of Commerce, bank, or university can be a source of local data. While such data may be appropriate, seldom will these data sources be able to provide forecasts of the same independent variables—a necessary component in an econometric revenue forecasting project.

Because of the lack of appropriate local data, forecasters often have to resort to proxy variables, e.g., the use of national income instead of local income to forecast sales tax revenues or national inflation rates rather than local price changes. While such substitutions may be adequate, users of these forecasts should recognize that this approach makes it unlikely that particular idiosyncrasies of a local economy will be captured in either the estimates or the forecasts. For example, the economy of Detroit or Pittsburgh may be more cyclical than that of the United States as a whole; thus substitution of U.S. personal income for a local measure of personal income can lead to less accurate forecasts of revenues in these localities than if truly local measures of income were available.

The problem of data availability, especially of forecasted independent variables, leads to the question of the desirability of subscriptions to a major national econometric forecasting model such as the Wharton Forecasting Project, Data Resources, Inc., etc. Such services could prove helpful in the model-building effort. First, they are a source of national, regional and local data that may require considerable effort to obtain if done by the forecasting staff. Second, they provide consistent forecasts of major national and possibly regional variables that can be used in the forecasts. Finally, contracts with these services usually provide for technical assistance in the construction of models. Nevertheless, few cities currently subscribe to such services, primarily because of their considerable costs.[12]

Estimation of the forecasting model   Estimation techniques usually center on some form of regression analysis, a discussion of which is beyond the scope of this article. Nevertheless, it should be noted that numerous theoretical statistical problems can arise with this technique. In turn, these statistical problems can lead to forecasts that may prove to be less than totally satisfactory. The existence of these potential problems is another reason that someone trained in statistics should play a major role in the overall forecasting effort.

Projections from the forecasting equation   Even in the absence of statistical problems associated with the estimation of forecasting equations, forecasts based on independent variables not known with certainty can also lead to prediction errors. For example, a forecaster may have specified that sales taxes are a function of national income and estimated the past relationship between local sales tax and national personal income. But forecasts of sales taxes must then be based upon *forecasted* future levels of this national personal income variable and thus the forecaster is faced with the need to obtain a suitable forecast of this variable. Unfortunately, even the major econometric forecasters are seldomly perfectly accurate in their projections of the national economy, e.g., many national forecasters have underestimated the national rate of inflation. To the extent that such forecasts are in error, forecasters of local sales taxes will also be in error, even if the relationship between national personal income and local sales tax receipts does not change in the future.

There is little that forecasters and forecast users can do to alleviate this problem other than recognize its existence and hope that the predictive accuracy of national forecasts improves. While judgmental adjustments can be made in the forecasts, such intervention destroys one of the original reasons for undertaking the econometric method—making systematic projections based upon a well-defined set of assumptions.

It can thus be seen that econometric revenue forecasting contains potential pitfalls which should be recognized before such an effort is undertaken. At the same time policy-makers and administrators should also recognize that a well-constructed econometric revenue model is capable of providing information not available in any other technique and, while costly, should be seriously considered as the major projection method if primary revenue sources are sensitive to local economic fluctuations and if reasonably accurate and systematic forecasts are desired from the effort.

Issues in multi-year expenditure projections

As suggested above, multi-year expenditure projections tend to be produced using deterministic or accounting-identity forecasting methods. That is, total expenditures in any one year are seen to be the simple product of the number of units of input (e.g., hours of labor, kilowatt hours of electricity, etc.) times the prices of the inputs (e.g., hourly wage, price per kilowatt hour, etc.). The problems of forecasting with this method center on the determination of the likely levels of these inputs and their corresponding prices. In this section we focus upon several issues associated with the derivation of these estimates, including the degree of disaggregation to be used, the service level assumptions to be applied, the derivation of input price forecasts and the methods by which the necessary information for carrying out such forecasts can be derived. Once again the utility of the forecasts can be critically affected by each of these issues.

The degree of disaggregation   One necessary decision when developing an expenditure forecasting model is the degree of disaggregation to be used in determining the projected amounts. Most cities undertaking forecasts perform some degree of disaggregation in the preparation of their long-term projections. Two natural levels of disaggregation are expenditures by agency (department) and by object.

More detailed disaggregation is obtained by considering subunits within agencies or subobjects within object codes. It is here that the practices of the various cities producing forecasts tend to differ greatly. Further disaggregation by expenditure subobjects is seldom performed primarily because of the difficulties inherent in projecting both the amounts and prices of highly detailed expenditure categories. Disaggregation by subunits is, however, carried out in at least some cities especially when the budgeting process is based on estimates made at the subunit level. For example, in Washington, D.C., some 500 "responsibility centers" identical to the units responsible for annual budget preparation have been identified and individual multi-year forecasts developed in each.[13] Both San Antonio and Dallas project expenditures on an agency basis, although within agencies the projections may be prepared by various subunits and then aggregated before being submitted to those preparing the forecast document.[14]

In general, the degree of disaggregation used will depend greatly upon the budgeting and accounting systems employed within a city. As suggested above, one of the attributes of a multi-year forecasting process is as a complement to the regular budgeting process. Especially important is the fact that it is likely to lengthen the time horizons of administrators as they contemplate the future. Disaggregation to the same level as is used in preparing the annual budget is most likely to facilitate this aspect of multi-year forecasting.

If particular subobject codes are anticipated to be of special interest, disaggregation of these inputs may also prove to be of sufficient utility to justify the additional efforts required. For example, recent energy price increases have prompted most cities to single out utility expenditure forecasts in their multi-year projections.

Service level assumptions   While disaggregation tends to be more or less a technical decision constrained primarily by the accounting and budgeting systems available for obtaining the necessary information, derivation of the assumptions underlying the forecasts is an important policy relevant decision. That is, what assumptions are to be used in projecting the levels of real inputs that are likely to be used during the projection period?

Nearly all cities undertaking multi-year forecasts indicate that their projections are based upon the assumption of "constant service levels."[15] There is, however, no general agreement as to what this really means. Presumably, the goal is to project what the expenditures will be in the absence of any major new policy initiatives (most forecasters recognize that they are not attempting to forecast *policy* but what expenditures would be under the current set of policies). Yet circumstances are constantly changing in any city environment—population may be increasing or decreasing, the socioeconomic composition of this population may be changing or there may be existing policies that mandate changes in the amount of services that will have to be provided in the near future. The question that arises is how the effects of these various changes are to be included in any forecast.

For some services systematic methods are available. For example, if there is some "standard" level of population per acre of park land deemed adequate, projected changes in population can be used to project future expansions of the park department.[16] Unfortunately, few public service outputs lend themselves to measurement in quite as systematic a manner as park lands. Furthermore, even in this case it may be felt that simply using population/acres of parks is an inadequate measure of the flow of service from these recreational sites since quality differences may vary greatly across different forms of publicly provided outdoor recreation. Nevertheless, many cities have attempted to devise procedures to address this problem in a systematic, if not totally analytical manner.

Possibly the most highly developed estimation process is used in the city of Dallas.[17] In Dallas, each department is required to estimate the workload effects of each of several exogenous changes that *are projected* (e.g., population changes) or *are scheduled* (e.g., policies in effect) that will likely affect operations in the future. It is important to note that this procedure does not attempt to anticipate or predict new policies that might be implemented between the time the forecast is made and the year that is being forecast. The exogenous changes include: changes in the absolute level of population (population trends, including scheduled annexations, are forecast centrally with the same set of assumptions used by all departments); scheduled changes in service levels already a part of city policy (e.g., if the city council has already passed a resolution calling for a decrease in police response times); state and federal mandates that will affect service levels during the projection period; operating and maintenance implications of capital projects scheduled to be completed during the projection period; and the effects of anticipated increases in productivity. It is only the last change that involves a great deal of discretion on the part of the forecaster and is not due to existing local, state or federal policies. While a classification of actions that are likely to affect the necessary levels of inputs still does not address the analytical question of the numerical effect of, say, an increase in population, the system approach does require that the departments give real thought to, and provide documentation for, their best guess of the impacts.

Some cities skirt the issue entirely by assuming that the level of real inputs will remain constant during the projection period.[18] In this manner only projected price increases will affect future expenditure levels. This method provides for an easier approach to forecasting and, perhaps, produces adequate results especially in a city experiencing stagnant population growth or actual population decline. Yet, even in these circumstances this approach precludes the possibility that the composition of services provided by the public sector will be altered during the projection period. For example, personnel additions in one function may just offset personnel reductions in another; but if average wages for these two groups differ there will be an impact on total expenditures that is not accounted for in this simple approach.

While one cannot specify categorically how cities *ought to* approach this question, it definitely is within the domain of policymakers to enter into discussions as to what approach to expenditure forecasting is likely to lead to the most useful set of estimates.[19] Therefore, the issues noted here must be considered early in the planning stages of a forecasting project.

Input price forecasts   The technical details associated with projecting prices of nonlabor inputs are comparatively few and not especially difficult. It is essential, however, that the input price projections be consistent with the underlying economic assumptions used on the revenue side of the forecasts if the two forecasts are to be strictly comparable.

An important policy question arises in the projection of wages. Because the multi-year forecasts being discussed here are likely to be matters of public record and not simply internal working memoranda, the question is which of a large number of possible wage rate changes should be used in the projections and, furthermore, whether differential changes in wages should be assumed for different classes of employees.

Different approaches to this issue have been taken. One is to assume that public employee wages will just keep pace with inflation; thus anticipated price increases are used to inflate labor expenditures. An alternative is simply to assume that wages will increase by some constant rate each year (e.g., 7 percent) without regard to national inflation rates. Finally, forecasts can be made under the assumption of no discretionary wage increases.[20] This assumption is used due to the fear that in a collective bargaining environment any information provided to union bargainers about the employer's expectations regarding wage settlements decreases the bargaining strength of the city. Obviously, omission of any wage increases will result in projections of expenditures that, in a period of rampant nationwide inflation, are likely to produce considerable underestimates of actual expenditures. Furthermore, it is inconsistent with the rest of the overall forecasting process where, for both revenues and nonlabor expenditures, care is taken to produce accurate projections under a set of well-defined assumptions.

Some argue that labor negotiations can be helped by the publication of a forecast that includes some projected increases in money wages. Their position is that a forecast of fiscal problems under some assumed increase in wages will encourage union negotiators to enter bargaining sessions with lower wage demands than in the absence of such bleak outlooks.

Resolution of this issue is likely to rest, at least in part, on the perceived sophistication of the labor negotiators. Nevertheless, the decision is obviously one of sufficient import to be considered at the highest policy-making levels of a city.

Administrative responsibility for the forecast   Several administrative questions arise when formulating plans for a multi-year forecasting project. One of these is where the responsibility is to lie for the forecast, and the second is the role to be played by individual departments.

The responsibility for expenditure forecasts is most naturally and most effectively placed within the agency responsible for preparation of the annual budget. Not only will this group be most familiar with expenditure decisions made at the agency level, but, in addition, multi-year forecasts can be made a part of the overall budget process. In this way longer term implications of decisions made in the current year can be analyzed immediately.

Whether or not the revenue forecasts should be made by the same group is less obvious. In at least some cities another agency (e.g., a finance department) is responsible for annual revenue forecasts. In such instances, it may be more efficient for this group to carry out the multi-year revenue projections as well. The potential problem in such an arrangement is that with two groups undertaking forecasts there may be less consistency in the assumptions used to generate the two sets of projections.

The second organizational question related to expenditure forecasts is the role to be played by individual agencies. On the one hand, projections can be made without any role played by these individuals. This is most feasible when the forecasts are based entirely upon projected increases in prices rather than the combination of price and real input changes. On the other hand, if effects of mandates, new capital projects, etc., are to be encompassed in the forecasts, the centralized approach is unlikely to yield projections that truly reflect the likely impact of these changes on individual departments since budget personnel are unlikely to be familiar enough with departmental operations to derive such forecasts. Second, centralized operations preclude one of the purported advantages of multi-year forecasting—requiring the departmental manager to take a longer time perspective in decision-making. At the same time, active participation by agency managers opens the possibilities for budgetary gaming. That is, they may strategically attempt to overestimate future budgetary needs in anticipation that, by doing so, it will be easier to obtain approvals of budget requests in subsequent years. Only through diligent centralized screening of even the longer term forecasts can this strategy be discouraged; however, this in turn adds to the overall cost of carrying out the forecast.

Summary

This article has reviewed the alternative uses of multi-year forecasts of revenues and expenditures, noting how such projections can fit into an overall financial management strategy. Although there are alternative techniques that can be applied to both expenditure and revenue projections, each has particular strengths and weaknesses that must be recognized when a forecasting project is undertaken. While econometric revenue forecasting is likely to contain the most information of any of the alternative techniques discussed, it was also shown that there are particular issues associated with this technique that are likely to cause potential problems and that must be resolved before it can be effectively applied. These problems include those associated with specifying the estimating equations, obtaining the data necessary to carry out the forecasts, statistical estimation of the relationship and obtaining accurate projections of the independent variables used. Finally, issues associated with expenditure projections were also discussed. These four issues include questions pertaining to the level of disaggregation, assumptions to be made about service levels, projecting prices of inputs (especially labor) and assignments of the administrative responsibilities for the forecast. In general, then, while techniques are important in determining the results of forecasts, there are other issues that must be considered before a forecasting effort can most effectively fit into an overall financial management strategy.

Note: Research for this article was supported by National Science Foundation grant no. DAR 78-20256. The author thanks Professor Bernard Jump, Jr., Marla Share, and Kurt Zorn, who made several helpful comments; the author, however, is responsible for any errors that remain.

1. Much of the information in this paper has been drawn from Roy Bahl and Larry Schroeder, *Forecasting Local Government Budgets*, Occasional Paper No. 38, Metropolitan Studies Program, The Maxwell School (Syracuse, New York: Syracuse University, December 1979); and, Larry Schroeder, "Forecasting Local Government Revenues and Expenditures," in *Management Policies in Local Government Finance*, ed. by J. R. Aronson and E. Schwartz, published by ICMA.

2. See, for example, Public Technology, Inc., *Multi-Year Revenue and Expenditure Forecasting: The State-of-the-Practice in Large Urban Jurisdictions*, Washington, D.C.: Public Technology Inc., 1979, which reports on a record HUD-financed study of multi-year forecasting that culminated in three well-attended two-day workshops.

3. See Roy Bahl and Larry Schroeder, *The New York State Economy: 1960-1978, and the Economy*, Occasional Paper No. 37, Metropolitan Studies Program, The Maxwell School (Syracuse, New York: Syracuse University, 1979).

4. Some cities may be essentially "recession-proof" or have revenues that are totally insensitive to economic conditions. In these cases, trend analysis may be quite accurate; nevertheless this assumes that similar conditions will hold in the future.

5. Given the apparent lack of respon-

siveness of assessed valuations to economic conditions, this combination of techniques is used in New York City to project the property tax. See New York City, *Four-Year Financial Plan: Fiscal Years 1979-1982* (New York City: 1979).

6. The Federation of Tax Administrators holds annual conferences on state revenue estimation and publishes proceedings. See, for example, National Association of Tax Administrators, *NATA Conference on Revenue Estimating, 1978* (Washington: undated).

7. Possibly the most highly developed econometric expenditure projection model is that of San Diego County, California. See County of San Diego, *Six-Year Revenue and Expenditure Forecasts: FY 1979-84* (San Diego: 1978).

8. Which of several available income measures to use is pursued below.

9. Such a variable is used in New York City's sales tax estimating equation. See Bahl and Schroeder, *Forecasting Local Government Budgets.*

10. It should be noted, however, that there are limitations to the alteration in forecasting equations to incorporate *all* possible policy questions. Data and statistical limitations are noted below: but in addition, one must recognize that no statistical method is likely to be sufficiently precise to ascertain the impact of all possible social, economic and political events that might have some minor effect on total revenues in a city.

11. See, for example, Roy Bahl, *Alternative Methods for Tax Revenue Forecasting in Developing Countries,* International Monetary Fund Department Paper, Fiscal Affairs Department (unpublished), 1972.

12. We are aware of only two cities currently using such subscriptions—New York City and San Diego. While subscription costs vary depending on the mix of services requested, they can add greatly to the costs of the forecasting effort.

13. Washington, D.C., *Multi-Year Financial Plan 1980-84* (Washington, D.C.: September 1978).

14. See City of San Antonio, Texas, *Long Range Financial Forecast FYU 1980-1985* (San Antonio: January 1980) or City of Dallas, Texas, *Long Range Financial Plan, 1978-1983* (Dallas: January 1979 revision).

15. This term, or some variant thereon is used in Dallas, *Long Range Financial Plan, 1978-1983;* San Antonio, *Long Range Financial Forecast FY 1980-1985;* and, Washington, D.C., *Multi-Year Financial Plan 1980-84.*

16. This technique is used by the Department of Parks and Recreation in San Antonio, Texas. See City of San Antonio, *Long Range Financial Forecast FY 1980-1985.*

17. City of Dallas, *Long Range Financial Plan, 1978-1983.*

18. This is the approach that has been used in New Orleans and, at least for some functional areas, in Washington, D.C. See New Orleans, Louisiana, *Municipal Budget Projections: Econometric Revenue Forecasting* (New Orleans: July 1977).

19. An even more active role in the forecasting exercise is played by policymakers in San Antonio. At the very start of the projection process the assumptions to be used are submitted to the City Council for their debate and approval.

20. See, for example, the multi-year forecast for New York City.

Fiscal Impact Analysis: A Practitioner's Guide

Robert W. Burchell and David Listokin

Introduction

The purpose of this article is to describe and demonstrate applications for the various techniques which have emerged to gauge the public costs of land development. These techniques are grouped under a common procedural description—*fiscal impact analysis*. All seek to predict both the municipal and educational servicing costs which accrue due to the public service demands of various forms of residential and nonresidential growth.

The technique, fiscal impact analysis, is not new—it is now close to fifty years old. Planners first employed this type of evaluation in the early public housing effort of the 1930s to justify the replacement of deteriorated structures due to their negative local fiscal effects. In the late 1940s it was used in the urban renewal movement to demonstrate the revenue generating superiority of the new land use that would replace the old. Since that time there has been steady growth in its employment through the 1950s, 1960s, into the 1970s. Fiscal impact analyses are now used to project the economic impact of alternative development proposals, major zoning or subdivision review plans, for boundary changes, municipal annexations, large scale, mixed-use developments or new communities, and as an integral part of the filing procedure for an environmental impact statement.

Today, there is a growing awareness that if it is possible to estimate the costs associated with growth, it may further be possible to dampen the short run service discontinuities usually associated

Reprinted from *The Fiscal Impact Guidebook: A Practitioner's Guide*, published by the U.S. Department of Housing and Urban Development, Office of Policy Development and Research, 1980.

with this growth and to allow the many public services which support development to be in place and available when they are needed. There is, as a result, a growing *demand* for straightforward, standardized methods to estimate the local public costs and revenues associated with land development.

Yet what is the *current* state of the art? In an analysis of 140 cost-revenue studies obtained from around the country, it was clear that in the majority of cases their quality was poor. Twenty percent of the studies were either incomplete, could not be followed or were conceptually or technically wrong. In over half the locations where the study was undertaken, the presiding local official could not gauge the study's accuracy. In 60 percent of the cases there was no way for technicians to use an existing fiscal impact analysis without the specific local consultants or staff planners who prepared the original report. This view of field practice indicated a pressing need for standardized methods, with explicit assumptions—and careful definitions as to the costs and revenues which were or were not being considered. Further, it was clear that there was now more than one fiscal impact method and sensitivity had to be paid to an appropriate pairing of method with task. This article is an attempt to answer these obvious field needs.

Definition of fiscal impact analysis   *Fiscal impact analysis*, as used here, is "a projection of the *direct, current, public costs and revenues* associated with *residential or nonresidential growth* to the *local jurisdiction(s)* in which this growth is taking place." Certain terms in this definition must be clearly understood. The following paragraphs discuss them in detail.

Fiscal impact analysis, as explained in this article, considers *direct* impact. It projects only the primary costs that will be incurred and the immediate revenues that will be generated. Direct or primary costs include, for example, salaries for instructors to teach new students generated by a large subdivision, or for policemen to control traffic at a new shopping center. Direct or primary revenues include property and sales taxes and intergovernmental monies generated as a consequence of the specific growth increment. Indirect impacts are not treated due to: (1) the near impossibility of predicting accurately the secondary consequences of growth; and (2) the recurring potential for double counting when primary and secondary impacts are viewed simultaneously. In the first case, will a shopping center increase real property values of adjacent parcels or does the presence of an immediate market enhance the value of the shopping center? In the second, should property tax revenues from an off-site nonresidential development, which in part is supported by a residential development, be considered the primary impact of the nonresidential development or the secondary impact of the residential development? This article considers no differential property value loss or gain relative to proximate development due to property or sales tax increases of a nonresidential facility benefitting from the nearby population. In the first case, it is assumed that the "contagion effects" of land uses in the long run will net to zero. In the second, the revenue contributions of any land use are considered only when that land use's primary fiscal impact is under scrutiny.

Fiscal impact analysis examines *current* costs and revenues. It tallies the financial effects of a planned unit development, urban renewal complex, new town, shopping center, etc., by considering the costs and revenues such facilities would generate if they were completed and operating today. This approach recognizes that development or redevelopment often requires several years and that inflation will increase costs and revenues over time. It also assumes, however, that the rising costs of providing public services will be matched by an essentially comparable increase in revenues—that the relative relationship of costs and revenues will change little over time.

Fiscal impact analysis is concerned with *public* (governmental) costs and revenues. It does not consider private costs of public actions, i.e., the costs passed on to developers or consumers through local land use regulations or building, health, and fire codes. Thus, special assessments on real property or the value of land dedications required of developers are considered private revenues. Private services provided are also considered private expenditures.

Tallying and comparing *costs and revenues* is a significant part of fiscal impact analysis. Costs include operating expenditures (salaries, statutory and material costs) and capital outlays, either directly incurred by a public jurisdiction or paid to others as a result of a specific development. Revenues comprise all monies a government receives from external sources as a result of the development or redevelopment. Revenues counted in a fiscal impact analysis include municipal and school district own source (local) contributions (taxes, charges, and miscellaneous revenue) and state and federal intergovernmental transfers.

Fiscal impact analysis is further concerned with the cost and revenue implications derived from *population and/or employment change*. These changes are broadly defined as residential and/or nonresidential entrance into or departure from a community. The fiscal impact analysis may be a prediction or a post hoc evaluation and may evaluate population and/or employment change in either the private or public sectors (i.e., a builder attempting to develop a mixed use planned unit development or a local authority seeking municipal approval for a public housing project or a civic center).

Finally, costs are projected to only the *local jurisdictions* in which the population or employment change is taking place. In most instances, the local jurisdiction is the town, township, borough, or parish for municipal costs and the school district(s) for primary and secondary school district expenditures. Fiscal impact analysis, as defined here, does not consider services administered by and revenues flowing to utilities, special districts, county governments, regional authorities, and states.

Emphasizing projections of exclusively local costs reflects user demand. Local governments—either municipal or school district— provide most services to residential and nonresidential properties. Police and fire protection, road maintenance and repair, education, etc., represent types of local government services. Local property owners must often share the cost of these services. Impacts on the cost are of vital interest to the local population; fiscal impact analyses volunteered by developers or required by local ordinances are the result. Services provided by special districts are usually paid for with user charges. They typically do not affect the local population directly. County government services in areas where local governments also provide services to property frequently involve major road construction or repair and institution or agency maintenance. The effect of change in their expenditures (related to a particular growth increment) on local residents is usually relatively small and not of vital concern.

Practitioner's notes

1. Emphasize the italicized portion of the definition.
2. Point out interchangeability of fiscal impact analysis and cost-revenue analysis yet differences between fiscal impact analysis and cost effective or cost benefit analysis.
3. Make clear that a development's secondary impacts are *not* ignored. Rather they are analyzed when they appear as their own primary impacts.'
4. Underscore analysts' concern with *publicly* funded activities and *publicly* raised revenues.

Methods of fiscal impact analysis and their application

Methods   There are two basic approaches to municipal cost allocation: average costing and marginal costing. Average costing is by far the more common field application. Costs are attributed to a new development according to average cost per unit of service (municipal and school district services) times the number of units the development is estimated to require. This method does not consider existing excess or deficient capacity that might exist for particular services or the possibility that a new development might fall at the threshold level, calling for major new capital construction to accommodate increased growth. Both of these deficiencies could invalidate an average cost assumption. Marginal costing, however, takes both of these potential deficiencies into account. Marginal costing relies heavily on careful analysis of existing demand/supply relationships for local governmental and school services.

The average cost and marginal cost approaches are two different ways to assess the cost of governmental services that growth imposes. Average costing views the relationships as linear while marginal costing views growth as having a more cyclical impact on local expenditures. In the extremely long run, however, the two techniques will yield similar estimates of growth impact. The difference is that at times the marginal cost estimate will lag behind the average cost projection, while in other instances the marginal cost estimate will lead or exceed the average cost figures. For example, marginal costs may be low in communities where unused facilities are available for an increased population; they are high when new facilities are to be built and new services provided that are greater than those immediately needed by the incoming population. Choosing either the average costing or marginal costing approaches will depend on what the fiscal impact analyst seeks—a best average estimate of the fiscal effects of growth, in which case the analyst will select the average costing approach, or a more intimate projection, in which case the analyst will opt for the marginal costing technique.

The following pages summarize six different methods to analyze cost-revenue impact. They are relatively simple and straightforward in nature, based on the derivation of either average or marginal cost-revenue characteristics from recent municipal and school district budgetary data. It is assumed that the recent cost-revenue characteristics of individual land uses will be maintained in the future. Because of their simplicity, these fiscal impact analysis techniques do not represent forecasting "models" of the more rigorous type (typically based upon sophisticated statistical analysis or mathematical modeling), rather, they represent ad hoc analysis techniques for estimating the likely cost-revenue impact of different land-use development patterns, based upon recent historical expenditure experience in the specific locality or in a suitably chosen likeness of that locality.

Three of the six fiscal impact analysis techniques—per capita multiplier, service standard, and proportional valuation—represent average costing approaches, while the three remaining techniques—case study, comparable city, and employment anticipation—represent marginal costing strategies.

All but two of the methods—proportional valuation and employment anticipation—are used for estimating the impacts of residential activity. The remaining two are applicable for nonresidential land uses, while the case study is used for both residential and nonresidential projections. Since the same methods for revenue estimation may be utilized under any technique, emphasis is given to differences in the estimation of public service costs.

Application Fiscal impact methods are applied to fiscal impact tasks based on: (1) fiscal conditions at the site of the analysis and (2) the type of problem with which the analyst is faced. In the first case, is the city's public service delivery system in tune with demand or is it drastically over- or under-utilized? If the services the city supplies are reasonably close to the level of demand that is being experienced, the assumption can be made that future costs are a reflection of current costs, and average costing methods (per capita multiplier, service standard, proportional valuation) can be employed. If, on the other hand, excess or deficient service capacity exists, the marginal strategies (case study, comparable city, employment anticipation) should be used.

In the second case (type of problem), if the analyst is faced with a small development proposal or several development alternatives, the simpler, usually average costing approaches, should be used. A large or unique development proposal will usually require one of the marginal costing methods.

For large, declining cities or small rapid growth suburbs, the case study method is almost always appropriate for large complex developments and even for smaller development or development alternatives. For mid-size, moderate growth suburbs, the per capita multiplier method is appropriate for smaller developments or alternative development scenarios, whereas the service standard method is more appropriate for the large, single development case.

For nonresidential impact analyses, the case study method should be used in large, declining cities or small, rapid-growth areas, and the proportional valuation method is almost always employed in mid-size, moderate growth communities, especially in situations where only a rough gauge of impact is desired.

Practitioner's notes

1. Emphasize that in some fiscal impact problems *multiple* methods may be used.
2. In borderline situations (fiscal conditions at impact site may not provide clear insight as to which method to use) two or more methods may be employed as a check against the accuracy of any one method.

Per capita multiplier method

Background The per capita multiplier method is the classic average costing approach for projecting the impact of population change on local municipal and school district costs and revenues. Due to its simplicity and ease of operation, the method has been applied to almost every type of fiscal impact situation.

The per capita multiplier method relies on detailed demographic information by housing type (total household size and number of school-age children) and the average cost, per person and per pupil, of municipal and school district operating expenses (including the amortization of capital expenditures) to project an annual (operating/capital) cost assignable to a particular population change. Using the proportional valuation method, the technique begins by sifting off the local costs assigned to nonresidential uses. Then it expresses all local municipal costs per person and school district costs per pupil. These per capita and per pupil costs, multiplied by an estimate of the population shift resulting from growth (partitioned by pupils and adults) are the incremental costs assigned to the specific growth generator.

To illustrate, assume that a midwestern municipality is attempting to analyze the local fiscal impact of 100 garden apartments (80 percent one-bedroom, 20 percent two-bedroom). Units in the proposed development will probably rent for an average of $250 and $300 monthly and are estimated to be valued at $15,000 and $21,000 per unit, respectively. Demographic profiles of garden apartments for the area indicate that an average 1.686 residents and 0.036 school-age children may be expected to reside in one-bedroom units and 2.685 residents and 0.232 school-age children in two-bedroom units. Information obtained from the city manager and superintendent of schools tabulates current total municipal operating costs per person at $250 annually and total school district costs per pupil at $1,500 annually. The development is assigned $33,720 (80 units × 1.686 persons per unit × $250 per person) in municipal costs and $4,320 (80 units × 0.036 children per unit × $1,500 per child) in school district costs for the local fiscal impact of a one-bedroom unit, and $13,425 in municipal costs (20 × 2.685 × $250), and $6,960 in school district costs (20 × 0.232 × $1,500) for a two-bedroom unit. The total cost to the municipality and school district for operations and capital additions for the 100-unit garden apartment development is thus estimated at approximately $58,000 annually ($33,720 + $4,320 + $13,425 + $6,960).

Assumptions A basic assumption of the per capita multiplier method is that over the long run, *current* average operating costs per capita and per student are the best estimates of *future* operating costs occasioned by growth. A second assumption is that current *local* service levels are the most accurate indicators of future service levels and that they will continue on the same scale in the future. A further premise is that the current composition of the population occasioning costs and the population contributing to future costs are sufficiently similar that the above scenario will remain unaltered.

A fourth and final premise is that the current distribution of expenditures among the various sectors of municipal service will remain constant in the short run and will serve as the primary indicator of the way in which additional expenditures will be subsequently allocated.

Advantages
Simplicity/low cost   The per capita multiplier method is comparable to the comparable city and service standard methods in terms of ease of implementation.

Acceptability   The per capita multiplier method is the most widely accepted fiscal impact procedure available, particularly for the private planning consultant.

Disadvantage
Richness of detail   Probably the single greatest disadvantage of this method is the detail to which results are available. Its most accurate indication of costs is only to the level of municipal and school district services.

Practitioner's notes
1. Emphasize that this is the most versatile, easily understood, simple to implement, and thus widely employed method.
2. Assumption that current costs per unit are the best indication of future costs is key to method.
3. Make point that method is inherently site-influenced—all information is obtained from historical local expenditure patterns.

Case study method
Background   The case study method is the classic marginal cost approach to project the effect of population change on municipal and school district costs.

The case study method employs intensive site-specific investigations to determine categories of *excess* or slack public service capacity (capacity beyond that needed to accommodate the existing service or target population at current public service levels) or *deficient* or overage capacity (capacity below that needed to accommodate the existing service or target population). The excess or deficient service capacities are subtracted from or added to best estimates of the operating and capital demands posed by growth for each service category. (Estimated changes in service population is the measure by which public officials gauge future operating and capital reactions.) The result of population-imposed need, mitigated by existing excess capacity or worsened by deficient capacity, is projected future public response for each service category.

For example, during an interview, the superintendent of schools reveals that both number of students per classroom and pupil-teacher ratios are significantly lower than in the past. He estimates that constructing a housing development will cause classroom size and pupil-teacher ratios to increase to previous levels but will not require new teachers to be hired or capital facilities to be expanded. In this case of obvious excess capacity, the new development is charged a minimal cost. In another example, however, new development requires that a rescue station must immediately be built, and additional firemen hired to serve an area already partially developed. In the case of existing deficient capacity, the new development is charged the *full* extent of these additional expenditures, even though previous development has contributed to the cost and will benefit from both the new facility and the additional personnel.

Assumptions   The case study approach is based on four assumptions. The first assumption is that communities differ in the degree to which they exhibit excess or deficient service capacity which significantly affects the level of local service extensions. The second assumption is that marginal changes in providing municipal and school district services, as a reaction to excess or deficient service capacity, are the most accurate indications of future local servicing costs.

The third premise is that while current local service levels may be altered slightly, they, and not national standards, represent the criteria against which local excess and deficient capacity are calculated. The fourth and final assumption is that local department heads, intimately familiar with the service delivery capacity of their departments, provide the most accurate gauge of future expenditure extensions in a particular category of municipal or school district service.

Data requirements   The basic data needed to implement the method—estimates of excess or deficient service capacity and expected local service responses—come from estimates made by local municipal employees. These factors are specific to each locality; they must be obtained through on-site interviews.

Advantage

Richness of detail   The other fiscal impact analysis methods omit the detailing of manpower and capital facility needs as a prerequisite for assigning costs. The case study method, however, not only predicts the financial consequences of growth, but also assigns the costs of growth to operating and capital facilities by component service category.

Disadvantage

Time and cost   The case study method is complex and costly. The method requires extensive interviews and other field work. It is more expensive than the other fiscal impact analysis methods. The relative ease and simplicity of most other methods stand in contrast to the considerable time and cost necessary to undertake the case study method.

Practitioner's notes

1.   Emphasize the time-consuming and, as such, costly aspects of implementing this method.
2.   Municipal officials' estimates may not always be accurate— use the service standard method as an accuracy check.
3.   Existing service excess or deficient capacity per municipal department will be the most difficult information to secure.
4.   There is no better method to employ for detailed results and intimate knowledge about the fiscal impact site.
5.   Municipal officials are often excellent sources of information for the distribution of service resources between residential and nonresidential uses.

Service standard method

Background   The service standard method is an average costing method which uses averages of manpower and capital facility service levels, obtained from the U.S. Census of Governments, for municipalities and school districts of similar size and geographic location. The service standard model determines the total number of additional employees by service function (financial administration, general control, police, fire, highways, sewerage, sanitation, water supply, parks and recreation, and libraries) that will be required as the result of growth. The analyst determines the local operating cost for additional personnel adding local operating outlays (salary, statutory and equipment expenditures) per employee by service function (e.g., $14,500 per policeman, $13,900 per fireman) to an annual expenditure for capital facilities specific to the service function. The annual capital expenditure is obtained through the use of capital-to-operating service ratios derived from Census information, and applied to the local total operating cost per employee.

To illustrate, a northeastern city of 33,000 residents will grow to 38,000 as a result of a new 1,600-unit single-family subdivision. Using service ratios of 2.33 policemen and 1.88 firemen per 1,000 population (for Northeastern municipalities of 25,000–49,999), if the community follows average service patterns specific to its population size and location, a service demand for 11.7 policemen (2.33 × 5.0) and 9.4 firemen (1.88 × 5.0) will be created locally as a result of the development. At the previously stated local average operating cost per policeman ($14,500) and fireman ($13,900), the operating costs assignable to the development for just these two functional areas is $300,310 ($169,650 [$14,500 × 11.7] + $130,660 [$13,900 × 9.4]). Using a 0.025 capital-to-operating ratio (Northeastern municipalities of 25,000–49,999 population) for police capital expenditures and applying this to the product of the number of policemen to be added locally, the average local operations cost per policeman will add $4,241 ($169,650 × 0.025); a 0.005 capital-to-operations ratio for fire protection capital expenditures, similarly applied to the product of the additional firemen, and the average local operations cost per fireman will add an additional $653 ($130,660 × 0.005). The total assignable cost (operating plus capital debt service) to the growth increment for these two functions is $305,204. This procedure is repeated for each functional area listed above to ascertain total costs assignable.

Assumptions   A fundamental assumption of the service standard approach is that over the long run average *existing* service levels for both manpower and capital facilities of comparable cities can be used to assign costs to future development.

Another premise of the technique is that service levels for both manpower and capital facilities vary according to the community's population. A further assumption is that after population size, geographic location also affects public service levels.

Data requirements   The basic data needed to implement the service standard method consist of multipliers for household size and school-age population for different types of housing; population estimates for municipalities and school districts; public employee service standards by service category; average operating costs per employee, and annual capital-to-operating expenditure ratios by service category.

Advantages

Richness of detail   The service standard method is second only to the case study method in the amount of detail it provides. The service standard technique not only predicts the financial consequences of population change but also traces specific growth-induced responses for each public service category.

Simplicity/low cost   The service standard technique is straightforward and inexpensive to use.

Disadvantage   To the extent that actual local performance differs from the average (due to variance in local wealth, excess or deficient service capacity, labor rules or traditions, public service emphases) the service standard projection will either overestimate or underestimate true local expenditures.

Practitioner's notes

1.   Point out to users the versatility of U.S. Census data as opposed to previously used trade union or employment association standards, etc.
2.   Method may be used when only rough gauges of future resident and school populations are available.
3.   Capital-to-operating ratios replace myriad standards for individual capital facilities.
4.   Standards are available for "common categories of municipal expenditure" as defined by Census of Governments. For service categories other than these other standards must be used.
5.   Standards are relatively stable over time. Multipliers appear to peak in 1968 and remain slightly lower and level from this period on.
6.   Local "standards," derived from the specific service experience of the city being analyzed, may be used in place of national standards.

Comparable city method
Background   The comparable city method is used to project marginal fiscal impact. It relies on expenditure multipliers that vary by size and growth rate of community or school district. The multipliers, presented in chart form, represent a proportional relationship of the average expenditures of cities of various size and growth rates to the average expenditures of cities of the most common population size and growth rate. As a community grows or declines at a certain pace, and in so doing changes population categories, its expenditure pattern is characterized by a different multiplier. The ratio of the new multiplier to the old multiplier is multiplied by existing per capita expenditures to determine the new local municipal and school district costs resulting from change. The expenditure multipliers have been derived from data compiled by the U.S. Cen-

sus of Governments and are available in sixteen increments for community size and growth rate. Briefly, the method projects increases or decreases in future gross expenditures for the five basic municipal services (general government, public safety, public works, health and welfare, recreation and culture) and school district services (primary and secondary education) by comparing the products of a community's expenditure ratios, per capita costs, and service populations before and after a projected growth increment.

To illustrate, a municipality with a population of 49,000 and a historical annual growth rate of 0.4 percent rezones land to accommodate a large planned development. This development will house 10,000 residents and be built over a five-year period. The community will thus grow to a level of 59,000 with a 4 percent annual growth rate over the period of its construction (10,000/49,000 = 0.20/5 yrs. = 0.04/yr.). Its pregrowth general government operating expenditure ratio is 0.97; its postgrowth operating expenditure ratio is 1.21. Assuming that before development the community exhibited a $20 per capita general government operating expenditure, then if this community behaves in a fashion similar to other communities of this postgrowth population size and growth rate, it may anticipate that future expenditures for general government purposes will be $25 per person ($20 × 1.21/0.97 = $25).

Multiplying this figure by the present plus the increment in service population, the community will experience (based on historic trends of the similar communities) $1,475,000 in total general government operating expenditures (59,000 × $25). Since prior to development it spent $980,000 annually for this service (49,000 × $20), the general government operating expense engendered by the large planned development, and thus assignable to this growth, is $495,000 annually ($1,475,000 minus $980,000). This projection procedure for operating and capital expenditures is repeated for each of the basic municipal and school district functions (i.e., public safety, public works, health/welfare, recreation/culture) to determine total costs assignable to future growth.

Assumptions   A basic assumption of the comparable city method is that public service expenditures vary significantly according to a community's size and growth rate.

A second assumption is that the direction of growth (positive or negative) also affects local service expenditures.

Data requirements   The most important data to implement the comparable city method are the expenditure multipliers for municipal and school district services, by community size and growth rate. These are available in the *Fiscal Impact Guidebook*, published by the U.S. Department of Housing and Urban Development.

Advantage

Time and cost   The comparable city method is relatively inexpensive to effect. Time requirements to employ this method are about the same as the service standard method.

Disadvantage

Validity of the expenditure multipliers   The comparable city method assumes that local operating and capital expenditures attributable to growth will, in the long run, emulate the expense patterns of communities of comparable size and growth rate. If local costs differ from the patterns indicated by the expenditure multipliers of comparable cities, average expenditure multipliers used to predict local response to population change may tend to either under- or overestimate the true reaction.

Practitioner's notes

1.   A precondition for employment of this method is future population levels and/or growth rates significantly different from what is currently being experienced.
2.   An assumption is that the service profile of communities of the size to which you will grow, via a growth rate different from the current one, is the best indication of future expected service loads.
3.   This is a severe view of cost impact as new servicing costs levels are assigned to the *entire* population.

Proportional valuation method

Background   The proportional valuation method is an average costing approach used to project the impact of *nonresidential (industrial and commercial)* development on local costs and revenues. Because data on real property value are almost universally maintained, analysts have regularly used this method, like the case study, to assess the municipal fiscal implications of commercial and industrial growth.

The proportional valuation method employs a two-step process to assign a share of municipal costs to a new commercial or industrial establishment. First, a share of total municipal costs is given to all local nonresidential uses. Second, a portion of these nonresidential costs is allocated to the incoming nonresidential facility. The method assumes that relative real property values represent shares of municipal costs. Experience has shown, however, that while the direction of this cost assignment procedure is relatively accurate, as the value of nonresidential property significantly differs from the average value of existing local property, the direct proportional assignment of costs tends either to overstate or understate the magnitude of assignable costs. Thus, the analyst must use refinement coefficients to compensate for this over- or understatement of costs, and to modify the direct proportional relationship in the allocation of municipal costs.

To illustrate, a local shopping center, valued at $5 million, is proposed for a Texas community whose total property valuation is $100 million ($80 million residential, farm and vacant land, and $20 million for commercial and industrial property). Annual municipal operating expenditures, including statutory and capital debt service costs, are $3.5 million.

The analyst using the proportional valuation method first assigns a share of the $3.5 million annual municipal operating expenditures to all local nonresidential uses. To do so, he multiplies all municipal costs by the product of local nonresidential real property valuation to total local real property valuation (in this example $20 million/$100 million or 0.20) and a refinement coefficient (1.38). The resulting share is $966,000. He next assigns a share of these costs to the incoming nonresidential facility by multiplying total nonresidential costs by the product of the real property valuation of the new facility to total local nonresidential valuation ($5 million/$20 million or 0.25) and a refinement coefficient (0.18). The result is $43,470. Costs are then partitioned into the six categories of municipal service, using percentage distributions which have been derived from case studies of other industrial and commercial fiscal impact.

Assumptions   A basic assumption of the proportional valuation method is that municipal costs increase with the intensity of land use, and change in real property value is a reasonable substitute for change in intensity of use. Further, as nonresidential real property value departs significantly from the average local real property value, the direct proportional relationship must be refined to avoid either overstating costs (where incremental or average nonresidential real property value significantly exceeds average local property values) or understating costs (where incremental or average nonresidential real property value is significantly less than average local property value).

Data requirements   The proportional valuation method requires a limited amount of data, most of it readily available. The most important segment of information is the equalized real property value—for the new nonresidential facility, for all nonresidential real property, and for all local real property. Refinement coefficients, to scale the costs to all nonresidential property and to the new nonresidential facility, are found in the *Fiscal Impact Guidebook.*

Advantage

Time and cost   The proportional valuation method may be completed quickly and inexpensively. Approximately thirty hours are required to implement this approach. This time factor, while comparable to the employment anticipation method, is far less than the time required to complete a case study.

Disadvantage

Validity of the refinement coefficients   Two sets of refinement coefficients are employed to improve the accuracy of the proportional valuation method. They are derived from retrospective analyses which compared the actual expenditures generated by nonresidential facilities to those projected using a simple proportional valuation strategy. The refinement coefficients are initial approximations which must be significantly expanded in the future.

Practitioner's notes

1. The proportional valuation method should *not* be used for residential analyses—more accurate methods are available for residential fiscal impact.
2. Refinement coefficients are necessary because this technique frequently understates the impact of low value facilities and overstates the impact of high value facilities.
3. The method provides only rough estimates; resources permitting, back-up should be undertaken with a case study.
4. Refinement coefficients can be replaced with a weighted average of department heads' estimates of the proportion of services allocated to nonresidential versus residential uses.

Employment anticipation method

Background   The employment anticipation method is a recently developed marginal costing technique for projecting the impact of *nonresidential (industrial and commercial)* growth on local municipal costs and revenues. The method relies on relationships between local commercial and industrial employment levels and per capita municipal costs. It predicts a change in municipal costs based on an anticipated change in local commercial or industrial employment levels and per capita municipal costs. Coefficients for the five categories of municipal service (general government, public safety, public works, health/welfare, recreation/culture) and for statutory/unclassified expenses and debt service have been developed using multivariate regression analysis to predict the change in municipal expenditures related to local employment variation. The coefficients may be read as "a change of one commercial or industrial employee will produce an increase in per capita local public service expenditures of x percent."

To illustrate, assume that a new industrial plant with 1,000 employees will be built in a growing community whose current population is 16,000 and whose current per capita public safety cost is $50.00. The cost for this service generated by the new facility is calculated by first multiplying the percentage increase per employee for public safety (0.00162) by the number of employees (1,000), which yields an increase in the per capita costs of public safety of 1.62 percent. Per capita outlays will therefore rise by $0.81 ($50 × 0.0162 = $0.81), from $50.00 to $50.81. Multiplying the resident population by the increase in costs (16,000 × $0.81) yields the total increase in operating costs ($12,960) for public safety assignable to the new industrial plant. This procedure is repeated for each of the remaining categories of municipal service and for aggregate statutory and capital (debt service) expenditures to determine total annual municipal costs related to growth. Revenues are tabulated in the same way as for the other methods and computed with costs to determine net fiscal impact.

Assumptions The employment anticipation method is based on three assumptions: (1) the level of local commercial or industrial employment directly affects the magnitude of local municipal expenditures; (2) the relationship viewed is the impact of commercial or industrial employment on municipal expenditures within a multivariate context, controlling for the confounding effects of other social, political, and economic factors; (3) the impact of additional employment will vary for communities of differing population and direction of growth.

Data requirements Data required for the employment anticipation method consists of four elements: (1) existing per capita expenditures by service category, (2) coefficients of per capita percent change per employee, (3) projections of future employees by nonresidential type, and (4) current municipal population estimates.

Advantages

Operational utility An obvious advantage of the employment anticipation method is that it expresses future municipal costs as a function of expected employees—the direct local product of nonresidential growth.

Simplicity/cost The employment anticipation method is inexpensive to use. It is similar in scope to the proportional valuation method.

Disadvantage   This method relies on coefficients to express changes in per capita municipal expenditures for categories of cities defined by population size and direction of growth. In so doing, a single multiplier is used for all cities within a particular population group. Since cities may vary by populations of close to 50,000 for the larger groups, the same nonresidential facility in a city of 149,000 may be shown to be significantly more costly than one in a city of 100,000. Obviously this is not the case. It is the grouping technique that limits the result.

Practitioner's notes

1. Emphasize that changes in a city's employment are viewed simultaneously with other changes taking place in city structure (i.e., income, wealth, tax basis, etc.). The specific effect of employment change on municipal expenditures is then segregated from other internal socioeconomic changes and specified as to magnitude.
2. The employment anticipation method does not provide coefficients for cities over 150,000. This is due to the data base that was used (New Jersey municipalities), which contained only a few cities in excess of 150,000 that were subsequently eliminated for insufficiency of sample. If nonresidential development is contemplated for cities over 150,000, the case study method should be used.
3. High impact costs in statutory/unclassified and debt service costs reflect liberal retirement benefits and capital facility expansions of the early 1970s.

Fiscal impact revenue projections

The U.S. Census Bureau recognizes four major types of revenue sources: general revenue, utility revenue, liquor store revenue, and insurance trust revenue. This article confines its interest to general revenue because the other sources are not major contributors to a local government's general fund. Utility revenue—the receipts from sales of water, electric service, transit service and gas—is often a large part of a municipality's gross revenues but an insignificant portion of net revenues. User charges (except for transit, which is usually a fiscal drain) typically reflect the unit cost of utility operations and do not provide significant local revenue outside the general fund. Similarly, insurance trust revenue, which comes from both contributions from employers and earnings on assets, and which provides income for social insurance and employee retirement benefits, usually can be used only to increase the insurance trust fund. Therefore, this type of revenue is also excluded from the discussion. Finally, liquor store revenues (in states that operate public liquor stores) provide such a small proportion of local revenues that they too have been excluded.

Revenues considered This article considers the two primary components of general revenue: (1) *own source revenue*, i.e., raised by the municipal and school district itself, and (2) *intergovernmental transfers* contributed to the locality by both the state and federal governments. *Own source revenues* include:

1. Taxes—real property, personal property, income sales, property transfer, occupation and business privilege, per capita, transient occupancy.
2. Charges/miscellaneous revenues—interest earnings, fees and permit revenue, fines, forfeitures and penalties.

Intergovernmental transfers come from:

1. State—sales tax redistribution, income tax distribution, motor fuels tax, cigarette and alcohol tax, educational basic assistance, educational categorical aid, etc.
2. Federal—revenue sharing, CETA, CDBG, Public Works Countercyclical, Federal Impact School Assistance, etc.

Revenue emphasis The revenue half of the fiscal impact calculation delves deeply into the array of local fiscal resources. When the user attempts to project revenues, the number of alternative local resources with which he is typically confronted is staggering. Two important segments of information help mitigate the arduous task of revenue tabulation. The first is a determination of which of these revenues will be affected. Information of this type permits the elimination of several categories of revenue from consideration, making the quantity of revenues with which the analyst must deal more manageable.

More important is a firm grasp by users on how revenues are generated locally. This may be obtained from close scrutiny of local municipal and school district operating budgets. The user will find, for instance, that the locality may depend heavily on the property tax or a locally levied income tax, or for that matter be supported to an extensive degree by intergovernmental transfers, i.e., from either the state or federal government. This knowledge of local revenue distribution permits the analyst to segregate those types of revenues which are important and, therefore, must undergo detailed calculations from those which are unimportant, capable of grouping and only worthy of estimation. Revenue distribution is shown in Table 1.

Revenue source	Revenue most often flows principally to:
I. Own source revenues	
Property, income and sales taxes	
1. Real property tax	Municipality/school district
2. Personal property tax	Municipality/school district
3. Income tax	Municipality/school district
4. Sales tax	Municipality/school district
Other taxes	
5. Property tax transfer	Municipality/school district
6. Occupation and business privilege tax	Municipality
7. Per capita tax	Municipality
8. Transient occupancy tax	Municipality
Miscellaneous revenues	
9. Interest earnings	Municipality
10. Fees and permit revenue	Municipality
11. Fines, forfeitures and penalty revenue	Municipality
User charges	
12. Recreation, health and property services	Municipality/school district
13. Water, sewerage and solid waste charges	Municipality
II. Intergovernmental transfers	
State	
1. Sales tax redistribution	Municipality
2. Income tax redistribution	Municipality
3. Motor fuels tax redistribution	Municipality

Table 1.

Projecting own source revenues—taxes

Real property tax   The real property tax is frequently the most significant source of local revenues. It is a percentage levy on the value of land and improvements. In most states, the municipality and the school district each levy a separate tax, even though a municipality often collects both revenues. The real property tax rate is expressed either in mills (one thousandth of a dollar) or as a dollar amount per hundred dollars of assessed valuation. A rate of forty mills thus equals a local tax rate of $40 per thousand or $4 per $100 of assessed valuation.

To project revenues from the real property tax, the analyst multiplies the expected assessed valuation by the local tax rate (expressed as a decimal). The local tax rate multiplied by the expected assessed valuation should always produce the same estimate of revenue as the product of the equalized tax rate and the market or true value of the property. Equalization is a process of estimating true

Revenue source	Revenue most often flows principally to:
4. Cigarettes and alcohol tax redistribution	Municipality
5. Incorporated/unincorporated business or business income tax redistribution	Municipality
6. Road and road lighting aid	Municipality
7. Public utilities franchise tax redistribution	Municipality
8. Aid to urban or rural areas	Municipality
9. Homestead and forgone tax rebate	Municipality
10. Educational basic support via flat grants	School district
11. Educational assistance via variable guarantees	School district
12. Educational categorical aid	School district
13. Elementary and secondary education act subsidies (ESEA Titles I-IV)	School district
Federal	
14. State/Local Fiscal Assistance Act (federal revenue sharing)	Municipality
15. Comprehensive Employment Training Act (CETA)	Municipality
16. Public Works Employment Act (anti-recession aid)	Municipality
17. Community development block grants (CDBGs)	Municipality
18. Educational Assistance in Federal Impact Areas (P.L. 815,874)	School district

Source: U.S. Census of Governments, 1972.

Table 1. Continued.

value of a property by applying a sales/assessment ratio to its assessed valuation. County or state governments often use this process because local municipalities often assess at different percentages of true values and frequently have dated assessments. In both cases the assessed value of a property is thus less than its true or market value.

Municipality $40,000 × $0.94/$100 × 1,000 residential units = $ 376,000

School district $40,000 × 2.81/$100 × 1,000 residential units = $1,124,000

Real property transfer tax Many municipalities levy a tax on the transfer of real property. This tax is often equally shared by municipality and school district. To project revenues from this source, the analyst multiplies the unit's sales price or market value by the transfer tax rate, the number of units, and the average frequency of unit transfer. A common mistake is to ignore the turnover factor and credit too large a revenue to the development as a result of applying the transfer tax rate to all new units rather than to the estimated annual portion of these units that will change ownership. The turnover figure in the example below is based on 1972 Census data, which indicate that, in general homeowners move once every five years. Put another way, 20 percent of the owner-occupied housing stock is transferred annually. Here are calculations for 1,000 single-family homes:

Market value/ unit	Transfer × tax rate	× No. of units	% of housing turnover/ × year	Total = revenues
$50,000	× 0.0100	× 1,000	× 0.20 (national figure)	= $100,000

Sales tax   As of 1977, 26 states imposed locally levied sales taxes. The tax most often applies to tangible personal property at the rate of 1 percent of the retail sales price. The tax is almost exclusively a source of municipal revenue, except in Louisiana, where school districts are also allowed to tax consumer durables.

Revenue from the local sales tax may be estimated for new residential development as follows (the resident proportion of total local sales may be obtained from comparative existing facilities in the area).

New development aggregate family income / Pre-development local aggregate family income	Current × revenues from local sales	Resident pro- × portion of total local sales	Additional local sales tax = attributable to growth
$\dfrac{\$30,000,000}{\$200,000,000}$ or 0.15	× $200,000	× 0.25	= $7,500

Per capita tax   The per capita tax is a lump sum tax levied on adults aged 18 to 65. It may be levied by municipalities and/or school districts. Revenues derived from new development are estimated by first subtracting dwelling unit estimates of pre-school and school-age children from similar estimates of total household size. This figure, the estimate of adult resident population, is multiplied by the per capita tax and by the number of anticipated occupied dwelling units.

Earned income tax   A significant number of localities throughout the country levy a tax on earned income. The levy is usually shared by municipalities and school districts. Typically the levy is on resident family *earned* income, without allowances for deductions. To project revenues from this source, the most frequent procedure is to convert estimated monthly housing costs (taxes, debt service, and insurance) or contract rental costs to family income. This procedure assumes that a family spends a given percentage of its monthly income on housing. The analyst then multiplies family income by the local income tax rate and the number of units in the development to estimate total revenue from this source.

Projecting own source revenues: user charges/miscellaneous

Interest earnings   Nationally, for units of local government, the largest single category of miscellaneous revenues is interest on investments. Many states allow municipalities to invest a share of their unused revenues during fertile cash flow periods (immediately after taxes are collected) in short-term marketable securities.

As population increases, general revenues increase and more tax money is available for investment. The per capita amount of revenues resulting from investment remains essentially the same, however. The reverse is also true. As a city begins to decline, the tax base diminishes; the city is not able to issue as many tax anticipation notes and instead must rely on its own cash revenues for lean periods, thus limiting short-term investment potential. The per capita amount also remains relatively constant. The additional revenue resulting from interest on investment may be projected as follows: for 1,000 single-family homes (value of assessment on existing vacant land not included):

Current estimate of annual interest on earnings, public property rentals and sales		Total assessed valuation of the new development / Total assessed valuation of all local properties		Increment on investment of earnings attributable to growth
$90,000	×	$\dfrac{\$ 40,000,000}{\$200,000,000}$		
$90,000	×	0.20	=	$18,000

Fees and permits   Most revenue fees and permits are the result of building, occupancy, electrical, explosive and landfill permissions or assurances. Revenue accruing from this source can be estimated via a two-step process. First, the current total annual revenue from this source is divided by the current estimate of the number of local dwelling units. Multiplying this figure by the estimated number of incoming dwelling units yields a projection of future development generated revenue from fees and permits.

Fines, forfeitures and penalties   Fines are levied locally for violation of traffic, safety (fire) building code and health ordinances. Penalties include payments for tax and library fund delinquency. This revenue resource is almost exclusively a municipal one. It may be estimated on a per capita basis for 1,000 single-family homes as shown in the following example:

Total annual revenues collected from fines and forfeitures	÷	*Current estimated population*	=	*Per capita revenue from fines and forfeitures*
$64,000	÷	16,000	=	$4.00

Per capita revenue from fines and forfeitures	×	*Anticipated development population*	=	*Total revenue from fines and forfeitures attributable to growth*
$ 4.00	×	4,300	=	$17,200

User charges for water, sewerage and sanitation services Contrary to the Census definition, municipalities frequently provide water, sewerage, and sanitation services which neither are operated as a distinct, separable authority (in which costs are assumed to equal revenues and thus the general treasury is unaffected) nor are privately operated (again the assumption is that general treasury remains unchanged). Frequently a municipality provides water, sewerage and sanitation services using public works personnel, and the taxes levied or flat fees charged enter the general treasury. The example below pertains to such a case:

Daily water consumption by type of facility (gallons/day)	×	*No. of days*	×	*No. of dwelling units*	=	*Total annual water consumption for domestic purposes (gallons)*
250 (single-family homes)	×	365	×	1,000	=	91,250,000
200 (apartments)	×	365	×	500	=	36,500,000

Total annual water consumption	×	*Water rate + sewer rate*	=	*Total revenue from water and sewerage charges attributable to growth*
91,250,000	×	$1.50/1,000 gal.+ 0.50/1,000 gal.	=	$182,500
36,500,000	×	$1.50/1,000 gal.+ 0.50/1,000 gal.	=	$ 73,000

Projecting intergovernmental transfers: state

State-levied sales tax redistribution   Sales tax levied by a state for the privilege of selling or renting tangible personal property at retail rates typically is returned to local governments as a flat and uniform percentage of the locality's taxable retail sales. The reapportionment rate is frequently less than 10 percent of total state taxes collected in a locality. This revenue flows almost exclusively to the general fund of municipalities. The key to predicting additional revenue from this source is to project the additional sales which will take place in the locality. Patterns of the new population's convenience and nonconvenience goods (or shopping goods) purchases and the proportions of income new residents will spend on taxable items in each of these categories are the basic data necessary for the calculation.

Several studies have documented that the great majority of shopping trips by automobile take no more than 7 minutes travel time (one way) for convenience goods nor 15 minutes for shopping goods. Consumer surveys report that, on average, residents commit 75 percent of their expenditures for convenience goods to local vendors (local is defined as within the area covered by the 7-minute shopping trip) but only 25 percent of their expenditures for shopping goods to local vendors. In addition, according to the Bureau of Labor Statistics, approximately 20 percent of family income is spent on convenience goods and approximately 10 percent on shopping goods. Other studies have estimated that, nationally, approximately 50 percent of consumer expenditures for convenience goods are for taxable goods; approximately 90 percent of consumer expenditures for shopping goods are for taxable items.

To calculate the state sales tax redistribution requires four steps. The analyst must first estimate the new increment of gross sales. From this figure, the analyst must then project the dollar amount of locally captured sales. Third, the analyst applies a tax rate. This figure, times the state-calculated or legislated reapportionment percentage, yields the state redistributed sales tax increment to the locality. The calculation for a development of 1,000 single-family homes is as follows:

New development aggregate family income	*% spent × on goods*	*$ spent = on goods*
$30 million	× 0.20 (convenience)	= $6 million
	× 0.10 (shopping)	= $3 million
$ spent on goods	*× Taxable share*	*Taxable share = of goods*
$6 million	× 0.50 (convenience)	= $3 million
$3 million	× 0.90 (shopping)	= $2.7 million
Value of taxable convenience goods	*% captured × locally*	*Value of taxable = goods purchased locally*
$3 million	× 0.75	= $2.25 million

Value of taxable shopping goods	% captured × locally	Value of taxable = goods purchased locally
$2.7 million	× 0.25	= $675,000

Value of taxable goods purchased locally (convenience plus shopping)	× Sales tax rate	Sales tax $ = sent to state
$2,925,000	× 0.05	= $146,250

Sales tax amount sent to state	Legislated or state determined percentage × of local return	Additional state sales tax revenues = flowing to locality
$146,250	× 0.10	= $ 14,625

State income tax redistribution   Several states redistribute state-levied income tax to local jurisdictions. In most cases, the direct fiscal flow is to the municipality rather than to the school district. The local reapportionment formula in the majority of cases is based strictly on the proportion of state population and seldom bears any relation to the amount of taxes collected locally. The analyst must remember certain important aspects about any redistribution formula which does not relate to a percentage share of revenues paid directly by the locality to the state but rather distributes a "pool" of revenues according to an ever-changing share of population, road miles or other criteria: (1) the gross amount of money to be apportioned is changing; (2) other localities within the state are changing their demands on the overall amount via population and/or apportionment criteria variations; and (3) changes in population and/or other apportionment criteria are taking place within the locality other than the development itself.

Practitioner's notes

1. Emphasize the importance of the analyst checking *current* entitlement guidelines and funding formulas of the intergovernmental aid programs as these guidelines/formulas are often modified.
2. Note that intergovernmental revenues are often more difficult to project than own-source funds: the allocation formulas are more complicated; eligibility for assistance changes as local wealth, unemployment or other indicators move upward or downward; and there are frequent overall community effects that must be considered. (Overall community changes are most likely with annexations and large projects as opposed to smaller scale growth.)

Projecting intergovernmental transfers: federal

Federal revenue sharing   The Treasury Department adminis-
ters funds authorized by the State-Local Fiscal Assistance Act of
1973. Funds are allocated directly to states and units of local government. Allocation of funds to local governments (two-thirds of the
total collected) is based on the local government population, multiplied by the general tax effort (adjusted taxes collected divided by
aggregate personal income), multiplied by the relative income factor (per capita income for the local government divided by the per
capita income for the county or municipality). Those municipalities
with more people, more tax money per dollar of personal income,
and larger shares of impoverished residents will receive more
money. For annexations, border changes, significant rezonings, or
changes in land use, the detailed calculation may prove worthwhile;
for most developments, per capita estimates based on the prior
year's allocation may be much more reasonable.

If the analyst wishes to use the detailed calculation, the analyst
must first estimate current local revenue sharing funds. To do so the
analyst multiplies the latest estimate of the aggregate statewide
revenue sharing funds to be apportioned locally by the locality's ratio (relative to state averages) of population, tax effort, and per capita income. The analyst then projects the amount of locally received
revenue sharing funds resulting from growth. To project this
amount, the analyst multiplies the most current estimate of the local amount of revenue sharing funds by the growth's ratio (relative
to local averages) of population, tax effort, and per capita income,
annexing areas in which 45,000 people reside.

Information on the current estimate of statewide federal revenue sharing funds to be distributed to localities is available from the
state treasurer's office. Some states have developed a simple, itera
tive computer program which allows state finance personnel to
gauge local changes in revenue sharing as a function of annual
changes in indices of local entitlement. Several states distribute to
municipalities an estimate of all future intergovernmental transfers in November of each year to be used in budget calculations for
the following March. This information (relative population, wealth,
tax effort, etc.) is often available from the state treasurer's office.

Educational Assistance in Federal Impact Areas   This sub-
sidy, commonly called impact aid, is given to "local educational
agencies upon which the United States has placed financial bur-
dens." The analyst should check with the local school district superintendent and the state department of education (federal grants
office) to help determine how many children in the housing being
constructed are likely to qualify for impact aid. Federal impact aid
per pupil typically equals the per student revenue derived from local

sources in a comparable nonimpacted district. Impact aid per pupil times the number of children qualifying for impact aid equals the projected revenue from this source.

Example calculation for federal revenue sharing

Current estimate of statewide federal revenue sharing funds to be distributed to localities	$\times$	New local population (including annexed area) / New state population	$\times$	New local tax effort (including annexed area) / New state tax effort	$\times$	New state per capita income / New local per capita income (including annexed area)	=	Total local revenues from federal revenue sharing funds
$40,000,000	$\times$	$\dfrac{415,000}{8,300,000}$	$\times$	$\dfrac{0.05}{0.04}$	$\times$	$\dfrac{\$4,350}{\$5,000}$		
$40,000,000	$\times$	0.050	$\times$	1.250	$\times$	0.870	=	$2,175,000

Current estimate of local revenues sharing	$\times$	Annexed area's population / New local population (including annexed area)	$\times$	Annexed area's tax effort / New local tax effort (including annexed area)	$\times$	New local per capita income (including annexed area) / Annexed area's per capita income	=	Total local revenues from revenue sharing attributable to growth
$2,175,000	$\times$	$\dfrac{45,000}{415,000}$ or 0.108	$\times$	$\dfrac{\$5,000}{\$8,000}$ or 0.63				
$2,175,000					$\times$	0.0351	=	$76,343

Practitioner's notes

1. Check the local budget to determine the presence and relative importance of the different federal intergovernmental revenues. Allocate time for projecting revenues accordingly.
2. Check current program entitlement guidelines and funding formulas.
3. Intergovernmental revenues are often more difficult to project than own-source funds: the allocation formulas are more complicated; eligibility for assistance changes as local wealth, unemployment or other indicators move upward or downward; and there are frequent overall community effects that must be considered.

Legal climate

Background   Fiscal impact considerations are either legally authorized or there are fertile grounds for authorization within the confines of numerous planning or planning related tasks. Economy and efficiency in the land development process have long been basic planning objectives. Fiscal impact calculations could thus easily be a part of a comprehensive planning process.

Fiscal impact analysis further can be used in cases of special exception or permitted use (for instance, as part of the PUD approval process) to assure local fiscal stability throughout the multiple stages of a large development. It may be used in variances or rezonings to provide documentation that undue hardship to an individual property owner is mitigated by general community economic benefit or that the fiscal situation has so changed in a community that the existing zoning bears no relationship to reality and, in fact, is counterproductive to orderly growth.

Fiscal impact considerations are similarly useful in annexations. They assess the likely financial outcome of convergence to both jurisdictions and prevent annexations which would be especially beneficial to the residents of one jurisdiction at the expense of the residents of the other.

Yet the user must realize that every land use cannot be a municipal benefit, and while we may assess relative fiscal merit, it does not follow that those land uses that either are not as beneficial as others or impose a liability can then necessarily be excluded.

Where fiscal impact analysis has had some history, the courts have in part specified its role. Fiscal considerations, while the concern of local land use policy, are neither the sole concern, nor may they be the basis on which to exclude totally a category of land use. The courts have indicated that localities may use this information to plan for the future; however, the fiscal implications of particular development are only one element in the planning process. Courts have recognized that municipalities also have to provide housing for those who work nearby, answer regional as well as local needs, and provide housing opportunities for those who are economically or racially disadvantaged.

Practitioner's note Jurisdictions with the most experience in fiscal impact analysis frequently have the largest representation in the case law. However, as fiscal impact analysis becomes a part of the planning process it has a tendency to be misused to permanently or totally exclude a category of land use because of its "negative" fiscal impact. This will be reacted to harshly by the courts. Exclusion need not be the outcome of a negative impact analysis. One may look to pair a more costly land use with concurrent or future less costly development. A negative analysis may be further used to gauge future revenue raising requirements.

Computerized models
Background Fiscal impact analyses are often time-consuming.

After completing an initial analysis the planner typically is faced with repeating the entire process should he desire to calculate either variations of a specific proposal or alternative growth strategies. The necessity to increase speed of computations and the desire for a more rigorous approach to fiscal impact analysis have led to the rise of cost-revenue models for computers. Since most calculations are routine and repetitive they lend themselves to computer use.

In addition to simplifying the task of performing sensitivity analysis, computer models usually have the capacity to store information such that the cumulative effect of historical development decisions becomes a part of each current fiscal impact analysis. For example, assume that a community has recently adopted a planned unit development (PUD) ordinance. Several development proposals are received, each containing multiple housing types and each having a specific fiscal impact on the community. Most computerized fiscal impact approaches are able to assess the impact of each development on the local fisc serially, taking into account the fiscal effects of previous developments. Further, it is possible through computerized approaches to view the impact of multiple proposals. Thus the impact of a development 70 percent completed may be viewed simultaneously with one 25 percent completed.

Computerized models are an important part of fiscal impact analysis. They simplify the tasks of county, regional and state agencies that must review locally submitted fiscal impact statements. They can provide small municipalities with quick and sophisticated analysis of a specific development. If used judiciously, models may become an intricate part of the everyday planning analysis performed in larger cities or counties where rapid growth is occurring or areas where there is a desire for more intensive econometric analyses than are currently available.

Practitioner's notes

1. Point out to users the considerable data gathering which must be undertaken prior to setting up the model. This is often many, many times the effort required to conduct a single fiscal impact analysis. Model employment should thus reflect a need for numerous fiscal impact analyses in a single jurisdiction or a desire for significant sensitivity analysis of a more limited set of development, zone change or annexation alternatives.
2. Most models are arithmetic, a few econometric. The latter, more sophisticated and more "black box," often make it more difficult to convey the results of an analysis to the public.
3. Model services from proprietors are usually available with ongoing consulting for both data gathering and analysis phases.

Demographic multipliers in fiscal impact analysis

Demographic multipliers are used to predict the municipal and school populations that will result from new housing development. When the number, type and configuration of incoming housing units and therefore the magnitude of the new population are known, estimates of public service requirements and costs (i.e., police, fire, public works, personnel/equipment, etc.) can easily be projected. The multipliers which describe the two principal users of local services (people for municipal services and school-age children for school services) are frequently expressed by number of rooms or bedrooms. Table 2 illustrates such multipliers.

These multipliers are developed from household surveys or from data found in the U.S. Census Public Use Samples for recently constructed housing. The example in Table 2 is interpreted: "An average of 3.94 residents and 1.13 school-age children live in a three-bedroom, single-family home in New England. An average of 1.50 residents and 0.038 school-age children are found to live in one-bedroom garden apartments in the same area." If three-bedroom, single-family homes or one-bedroom garden apartments are proposed to be developed locally, the product of demographic multipliers and the number of forthcoming housing units provides an estimate of the magnitude of new residents and school-age children for whom municipal and school services must be provided.

Assume, for example, that 100 one-bedroom garden apartments are being considered for an area. Assume also that locally it costs $200 per person to provide municipal (general government, public safety, public works, health/welfare, recreation) services and $2,000 per pupil to provide school (primary and secondary education) services. Using the demographic multipliers shown in Table 2, 100 one-bedroom garden apartments would, on the average, generate 150 people (1.500 × 100) and four school-age children (0.038 × 100). Multiplying these population estimates by per capita and per pupil servicing costs indicates that roughly $38,000 will be the cost to provide public services to the new apartments [(150 × $200) plus (4 × $2000)].

Demographic characteristic	Single family homes, no. of bedrooms			Garden apartments, no. of bedrooms	
Northeast/New England	*Two*	*Three*	*Four*	*One*	*Two*
Total household size*	2.485	3.940	4.965	1.500	2.430
School-age children	0.246	1.130	2.068	0.038	0.150

*Total household size is the total number of persons, both related and unrelated, residing in a housing unit.

School-age children includes all persons aged 5 to 18 residing in the housing unit.

Table 2.

Calculating demographic multipliers   Until recently practitioners have depended on demographic multipliers determined from local field surveys to project future population. Often sample sizes, procedures, specific characteristics of occupants, etc., allowed the results of the surveys to be applicable in only limited areas. One of the larger samples was a 1973 Rutgers University survey. Results were reported for four structure types (garden apartments, highrise apartments, single-family homes and townhouses).

A better procedure for determining demographic multipliers has also begun to emerge, however. This procedure uses U.S. Census Public Use Samples to estimate demographic multipliers by housing type. The analyst can obtain an appropriate state or county group Census tape for an area, use certain programming to define housing types and convert age group distributions to school-age children, and thus estimate the number of people and pupils by housing type. Due to the rising costs of sample surveys and the possibility of bias due to sample design or administration, employment of the U.S. Census Public Use Samples is receiving increasing attention.

Practitioner's notes

1. Discuss the definitions of total household size and school-age children. Be sure to distinguish between school-age children and *public* school-age children.
2. Discuss studies involving regional and temporal variation of demographic multipliers. Emphasize that lack of temporal variation does not hold for the post-1970 period.
3. Point out how demographic multipliers can be tallied and the advantages/disadvantages of both local survey sampling and the national Public Use Sample.
4. Cover the historical evolution of demographic multipliers and the studies which have led them to be presented in their current format.

Note: The preparation of this material has been supported by the Office of Policy Development and Research, U.S. Department of Housing and Urban Development, under Purchase Order #603-80. The statements and conclusions contained herein are those of the authors and do not necessarily reflect the views of the U.S. government in general or particularly the U.S. Department of Housing and Urban Development. Neither the federal government nor the Department of Housing and Urban Development makes any warranty, expressed or implied, or assumes responsibility for the accuracy or completeness of the information herein.

Beware the Pitfalls in Fiscal Impact Analysis

Richard B. Stern and Darwin G. Stuart

More and more these days, local governments are confronted with development proposals that may require expansion of public services. At the same time, money for expansion is in short supply. The obvious solution is to determine the fiscal consequences of each development proposal. This is not to say that other criteria should be overlooked but that analysis of fiscal impact be a prerequisite for approval.

Using the tool

Planning agencies use fiscal impact analysis in four ways:

1. As a growth management tool to evaluate areawide land-use alternatives. (Examples: Phoenix, San Diego, Tucson, San Antonio, and Minneapolis–St. Paul.)
2. As an integral part of budget forecasting in central cities.
3. As part of redevelopment programs in declining portions of central cities. (Here fiscal impact analysis is used to identify slack or underutilized capacity and to streamline and improve established public services. It can also be used to find out the extent to which major projects will pay their own way through tax increment financing, value capture, and similar techniques.)
4. As a way to evaluate the fiscal consequences of a specific development proposal. (In this case, the analysis is prepared either by a local government or a developer in response to local zoning, annexation, or subdivision requirements.)

Types of analysis

Six fiscal impact analysis techniques—actually cost analysis techniques, since the method of evaluating revenues is the same in all cases—are defined by R. W. Burchell and David Listokin in *The Fiscal Impact Handbook.*[1]

These techniques are:

1. The per capita multiplier method, which applies only to residential development and considers average municipal costs per person and average school costs per pupil
2. The case study method, which projects future local costs associated with specific demands for services
3. The service standard method, which estimates manpower needs for specific services required by new development
4. The comparable city method, which estimates the impact of large-scale development by comparing the impacts of comparable developments on similar communities
5. The proportional valuation method, which assigns municipal costs to a proposed nonresidential development according to its proportion of total local property valuation
6. The employment anticipation method, which estimates costs associated with new employees generated by nonresidential development

Three of these fiscal impact methods—case study, comparable city, and employment anticipation—use marginal costing; the others use average costing.

The eight pitfalls

Experience indicates that there are potential stumbling blocks in all six methods. In some cases, the danger lurks in the underlying assumptions; in others, it stems from a misunderstanding of method. Not all the pitfalls lie in wait for every fiscal impact analyst, but most analysts will encounter at least one; and each one could result in inaccurate or unintelligible results or severe misunderstandings when conclusions are conveyed to officials or the public.

Making inappropriate assumptions about the ratios of residential to nonresidential land uses   Homeowners in communities with lots of business and industry in general pay lower property taxes than homeowners in communities that are largely residential. In the first instance, nonresidential land uses produce tax revenue without making major demands on schools and other public services. Thus, the mix between residential and nonresidential land uses that is assumed as a context for analyzing any given development project is critical to the analysis of fiscal feasibility. The analyst needs accurate answers to these questions: What are the overall development trends within the community? Will the present ratios of residential to nonresidential land uses persist? Will pre-project and post-project land-use ratios be the same?

The intent here is not that every project produce a surplus of revenue but that land uses remain balanced. Nonresidential uses that have "carried" residential land uses in the past should continue to carry them in the future. In sum, the analyst needs an understanding of the entire range of projects taking place within the community so that the surpluses of some can offset the deficits of others.

Overestimating or underestimating intergovernmental transfers In the 1976 fiscal year, fully 40 percent of all general revenues received by local governments took the form of intergovernmental transfers. Chief among the sources were state and federal aid to public schools. However, the stagnant or declining enrollments that now characterize many school districts should cause concern about the impact of new development on intergovernmental transfers. In many states, a development that causes an increase in assessed valuation but no appreciable increase in school enrollment will result in a net reduction of school aid to the community.

Perpetuating the mystique of computerized models Too often, elected officials, planners, administrators, and citizen commissioners regard computer analyses as more precise and credible than analyses performed by hand. This assignment of magical powers is unfortunate, since all fiscal impact analyses require the same computations. Computers simply perform them faster.

Further, the use of computerized models tends to hide the high degree of uncertainty involved in all fiscal impact analysis. Fiscal impact methods are all ad hoc in nature, with very little in the way of statistical precision.

If the problems to be analyzed are massive and detailed, a computer can make sense. But for small-scale, relatively straightforward fiscal impact analyses—the great majority—such models tend to be cumbersome and inflexible. Data requirements tend to be too expensive, and the workings of the models are often difficult to understand.

Computer analysis does have a particular virtue, however. That is its potential for sensitivity analysis. Sensitivity analysis makes it possible to explore different land-use mixtures and to assess various revenue sources and the costs associated with different public service systems.

Neglecting to weigh fiscal impacts against other impacts A common pitfall involves placing too much weight on fiscal factors and ignoring factors that are less easily quantified. Other kinds of impacts include those typically considered in environmental impact statements: environmental impacts on air, water, flora, and fauna; traffic impacts; social consequences for neighborhoods, housing markets, racial balance; economic impacts; land-use and transportation impacts.

One way to gain a better perspective on the relative importance of fiscal consequences is to relate all the impacts in a broader cost-effectiveness or cost-benefit framework. Monetary impacts—those involving public costs and revenues—then become only one of several important consequences that must be assessed, compared, and traded off.

Not knowing when to use average costing approaches   Average costing is by far the most commonly used approach in fiscal impact analysis. This approach assumes that the average costs of municipal services will remain stable in the future, with some adjustment for inflation. That assumption is fair in relatively slow-growing communities where the supply of public services matches demand and financing systems are stable. The most popular analysis method, the per capita multiplier technique, is based on this assumption.

However, in communities with population decline or rapid growth, a different situation pertains. Public service capacity is then likely to be either underutilized or deficient.

In these situations, marginal costing makes the most sense. Here, the costs associated with public services needed for new developments should reflect the amount of excess capacity available (in which case marginal costs will be relatively low) or the degree of overcrowding (in which case there will be higher marginal costs). Basic to the use of marginal costing is an understanding of the existing supply of and demand for local public services. Highly misleading results may emerge if the inappropriate fiscal impact technique is used.

Using fiscal impact analysis to support exclusionary zoning   Fiscal impact analysis can be used to exclude certain land uses: low- and moderate-income housing, for example. This application is invalid and has been banned in court in certain states. New Jersey, which has paid more attention to fiscal zoning than any other state, is an example.

As a type of land-use regulation, fiscal impact analysis can be a valid exercise of the police power; but, like other forms of land-use management, it must be used in support of a comprehensive plan. In general, the courts have held that fiscal impact analyses that favor certain land uses—while explicitly excluding others—are invalid.

The courts have concluded that zoning based on fiscal well-being may be considered locally but that it may be neither the sole basis for zoning nor a means to exclude certain groups.

Risking the increasing skepticism of public officials by not using standardized methods Many communities that have included requirements for fiscal impact analysis in their zoning codes or subdivision regulations have become disenchanted with the effectiveness of such requirements. The reason is that virtually every analysis has turned up a positive fiscal impact regardless of the type of development, density, or land-use mix. In other words, analysts have tinkered with the various techniques until they have found one that presents the development in a favorable fiscal light.

Public officials become skeptical when confronted with lack of standardization among the various fiscal impact methods. Depending on local growth and development conditions, as well as fiscal relationships and data, different methods can produce dramatically different cost-revenue ratios. It then appears that the methods have been manipulated to produce desired results. The *Fiscal Impact Handbook*, developed with HUD funding, represents a major step forward in the standardization of methods, but more needs to be done.

Neglecting to devote enough time to the presentation of conclusions Most planners prefer the simplest methods of fiscal impact analysis. The per capita multiplier method, which is the easiest to understand and most logical, seems to be the most credible. But it is also the most simplistic, making many shaky assumptions about average costing, land-use mixes, and so on.

Because they are harder to understand, more sophisticated techniques require more effective communication of methods and results. It is particularly important to match the results of fiscal impact analysis with other pertinent impact analyses. Too often, local officials cannot determine how the results of fiscal impact analysis should be weighted.

Future trends

The governments most likely to use fiscal impact analysis are those that are well versed in budgeting procedures, recognize how fiscal impacts fit into the overall evaluation of development, and have the in-house capability to understand the nuances of fiscal impact analysis in the first place.

Private developers are likely to submit analyses only if they are required to do so. Even then, developers will keep analysis costs down by using average costing, as opposed to marginal costing, approaches. Thus local governments must do such studies themselves, or they must use the resources of regional councils, consultants, and university extensions. At the very least, they should be able to evaluate the analyses that developers submit to identify deficiencies.

Even communities that cannot afford an in-house fiscal impact evaluation system will begin to guide (rather than react to) major land-development proposals by requiring more than one analysis for a given site. In so doing, they will be able to assess the fiscal implications of alternative land uses for a given parcel.

Following a few guidelines can help avoid the eight pitfalls. Of key importance is the need to present the results of analysis in the simplest terms. Presentations of conclusions should include a statement of assumptions, the methodology used, and pertinent findings. Also important is the need to use the appropriate fiscal impact technique for each project.

Finally, it is important to be aware of the analytical capabilities of the local community. If a local public agency is responsible for determining a project's fiscal impact, the staff must know about alternative methodologies and should choose a system that can be implemented locally and explained easily.

1.   Portions of this publication are reprinted in the preceding article.

PART 3

Infrastructure Programming and Financing Techniques

Capital Planning and Programming Techniques

Local governments are facing an infrastructure crisis. The decline of federal funding, escalating debt service costs, maintenance deferred because of insufficient local revenues, and caps on taxes and expenditures have caused a deterioration of the infrastructure in many cities. Meanwhile, requirements for new capital facilities have increased because of population growth, economic develop ment, and rising standards regarding such factors as the environment. Estimated costs over the next ten years for the maintenance, repair, and rebuilding of public facilities in the United States range from $3 to $4 trillion.

A recent study for the National League of Cities and the U.S. Conference of Mayors revealed that local officials rank streets, storm-water collection, wastewater treatment, sewage collection, public buildings, and water distribution as the top six infrastruc ture needs. Criteria cited included protecting public health and safety, providing essential residential services, facilitating economic development, retaining public sector jobs, and federal and state mandates.

Local concern over the crumbling infrastructure has focused attention on capital planning and programming as a means to improve capital investment decisions. An effective capital planning and programming process involves the establishment of an appropriate organizational structure and administrative procedures, a system for assessing the condition of the existing infrastructure, a formal method of collecting and ranking capital project information, an evaluation of the impact on the operating budget, an analysis of alternative methods of financing, and an effective monitoring system. A local government must also recognize the limitations as well as the benefits of capital planning and programming.

Definitions

Capital programming terminology can be confusing. The term *infrastructure* refers to public facilities such as streets, bridges, water and sewer systems, parks, jails, and wastewater treatment facilities. A *capital project* or improvement is a major nonrecurring tangible fixed asset with a useful life of at least one year (often five years) and a significant value. The term includes property acquisition, major improvements to an existing facility, and purchases of equipment over a stipulated value. Whether a project is a "capital project" based on its life span and value depends on the size of the jurisdiction and its budget. Some smaller cities use a value cutoff point of $5,000, while larger cities may use cutoff points of $50,000 or higher. Supplies, maintenance and repair projects below a certain dollar amount such as $5,000 or $10,000, and equipment and furnishings for existing buildings or with a useful life of less than five years are often excluded from the capital project definition.

A *capital program* is a schedule of capital projects listed in order of priority for a five- or six-year period with their estimated costs and sources of financing. The *capital budget* covers projects in the first year of the multi-year capital program and may be incorporated into the annual operating budget. Capital expenditures to be incurred during the budget year from funds appropriated by the legislative body are included in the capital budget. Capital programming covers the implementation of projects through the capital budget, the annual addition of another year to the multi-year program, and necessary revisions to project scheduling and financing.

Benefits and limitations of capital planning

Capital planning and programming provides a structured system for establishing capital needs, setting priorities, and allocating financial resources for a multi-year period. It:

1. Serves as a major tool for linking the master and financial plans to physical development
2. Relates public facilities to public and private development and redevelopment policies and plans
3. Focuses attention on community objectives and financial capabilities
4. Keeps the public informed about future needs and projects
5. Coordinates the activities of neighboring and overlapping units of local government and private agencies in project planning and scheduling, thereby reducing project duplication and costs
6. Allows time for careful planning and design so that land can be acquired and costly mistakes can be avoided
7. Enhances credit ratings and helps to control tax rates and avoid sharp changes in debt service requirements

8. Identifies the most economical means of financing capital projects
9. Increases opportunities for obtaining federal and state financial assistance
10. Facilitates coordination of capital and operating budgets.

Despite the benefits accruing from capital planning and programming it has several limitations. Some critics contend the process introduces excessive rigidity into policy making because plans for projects become solidified and are difficult to change. Other critics note that the scheduling of one improvement may precipitate a demand for other improvements. Some say too much is involved in the process. Elected officials may contend that it is not practical to project too far into the future because expectations are raised and funding is uncertain. The competence of planning commissions and citizen committees to review engineering and other technical details is questioned. Criticism is aimed at the subjectivity associated with priority setting on the one hand, and a lack of active citizen involvement on the other. Some dislike the centralization of the planning process. Finally, critics point to the limited use made of up-to-date techniques to assess the condition of public facilities, analyze replacement options, and make investment decisions.

Organizing for capital planning and programming

The chief executive is customarily responsible for overseeing the capital planning and programming process and making recommendations to the legislative body, but the role varies according to statutory requirements and the form and size of government. The legislative body usually establishes the length of the program, project eligibility criteria, financing guidelines, and the amount of citizen participation desired, and assigns planning and administrative responsibilities. Legislative support and willingness to adopt and implement a proposed program are critical to its success.

Traditionally, planning departments or the central budget staff direct the capital planning and programming process. Planning departments have played a prominent role because they have access to data on population, land use, traffic and transportation, and the economic base and are able to relate capital plans to the community comprehensive plan and other plans. Planning commissions typically are assigned the responsibility for reviewing capital project requests and making recommendations.

In some cases public works departments are assigned the responsibility for coordinating capital programming. The finance department is usually responsible for conducting financial analysis, reviewing the impact of the capital program on the operating budget, and recommending methods of financing. Financial consultants and other experts are entering the picture because of the diversity and complexity of financing options. Some jurisdictions utilize interdepartmental committees to review and rank projects. There is a growing use of citizen advisory committees, including neighborhood committees and citizen surveys. Project requests are usually prepared by the operating departments.

Although too much centralization is counterproductive, central coordination and oversight are necessary to provide uniformity and consistency between the capital program and budget and the operating budget. For this reason, there is considerable merit in assigning the responsibility for preparing the capital program and budget to the operating budget staff. Operating departments can continue to play a major role in generating project requests.

Forms and instructions

The agency or individual assigned the responsibility for capital planning and programming prepares a calendar, forms, and instructions. Dates for each step of the process are listed on the calendar. Capital programming should be scheduled around the operating budget cycle to avoid an excessive workload and provide time for review and analysis. If capital planning begins several months prior to the operating budget cycle, information will be available on capital costs and their potential impact on the operating budget when the budget is prepared.

Forms commonly used in capital programming include summary forms, project request forms, and equipment forms. Summary forms list projects in order of priority by year, the annual and total costs for projects, and the method of financing. Project request forms are used to gather detailed information on specific projects: name, description, location, purpose and justification, who benefits, how needs are currently met, detailed cost breakdown, status in the last program, current status of planning and engineering, proposed expenditure by year, construction data, effect on operating budget and budgets of other departments, relationship to other projects, conformance to master plan and other plans, scheduling of construction phases and project expenditures, priority, and recommended method of financing. This information is then used to evaluate and rank requests.

In some cases, a separate equipment form is used to gather information on equipment to be purchased: its proposed use, form of acquisition (purchase, lease, rent), number of units, purpose of expenditure, gross and net cost, number of similar items in inventory, proposed period of usage, estimated useful life and information on the equipment to be replaced (including make, serial number, age, condition and maintenance cost and downtime in prior years). Information is also gathered on the recommended disposition of the equipment to be replaced: transfer to other agencies, trade in, salvage or sale.

Maintenance impact statements, which present the life-cycle operating and maintenance costs of proposed projects, are required by a number of jurisdictions because such costs are significant in prioritizing projects.

Standard forms provide uniform and complete information and facilitate analysis. Detailed instructions and samples of completed forms should accompany the forms when they are distributed to operating departments or others responsible for completing them. Training sessions are essential to teach personnel how to use the forms.

Inventory and condition assessment

Just as important as detailed project information is an inventory of existing public facilities and an assessment of their condition. Basic inventory information consists of a description of the asset, its location, age, condition, original cost, current value, maintenance and operating costs, type and extent of use, depreciation, estimated replacement cost, and the proposed date for rehabilitation or replacement. A real and personal property inventory system and fixed asset accounting will simplify the accumulation of the relevant information, which is valuable for insurance purposes, internal control of property, and financial reporting, as well as for planning.

Most local governments make only limited use of quantitative techniques to determine the condition of existing facilities. In many instances condition is judged subjectively. Condition indicators are available: Engineering measures include street and bridge rating scales, age, and pipe size. Federal agencies and some cities have developed rating systems for evaluating the condition of streets, bridges, sewers, and waste treatment facilities. Mechanical devices such as rough-o-meters are used to measure the roughness of streets. Other measuring equipment is available to evaluate the condition of streets, sewers, and bridges. Television equipment is being used to inspect sewers.

Another way to assess condition is to gather information on such indicators as number of sewer line stoppages, equipment downtime, and sewer or water main failures. Maintenance unit costs are another indicator for measuring condition. Computerized maintenance systems are ideal for accumulating maintenance cost data and assisting in making repair or replace decisions. Service level indicators include service complaints, basement flooding, service interruptions, and claims for vehicle damage due to deteriorated streets. All of these indicators provide a factual basis for making capital investment decisions.

Local officials can use replacement analysis techniques to decide whether to defer maintenance and repairs, continue to provide maintenance, rehabilitate, or replace. To determine which option is most cost effective, one needs to know the life-cycle cost of the item or facility, the impact on service level and quality of each option, the amount of uncertainty or risk attached to projected costs and impacts, the availability of alternative financing sources, and the projected consequences of taking no action. The calculation of risk is important because of the difficulty of projecting costs into the future and estimating such factors as amount of rainfall or potential infiltration that may affect design success.

Techniques for evaluating the various options include equipment replacement analysis techniques used in the private sector, cost benefit and cost effectiveness analysis, value engineering, and sensitivity analysis. Specialized knowledge and skill are required to employ the techniques. Each has its limitations, and data collection and analysis can be expensive. Nevertheless, a formal system can help evaluate the condition of public facilities and determine the most appropriate method of addressing infrastructure problems.

Review of project requests

After the capital project request forms are completed by the departments, they must be reviewed for accuracy and completeness. Project eligibility and need are determined along with any legal impediments. Cost estimates are compared with previous estimates and are reviewed for completeness. Projects submitted in previous years are again evaluated. Proposed scheduling and financing recommendations are examined. Cost estimates are adjusted for inflation. Projects are listed in a tentative schedule along with proposed financing. In some cases the reviewer may wish to make site visits or request additional information for clarification. Particular attention is directed at this stage to the need and justification for the project and its impact on the operating budget.

Project requests are also reviewed in a planning context. Conformity of the requests with the comprehensive plan and other plans is checked, as well as the interrelationships among projects and their proposed timing. If community goals and objectives have been established, the projects are compared against them. Design criteria are examined. Environmental impacts are considered along with neighborhood population changes and trends.

Engineering and architectural experts review the project proposals for general feasibility, adequacy of plans, design and specifications, availability of alternative design methods, appropriateness of cost estimates, and feasibility of proposed scheduling. Project proposals are compared with related projects of other public and private agencies in order to improve coordination and reduce costs.

Finance officials analyze the total cost of capital projects, including direct, indirect, operating, and maintenance costs, and analyze their effect on the jurisdiction's financial condition. Cash flow projections are made based on estimated work completion dates. Impact on the tax rate and the availability of fiscal resources are considered. Alternative methods of financing are carefully studied. Potential revenue forecasts are confirmed and debt capacity is determined. Fiscal impact techniques may be used to relate the proposed projects to other development activities.

Citizens are usually involved during the review stage. A planning commission or citizen capital improvements committee may hold public hearings on project proposals. Comments from the hearings and, in some cases, citizen surveys are used to formulate recommendations, which are generally presented to the chief executive. Several local governments obtain feedback from elaborate networks of neighborhood organizations.

Prioritizing projects

The most difficult aspect of project review is the prioritization of projects. Many different systems are in use. One approach is to establish several ratings, such as Priority 1, 2, 3, 4, and 5, and put each project in the appropriate category. Priority 1 projects might include an approved program to which the city is committed and for which timing and funding are not flexible. Priority 2 might include projects needed now but for which funding is flexible. Priority 3 can include highly desirable projects that have both funding and timing flexibility. Priority 4 projects might lack immediate justification but may be needed in the future. Priority 5 projects require more analysis.

Another type of rating system is based on values such as preservation of life, health, or property. Consideration is given to how essential the project is, the extent of the existing deficiency, and the availability of funds. Urgent or essential projects remedy a condition dangerous to safety, health, or property; are needed for a critical community service; or are required to complete a started project. Necessary projects are those for which funds are available for only a limited period of time, those needed to conserve or replace existing facilities within a few years, and those required to provide a minimum essential service. Desirable projects are adequately planned projects needed for expansion, to induce new development, or to make the community more aesthetically attractive. Deferrable projects are those with inadequate planning or justification, those benefiting only a small portion of the community, and those aimed at improving convenience or cultural values.

Another type of rating system uses a list of questions as a basis for setting priorities: What is the relationship of the project to the welfare and progress of the entire city? How many citizens will be helped and how many will be harmed or inconvenienced? Will the project replace an outworn structure or equipment or is it new? Will the construction of the project add to or reduce the operation and maintenance budget or will it be self-supporting? Will the project add to the value of the area or stimulate economic development? What will be the extent of citizen or political opposition? Does the project serve the entire community or a single neighborhood? Are there any legal problems? Does the project produce revenue? Are sources of funds immediately available to finance the project? Will the project increase employment? Will the project stimulate residential development?

There is a trend toward the use of more sophisticated rating systems that use numerical points to rank projects against established criteria such as conformance with plans, impact on economic development, neighborhood involvement, special need, public benefit, environmental quality, useful life expectancy, extent of neighborhood deterioration, impact on revenues, and so on. Minneapolis rates projects on a scale of zero to fifty points on fourteen factors. Dayton, Ohio; Dade County, Florida; Montgomery County, Maryland; St. Paul, Minnesota; and Winston-Salem, North Carolina, are a few of the cities that employ similar weighting systems. These systems appear to be objective, but the method used to assign points is in fact subjective. Nevertheless, the systems demonstrate that consideration is given to important factors in assigning priorities, and they serve to sharpen the distinctions between alternatives.

If projects are ranked by a committee, an effort should be made to establish standards for assigning points to each criterion. Standards help to reduce the degree of subjectivity. Creative group problem-solving techniques such as the nominal group technique offer a means of identifying significant criteria in a short period of time, without inhibiting the participants. The technique involves voting and limits discussion and criticism. A decision matrix is another effective tool for comparing projects against established criteria.

Evaluation and prioritization will be substantially improved if hard data are available on the condition of existing public facilities and equipment. Condition assessment and replacement analysis techniques can make available high-quality data for establishing priorities. Capital investment decision making is also aided by the use of such techniques and concepts as rate of return, payback period, opportunity costs, life-cycle costs, net present value, and discounted cash flow. Although quantitative techniques will improve the art of capital programming, users must recognize their limitations and the fact that priorities are often set by the political process of compromise.

Capital financing alternatives

Capital planning and programming require the identification and evaluation of alternative financing strategies. Little information is available about procedures for selecting among financing options. The finance department must carefully examine the implications of each financing alternative in terms of cost, administrative feasibility, timing, legality, and yield. Changes in federal tax policies, borrowing restrictions, the volatile bond market, and the vast number of financing options available complicate the selection of the most appropriate financing strategy.

Capital financing options are numerous. Federal loans and grants including revenue sharing and community development funds are available, although categorical grants are diminishing. Proposals are being considered in Congress for a federal infrastructure bank and a taxable bond option. State assistance is available in the form of economic development funds, loans, grants, dedicated revenues such as motor vehicle revenues, state bond issues for such purposes as parks, and state bond banks that enable smaller cities to obtain funds at reduced interest rates. Infrastructure banks are being considered in a number of states. The banks would consist of permanent revolving funds that would provide low-interest or zero-interest loans.

Long-term financing options consist of general obligation, revenue, industrial development, tax increment, and special assessment bonds. Short-term borrowing instruments include commercial paper, bond anticipation notes, grant anticipation notes, variable interest notes, and project demand notes. These options are particularly attractive when interest rates for long-term borrowing are high. Borrowing costs can be reduced by as much as five percent through the use of credit enhancements such as bond insurance and bank letters of credit.

New capital financing approaches have been developed to make it easier for borrowers to reach the market and obtain lower interest rates. Examples of these techniques are zero coupon bonds, stepped coupon bonds, tender option bonds, floating rate bonds, adjustable floating rate bonds, floating fixed rate bonds, and bonds with warrants. These techniques are complex and require caution in their use because of the risks associated with them.

Leasing has become a popular financing tool because it does not affect the jurisdiction's debt limit and does not require voter approval. Types of leases include operating, financing, sale-leaseback, and leveraged leases as well as certificates of participation. Other possible financing alternatives include developer fees and exactions, charitable contributions, joint power authorities, special districts and other authorities, user charges, and capital improvement funds.

Privatization is receiving considerable attention in such areas as the construction of wastewater facilities. Under this concept private firms construct and operate public facilities through licensing, service contracts, or sale-leaseback arrangements. The private firms receive tax benefits in the form of accelerated depreciation, tax credits, and deductibility of interest on debt.

Innovative capital financing may use various combinations of the above techniques. In all cases, the local government must exercise caution, recognize the limitations of creative financing, and consider thoroughly all of the implications of a project, including the impact of credit ratings, long-term liabilities, equity, cost, marketability, and residential and economic development. A matrix helps to compare various financing options against pre-established criteria such as legality, yield, cost, administrative feasibility, equity, applicability, and economic impact.

Adoption of capital program and budget

After the completion of the review process the proposed capital program and budget is presented to the legislative body. The completed document may include a capital program message, which reviews the general basis of the planning and discusses costs, benefits, impacts, and financing proposals. Projects are listed in recommended order of priority by year with proposed method of financing. It is helpful if separate pages are provided for each project including a description, justification, proposed timing, summary of capital and operating costs, and recommended financing. A map showing the location of each project can be very beneficial. Some program documents group projects in general categories such as streets, sewers, water, parks, fire stations, and public buildings.

The legislative body usually holds public hearings and study sessions to review the program. Departmental presentations are made and citizen comments solicited. Modifications may be made to the capital program based on the feedback received at the hearings. At this stage political and public policy considerations play an important role in the process. Once its review is completed the governing body should adopt the capital program and budget to demonstrate commitment to the program and provide overall policy guidance. Failure of the legislative body to formally adopt the program does not reduce its value as a management tool. Information that has been gathered can be used for planning and in the discussion of specific project needs.

Implementation and monitoring

The adoption of the capital program and budget does not complete the process. Since a capital program is a moving program, annual review and revision are essential to accommodate changing needs and resources. Approved projects in the capital budget must be implemented. This requires the preparation of plans and specifications, the letting of contracts, and the supervision of the project. Project implementation is facilitated by the use of such techniques as design review, value engineering, cost analysis, materials management and planning, and control and scheduling techniques such as the critical path method and the program evaluation review technique. A project control log showing a description of the project, its status, and key events such as plan approval, bid approval, groundbreaking, and major construction phases is a useful construction management tool. Special attention should be given to the selection of the most appropriate type of construction contract. Lump sum, guaranteed maximum price, construction management, design/build, and turnkey contracts each have distinct advantages and disadvantages.

Careful design and vigilant monitoring are crucial to controlling construction and operating costs. Value engineering can substantially reduce costs. Although the initial cost of energy-efficient buildings may be high, the long-term savings on energy costs more than offset the initial costs. Improved maintenance, rehabilitation, and replacement techniques will lower capital expenditures.

Critical to the success of a capital monitoring program is the existence of an accounting system that can record and report the status of capital expenditures. Good communication between project managers and finance personnel is necessary for strict accounting and cash flow analysis, which in turn is needed to maximize the funds available for investment while providing cash when required. Throughout the implementation phase, progress reports should provide a comparison of estimated and actual costs and timeframes. A final accounting is made when a project is completed. Written procedures are the best method of ensuring proper implementation and monitoring.

Conclusion

The issue of infrastructure will continue to be a problem of critical importance to local government. In their search for ways to address the problem, local officials will recognize the value of capital planning and programming. Their attention will be focused on how to improve and modernize their capital programming and budgeting systems. Following are suggestions for strengthening these systems:

1. Review the organization framework and procedures to determine if they meet current needs.
2. Identify and employ the most useful indicators for assessing the condition of public facilities.

3. Experiment with replacement analysis and capital invest-
    ment techniques.
4. Develop a system for evaluating maintenance/repair, re-
    habilitation, and replacement trade-offs.
5. Consider the life-cycle costs of capital projects.
6. Examine alternative designs and construction methods.
7. Form a public/private partnership to address the infrastruc-
    ture problem.
8. Require maintenance impact statements for capital projects.
9. Integrate the capital and operating budgets.
10. Use objective techniques to help set priorities for capital
    projects.
11. Develop criteria for evaluating alternative financing strate-
    gies.
12. Implement state-of-the-art project monitoring techniques.
13. Identify new ways to promote citizen participation and sup-
    port.

A formal capital programming and budgeting system can reduce current and future capital and operating costs, prevent deterioration of the physical plant, and promote economic development.

Capital Financing: A New Look at an Old Idea

Ronald Chapman

Capital budgeting within local government has not received the serious attention it deserves by practitioners or academicians. Theoretically, municipal capital budgeting involves the preparation of cost and revenue estimates for all proposed projects, an examination of the need for each, both politically and economically, and a choice of those worthy of capital investment.

In reality, few municipalities use financial decision making tools when evaluating capital projects. Instead, they rely too heavily on political considerations to determine which, if any, capital investment is worthwhile.

Political considerations are needed. Often they are valuable decision making tools. With respect to capital budgeting, they should enter the picture after the proposed capital investment has been financially tested using traditional capital financing approaches. This will ensure the investment is truly good for the municipality.

Three traditional business techniques are available for local governments to use in order to reach these decisions. Each will be briefly described. The reader can judge which one would best fit his situation.

The techniques have been modified some to fit the municipal government environment. They include: payback period, rate of return on average investment, and discounted cash flow.

The simple payback method evaluates the time required to recover the capital investment through net annual cash flow savings. These are the monies the municipality expects to save by making the capital investment minus expected expenditures.

Reprinted with permission from the June 1983 issue of *American City & County* magazine.

For example, suppose the municipality is evaluating the purchase of a $100,000 computer system expected to have a gross annual savings of $50,000 and an annual operating cost of $15,000. The net annual cash flow savings is $35,000 ($50,000 minus $15,000).

To fully utilize this method, the municipality must determine the total investment required to purchase the capital asset. In the example, the municipality has received open competitive bids for a computer with the lowest bid being $100,000. For our purposes, we will assume the lowest bid is offering the better package.

Second, the municipality must determine the expected life of the asset. Also for this purpose, we will adopt the traditional life of five years for high technology assets.

The payback period (PP) can then be determined by dividing the annual investment (I) by the net annual cash flow savings (AS) as follows:

$$I/AS = PP$$
$$\text{or}$$
$$\$100,000/\$35,000 = 2.86 \text{ years}$$

A further refinement of this method takes into account the expected life of the asset in determining actual savings. The expected life (EL) minus the payback period equals the remaining asset life:

$$EL - PP = RL$$

The remaining life is multiplied by the annual savings (AS) to determine the actual savings (aS) or

$$RL \times AS = aS$$

To determine the payback period and actual savings, apply this composite formula:

$$I/AS = \text{Payback period}$$
$$\text{while}$$
$$(EL - PP) \times AS = aS$$

A word of caution. The payback method does not address the time value of money. It should only be applied where the annual savings flow evenly.

This approach becomes more useful the further into the future the municipality is predicting. Where future predicting is extreme and interests are unpredictable, this method is superior. For comparative purposes, the project with the shortest payback period is generally considered the best.

The second technique, rate of return on average capital investment, is calculated by dividing the net annual savings by the average investment in the capital asset. It assumes the municipality depreciates its assets each year. Also, a sum equal to the yearly depreciation in a capital replacement fund should be invested to ensure available replacement revenue at the end of the asset's useful life. If this is not practiced, don't use this technique as it does not address the time value of money.

In our earlier example, the municipality estimated its net annual savings to be $35,000 through investing $100,000 in a computer system. The average investment method assumes each year's depreciation will reduce the book value of the asset by $20,000. The formula looks like this:

$$\frac{\text{I (initial investment)}}{\text{EL (expected asset life)}} = \text{Annual depreciation}$$

Consequently, the municipality assumes it will have a $100,000 book value the first year of investment (FI) and a $20,000 book value the last or fifth year (LI). Therefore, the municipality will have an amount invested equal to the computer system book value each year, or an average investment (AI) of $60,000. This is calculated as follows:

$$\frac{\text{FI+LI}}{2} = \text{AI}$$
$$\text{or}$$
$$\frac{\$100,000 + \$20,000}{2} = \$60,000$$

Once the average investment is determined, the rate of return on average investment (RI) may be calculated by dividing the net annual savings (AS) by the average investment (AI) as follows:

$$\text{AS/AI} = \text{RI}$$
$$\text{or}$$
$$\$35,000/\$60,000 = 58.3\%$$

Whether a return on average investment of 58.3 percent is good or not relates to other municipal investments. Such a return is better than 12 percent, but not as good as 75 percent. Therefore, a basic rule may be applied. If the return on average investment is higher than current investment returns on invested capital, and the net annual savings represent uniform savings, the investment opportunity should be seriously considered.

The third technique, discounted cash flow, when compared with amounts to be invested, offers a better means of selection.

A Central American saying "a bird in hand is worth a thousand flying" resembles our "a bird in the hand is worth two in the bush," only more so. The first maxim places a higher value on money in hand today over future promises.

Present day interest rates provide a typical example. In fact, interest rates represent a ratio of exchange between today and tomorrow.

The higher the value placed on today, the higher the present day interest. In other words, how much will the principal be worth in year "n"? This may be determined using this formula:

$$F = P (1 + i)^n$$

where F is the sum at the end of year "n," "P" the principal, "i" the interest rate, and "n" the number of years invested.

On the other hand, discounting is compounding interest in the reverse. With the present value concept, a future sum of money discounted at an appropriate interest rate determines its equivalent present sum. It looks from the future back to the present. It asks what is present value (PV) of future sum invested for years "n," at interest "i," compounded annually? The formula works like this:

$$PV = \frac{F}{(1 + I)^n}$$
$$\text{or}$$
$$PV = F (1 + i)^{-n}$$

Adopting the discounted cash flow or present value model to municipal budgeting is an excellent way to evaluate investments with uniform and nonuniform net annual cash flow savings. It works equally well for phased capital investments. Here's a look at each of these.

When a municipality makes a capital investment, it expects to secure from it a stream of future savings or net annual savings. Normally, it should not invest in the capital asset unless the annual savings discounted to present dollars are sufficient to return the amount invested, plus a satisfactory return on investment. The return sought should equal present investment earnings. This uniform discounted cash flow method is shown in Table 1.

The table shows that the capital investment of $100,000 in a computer system with a net annual savings of $35,000 will recover

n Years	F Net annual savings	(l-i) Present value of $1 at 10%	P Present value of annual savings
1	$35,000	.909	$31,815
2	35,000	.826	28,910
3	35,000	.751	26,285
4	35,000	.683	23,905
5	35,000	.621	21,735

Total present value.. $132,650
Amount to be invested.. 100,000

Positive net present value.............................. $32,650

Table 1. Uniform discounted cash flow method.

the initial investment. It will also result in a 10 percent annually compounded return on investment. Moreover, it produces an added $32,650 positive net present value. If the municipality considers this return a good investment, the system should be purchased.

Using this method, several investment opportunities can be compared. If each has the same initial investment and risk, the one having the highest positive net present value is preferred.

Often the municipality must select between two or more investment opportunities with varying investments required and nonuniform net annual savings. Here again, the discounted cash flow method is the best to use.

Assume, for example, the municipality has three capital projects to choose from: A, B, and C. Project A requires an initial investment of $80,000 and has net annual savings of $35,000, $35,000 and $35,000. Project B requires an initial investment of $80,000 and has a net annual savings of $40,000, $30,000, and $25,000. Project C requires an initial investment of $50,000 and has net annual savings of $10,000, $15,000, and $20,000.

To determine which asset is the better investment, the discounted cash flow method should be applied to each project as shown in Table 2. In this case, AS equals the net amount cash flow savings, Factor the discounted rate (10 percent annually) and PV the present value of AS.

In Table 2, capital projects B and C result in a negative net present value. They should be rejected. Project A, on the other hand, has a return on investment of 10 percent, plus an added return of $7,010. This makes it the better investment.

All capital investments cited were assumed to have no salvage value at the end of their expected life. If a salvage value is present, the cost analysis remains the same. The salvage value is added to the last year's net annual savings prior to the present value calculation.

Suppose the municipality is investigating the purchase of a new computer system with an initial investment of $50,000. Further investments would require outlays of $100,000 and $125,000 in years two and three. Also, assume the net annual cash flow savings are $75,000, $100,000, and $125,000 in years one through three. Present

	Project A			Project B			Project C		
Period	AS	Factor	PV	AS	Factor	PV	AS	Factor	PV
1	$35,000	.909	$31,815	$40,000	.909	$36,360	$10,000	.909	$ 9,090
2	35,000	.826	28,910	30,000	.826	24,780	15,000	.826	12,390
3	35,000	.751	26,285	25,000	.751	18,755	20,000	.751	15,020

Table 2. Nonuniform discounted cash flow method.

	Annual cash flow savings discounted by 10%			Phased investment discounted by 10%		
Period	AS	Factor	PV	AS	Factor	PV
1	$ 75,000	.909	$68,175	$ 50,000	1.000	$50,000
2	100,000	.826	82,600	100,000	.909	90,900
3	125,000	.751	93,875	100,000	.826	82,644

Total PV (savings)... $244,650
Total PV (investments).. 223,544
Net PV .... $ 21,106

Table 3. Phased discounted cash flow method.

value calculations for this project are presented in Table 3.

Using this table, we can see the capital project has a total present value savings of $244,650, a total present value investment of $223,544, and a net present value of $21,106. Assuming a 10 percent return on investment is desirable, the municipality should go forward with the project.

The phased investment plan requires the same 10 percent discounting as is used in annual cash flow savings. This reduces the total required investment to its present value.

In phased investment projects, the total investment is not required in the initial stage. Therefore, the amounts required in years two and three must be discounted to their respective present values.

For example, suppose a planned investment equal to $100,00 is to be made in the second period. The municipality only needs to invest $90,900 at 10 percent interest today to realize $100,000 at the end of one period.

The initial investment in period one is never discounted because it already reflects present value. As a result, when discounting phased investments this formula should be applied to all except the initial investment:

$$PV = \frac{F\,(n-1)}{(1+i)}$$
$$\text{or}$$
$$PV = F\,(1+i)\,(n-1)$$

Of the three techniques, discounted cash flow often produces the better decision making data. However, the payback period and return on investment methods should be used instead where interest rates cannot be accurately predicted.

In reality, the discounted cash flow analysis places each proposed project on an equal footing.

The assessing of current budget impact is important in this era of cutback management. This is especially true when one assumes future years will not produce large and lavish budgets.

In the final analysis, the chief executive must ask if the project is financially proven; does the municipality have the current finances needed to invest in the project; and, if the project is not financially proven and the municipality does not have the current resources available, are the political factors important enough to tip the scales in favor of the project?

If the decision is made on purely political factors, the chief executive is like a blind man leading the blind. He simply has no idea of the present or future impact the project might have on the budgetary structure. As the saying goes: "A bird in hand is worth a thousand flying."

Dangers in Discounting

C. Torben Thomsen

Present value tables are omnipresent in accounting. Whether it is a problem of bond value, mortgages, leasing, pensions, installment sales, or capital budgeting, present value concepts are used. The specific application may be either by reference to present value tables, by special keys on a calculator, or by a part of computer programs. By understanding the time distortions induced by discounting, the user of present value calculations guards against applying discounting where it is not warranted.

Figure 1 shows the traditional method of discounting. A future payment of $1 is discounted more the further it is in the future. If one views each payment as consisting of a flow of $1 for one year, one has $1/year $\times$ 1 year discount factor = present value. It is irrelevant whether the discount factor is applied to the $1 or to the one year, because the present value is the same. That is,

$$(\$1/\text{year} \times \text{discount factor}) \times 1 \text{ year} = \$1/\text{year} \\ \times (\text{discount factor} \times 1 \text{ year})$$

because of the mathematical rules for multiplication. In Figure 1, we show that equivalency by rotating each block (representing present value) in the upper part of the diagram and placing it on the lower part of the diagram where the discount dimension is along the time axis. The shaded areas in the two diagrams are exactly equal because the only operation that has been performed is rotation. The time axis on the lower diagram in effect shows "discounted time." In other words, the present value of $1 per year for three years is the same as $1 per year for 1.95 years. The first year has been contracted to .8 of a year, the second year to .64 of a year, and the third year to .51 of a year. The total of these three contracted years is of

Reprinted with permission from the January 1984 issue of *Management Accounting*.

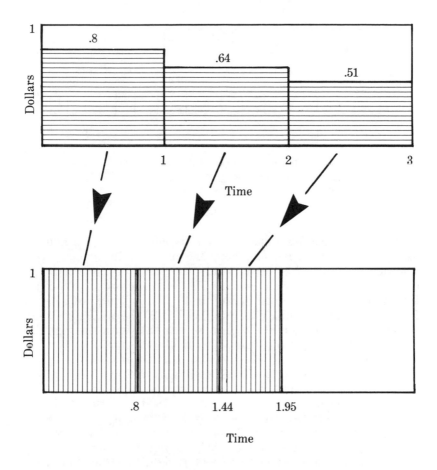

Figure 1. The equivalence of discounting dollars and discounting time. The top diagram represents discounted dollars at 20% per year. Each block is rotated 90° to produce discounted time in the lower diagram. The shaded area representing present value is the same in both cases.

course 1.95 years, the numerical value of which is equal to the present value of an annuity of $1 for three years.

A decision maker's time horizon

Figure 2 illustrates the dramatic difference in time horizons for discount rates of 5% and 20%. (For the balance of this article continuous discounting will be used for consistency and simplicity.) In both cases the time horizon is finite, because the present value of the perpetuity is 1/i. The two different scales show the different time per-

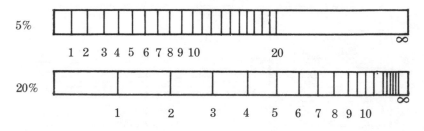

Figure 2. Comparative total time horizons for decision makers using a discount rate of 5% and 20%. Note how much more important the present is at the 20% rate than at the 5% rate.

spectives of a decision maker using a discount rate of 5% and one using a rate of 20%. The one using the 20% rate is obviously very nearsighted. With a 5% discount rate, the first 20 years occupy just over 60% of the total time horizon (63.2%). (The proportion of the total time horizon occupied by the first t years at interest rate i is $1 - e^{-it}$.) With a 20% discount rate the first 20 years occupy almost the entire time horizon (98.2%). It is clear that with the high discount rate the distant future has practically no significance to the decision maker who uses present value calculations.

Consider, for example, a bank lending by taking a 30-year, 13% mortgage. The 30-year term of the mortgage occupies 98% of the bank's time horizon—that is, for all practical purposes, the bank does not look much further ahead than 30 years. Ten years ago when mortgage rates were around 8%, the 30 years would have occupied 91% of the bank's time horizon. This example illustrates that relatively long periods of time cover a very significant portion of the time horizon even at different interest rates.

But it is surprising to realize that for the bank lending at 13%, the first 5.2 years of the loan count the same as the last 24.8 years— the present values of the receipts during those two time periods are equal! This is especially surprising because after 5.2 years, 98% of the loan principal remains on the books of the bank. (For an 8%, 30-year loan the first 7.6 years count the same as the last 22.4 years.)

Looking at it another way, a 30-year, 13% mortgage for $100,000 is paid off by a monthly payment of roughly $1,100. If that same payment is made for only 5.2 years, the bank would extend a loan for $50,000. The first 5.2 years of payments get a loan of $50,000. The last 24.8 years of payment induce the bank to add another $50,000 to the loan.

In capital budgeting an understanding of the distorted time horizon is especially significant. The indiscriminate use of discounting may lead to such a myopic view that long-run strategic errors are made.

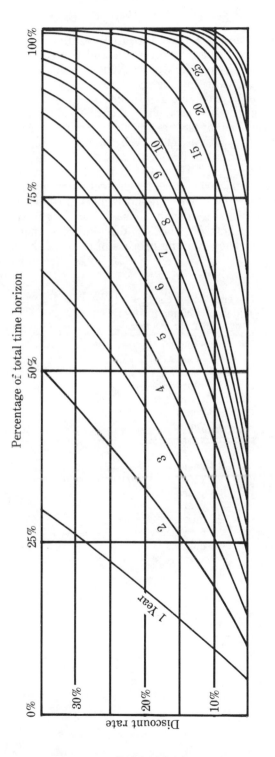

Figure 3. Relative importance of time using different discount rates.

Consider a firm that uses a 20% discount rate in valuing capital projects. The firm is comparing two projects, A and B. Project A costs $100,000 and results in a cash flow of $32,000 per year for the next 5 years. Its net present value is roughly $1,100. Project B also costs $100,000, but the cost is paid out as $10,000 per year for the next 10 years. At the end of the 10-year development period a yearly cash flow of $60,000 is produced for the next 50 years. Project B's net present value is roughly a negative $2,600. Why should project B, with a cash flow about twice that of project A and a life span of 10 times that of project A, be rejected? The answer is simply that at a 20% discount rate the first 10 years (which for project B are years of negative cash flow) count as 86% of the time horizon. While positive cash flows occur over a 50-year time span, those 50 years lie in the tiny 14% portion of the time horizon. The 20% discount rate, therefore, strongly biases the decision-making process in favor of short-term projects.

At interest rate	The entire 21st century is equal to this much time from a 1984 perspective
1%	77.4 years
2%	49.4 years
3%	29.6 years
4%	18.2 years
5%	11.8 years
6%	8.0 years
7%	5.6 years
8%	4.1 years
9%	3.0 years
10%	2.3 years
11%	1.7 years
12%	1.3 years
13%	1.0 years
14%	10 months
15%	7.7 months
16%	6.1 months
17%	4.9 months
18%	3.9 months
19%	94 days
20%	76 days
25%	27 days
30%	10 days

* Solve for t in

$$\frac{1 - e^{-it}}{i} = e^{-16i} \ \left(\frac{1-e^{-100i}}{i}\right)$$

Table 1.

Figure 3 shows in more detail the effect of time distortion for discount rates ranging between 5% and 35%. Each curved line represents a number of years and the percentage of the total time horizon that those years occupy. For example, looking at the two-year curve one sees that the first two years of the future occupy about 10% of the time horizon at a 5% discount rate. Moving up the curve to the 35% discount rate, the first two years now occupy about 50% of the time horizon. Note on the right side of the graph how time beyond 20 years almost completely vanishes in significance at high discount rates.

Table 1 presents the effect of time distortion in a different way by asking how much of the *immediate* future starting in 1984 is equivalent to the entire 21st century. The results are startling! Even at a modest rate of 13% the entire 21st century counts the same as about one year in 1984. Severe time distortion like that makes present value calculations unsuitable for strategic planning. It is not that the present value technique is wrong, but rather that it is unrealistic to assume that high discount rates can continue over an extended period of time.

This view of discount rate–induced time distortion also leads to the conclusion that high interest rates serve as a destabilizing factor in the economy as a whole. The high interest rates encourage and even demand that decision makers use high discount rates in their planning. The high discount rates, in turn, tremendously increase the importance of the present—the time horizon becomes biased toward the *near* future—and the comparative neglect of the long run makes the short run even more unstable.

Knowledge of these time distortions will enable the decision maker to become a judicious user of present value models.

Local Government Financing: The Shirttails or the Alternatives

————— Harvey Goldman and Sandra Mokuvos

The decline of federally funded programs, the tightening of federal and state purse strings, and local concern over tax rates and user fees have many communities seeking innovative financing alternatives to fund needed capital intensive projects. What local governments seek, professional advisors are starting to provide.

The responses have ranged from creative applications of conventional financing mechanisms to relatively new uses of leasing concepts and full-service delivery methods such as privatization. In some cases, private credit in the form of service agreements has been used by the public sector to secure needed financial resources.

Given the panorama of new financing approaches and resultant emergence of new and often confusing terms describing them, local leaders need guidance on various approaches to financing and providing delivery of needed services. These include:

1. Actions at the state government level
2. Short- and long-term financing options for local governments
3. Leasing concepts
4. Privatization.

An important point to note is that often the most cost-effective project financing method incorporates a combination of specific approaches from within several of the above categories.

In a report prepared for Congress, the money necessary to meet infrastructure needs through the early 1990s was cited at $2.5 trillion to $3 trillion. Among the capital intensive needs that exist are municipal water systems, wastewater treatment facilities, schools,

---

transportation networks and prisons. According to statistics cited in the report, at current expenditure levels, less than one-third of these needs will be met through conventional approaches. Given the limitations of capital markets to fund all the needed projects, new approaches to financing facilities must be developed.

As federal funds decrease, local governments have traditionally looked toward two places for assistance: their state governments and their own credit worthiness in terms of local access to the bond market. There are traditional and innovative alternatives available under each of these options.

State assistance

At the state level, as less money comes down the federal pipeline, more responsibility for meeting statewide needs falls to each individual state. With an increasing fiscal burden on state shoulders, the amount of money that passes through to the local level will continually decrease. However, there are some alternatives available for communities seeking local assistance from their state governments.

Economic development funds   The purpose of these funds is to provide state assistance to local governments or private sponsors in the development of projects. Assistance takes the form of state loans, grants or below-market interest rates for a portion or all of the costs of a local project.

General fund appropriations   General use funds include property taxes, sales tax, cigarette taxes and federal general revenue sharing funds. Typically, these taxes and revenue streams are dedicated for specific purposes.

Direct state purchase   As an alternative to grants and loans, some states buy municipal bonds for specific local projects. Local governments benefit by paying a lower interest rate. Another alternative is for the state to use the funds to pay for a portion of construction costs, take title to the project and then sell it back to the sponsor over a long period of time.

Bond banks   A state or federal bond bank could be empowered to issue bonds and notes in its own name, the proceeds being used to purchase the bonds and notes of local government units, hopefully driving down the interest costs by trading upon the credit of the state or the credit of multiple rather than individual projects. In addition, state loan funds are also being conceived. Commonly referred to as an "Infrastructure Bank," the program would combine state and federal grant money and provide local government with zero interest or low interest loans that would eventually be repaid out of project revenues.

Tax-exempt debt offerings

Communities have traditionally used bonds to finance construction of needed facilities, although in some portions of the country "pay-as-you-go" approaches have been utilized. While pay-as-you-go avoids interest charges by accumulating the capital requirements for a project in advance of construction, it typically is limited to more affluent or fiscally conservative areas.

The volume of both short- and long-term, tax-exempt debt offerings has increased dramatically in recent years. Long-term municipal debt issuance averaged $45 billion per year between 1977 and 1981. In 1982, long-term financing volume totaled $77 billion— amounting to a 67 percent increase in one year. Short-term financing volume has similarly risen, more than doubling from $21 billion in 1979 to $43 billion in 1982.

Up until a few years ago, there were relatively few options for a community seeking to finance capital-intensive projects with bonds, and credit worthiness has always been a limiting factor. Often, a community's ability to issue bonds is limited by a statutory ceiling on outstanding debt capacity or the community's credit rating is not high enough to be competitive with other issues at a given interest rate. Many growing communities do not have current revenues sufficient to meet debt service requirements for the large volume of debt issuance needed for capital projects.

While a number of new financing alternatives have become available, with them have come new problems associated with the complexities of the credit market. Traditional investors, banks and insurance companies are being replaced by money market funds and private individuals. Investors want more security and more acceptance of risks, such as interest rate fluctuations, by the issuer instead of the investor.

An area that is still of concern to issuers is how to improve their credit rating, which has an impact on the interest rate that will need to be offered to successfully market the securities. Financial analysts have provided local communities with a number of alternative mechanisms to increase their ratings.

Users of municipal bond insurance (MBI) have the ability to repay debt, but use MBI to enhance their credit rating, lower interest costs and expand their access to the market. Prior to marketing the bonds, an issuer obtains an insurance policy for a one-time premium of approximately 0.6 percent to 1.5 percent of the aggregate principal and interest due on the bonds from the delivery date to the final maturity date. The insurance, in effect, guarantees to the bond holders timely payment of interest and principal.

There are several firms that provide bond insurance with the American Municipal Bond Assurance Corporation (AMBAC) and Municipal Bond Insurance Association (MBIA) being the most well known. Standard & Poor's rates both AMBAC-insured and MBIA-insured bonds as triple-A. Moody's tends to ignore the insurance when assigning the rating.

Another method for a community to improve its bond rating is to secure an issue with a bank letter of credit. The cost of obtaining a letter of credit is usually an annual fee of approximately 0.75 percent to 1.25 percent of the amount of notes outstanding. If a letter of credit is used to repay any or all of the issue, then the obligation converts to a direct bank loan.

These alternatives provide lower borrowing costs, presently up to 500 basis points, or 5 percent, lower than long-term debt. While these alternatives usually provide lower initial costs, there are important risks to consider. For example, financial markets may change and subsequent long-term borrowing costs could be higher than if long-term financing was initially used. An adequate strategy to protect the issuer against this potential risk should be developed before going forward. Some of the more prevalent short-term financial approaches, which can later be converted to long-term debt, include:

1. Tax-exempt commercial paper
2. Bond anticipation notes
3. Variable rate demand notes.

Tax-exempt commercial paper (TECP) Can be used during construction to allow the issuer to select a better market for long-term financing. TECP usually matures between 15 days and 45 days. Additional costs associated with TECP should be given consideration. These include a fee of 0.75 percent or more for a letter of credit and a fee of 0.125 percent or more for the agent who places the commercial paper.

Bond anticipation notes (BANs) These bonds are issued in anticipation of a long-term bond issue. BANs typically mature in one year to three years and are payable from the proceeds of the long-term bond issue. Prior to the refinancing, interest on the BANs may be capitalized from the proceeds of the notes or paid from revenues of the project. The principal is payable in one lump sum. Grant anticipation notes (GANs) are a variation of this theme and are used when a grant, rather than a bond, is expected to provide long-term financing.

Variable rate demand notes (VRDNs) Usually having a maturity of two years or three years, the interest rate on these notes fluctuates periodically with a prescribed municipal bond market index or an alternative index based on a major bank's prime lending rate. As in any demand note, the holder has the option of holding the note to maturity or tendering the note to the issuer for redemption at the original par value upon seven days notice.

Long-term financing

There have been a number of innovative approaches and variations of traditional long-term financing methods. General obligation bonds, revenue bonds and special assessment bonds have traditionally been used, but are now being supplemented by creative concepts to tailor repayment schedules and renegotiation options to project-specific and community-specific needs. Care must be taken to ensure that the proper long-term financing approach is matched to the circumstances at hand.

General obligation bonds (GO bonds)   Backed by the general credit and taxing authority of the issuing agency, GO bonds are typically at somewhat lower interest rates compared to less conventional bonds. Their use "draws down" a community's borrowing capacity and credit standing, because they are backed by the full faith and credit of the issuer. GO bonds are becoming a limited source of funding due to bond market fluctuations, interest rate increases, statutory and constitutional limitations on municipal debt, and referendum requirements.

Revenue bonds   Revenue bonds are repaid exclusively from the earnings of a specific enterprise, e.g., a water system, a toll road, etc., and are normally used for capital-intensive projects, which generate their own revenue streams from users served by the project. The interest rate is generally not as favorable as that of general obligation bonds, although the security of the project's revenue stream will influence the rate. Limitations on revenue bond issues are: (1) typical underwriters' requirements that service charges be set at 120 percent to 150 percent of the level required to meet annual debt service costs, and (2) the capability of service users to pay the user charges.

Industrial development bonds (IDBs)   IDBs are a specific type of bond used to encourage private investment in a particular area. A municipality, a nonprofit authority or other governmental unit issues an IDB for a private sector firm, which uses the proceeds of the bond sale to build a facility. IDBs provide private sector groups with tax-exempt financing rates for projects.

Limitations exist on the size of the issue allowable to still be eligible for the tax-exempt status and on the types of facilities for which IDBs can be used. There has been recent concern about potential abuses of the use of IDBs and one should exercise due care when planning on their future use. Infrastructure projects in the water, wastewater and resource recovery field receive special favorable treatment under current legislation.

Special assessment bonds   These bonds are used to finance elements of a project, e.g., the collection system of a wastewater treatment facility, which benefit individual properties. Usually, these bonds are sold locally or regionally by the issuing political subdivision and discharged by the individual property owner over a five-year to 20-year term. The issuer's taxpaying power may or may not be pledged as additional security.

Innovative approaches

There are a number of creative concepts that have been applied in the field of long-term financing. These innovative, long-term bonding options include:

1. Deferred interest approaches (zero coupon bonds, stepped coupon bonds)
2. Tender option bonds
3. Floating rate bonds (floating rate bonds, adjustable floating rate bonds, floating fixed rate bonds).

Zero coupon bonds (zeros)   These bonds pay no current interest coupon and are sold at a deep discount. Investors in these bonds forgo current interest income for appreciation in principal. The attraction to investors is the ability to lock in a guaranteed yield to maturity based on the discounted price at the time of purchase.

Stepped coupon bonds   Like zeros, these bonds provide lower than normal interest rates in the early years and higher rates in later years. Their use can produce a lower total debt service, because more principal is repaid earlier in the term. The bonds attract investors desiring an increasing rate of return. A lower interest rate in early years can mean substantial savings on projects for which interest is capitalized during the construction period, because the capitalized interest is based on the lower coupon rate. However, the call premiums are unusually high to offset the investors' loss of coupon income in the early years, making it costly to refinance the debt.

Tender option bonds (put bonds)   Having a maturity of 25 years to 30 years, these bonds also give the holder the option to tender the bonds to the issuer for repayment at par value at the end of a specified period, usually at least three years to five years. Thereafter, the option can be exercised periodically at either one-year or three-year intervals. Because of this liquidity feature, investors will accept significantly lower yields on put bonds than on standard 30-year bonds.

Floating rate bonds (FRBs)   As indicated in the name, these bonds bear a varying or "floating" interest rate. These are typically issued by those who want to take advantage of current interest expense savings, compared to long-term rates. Issuers might expect interest rates to decline in the near future, whereas purchasers might anticipate that rates may rise and do not want to be locked into a fixed rate at the current level.

Adjustable floating rate bonds (AFRBs)   An AFRB, which functions like a tender option bond, is a combination of the option bond and the floating rate bond. If, prior to any option date, the interest rate for short-term bonds is higher than the coupon rate on put bonds, it is very likely an issuer can expect that a large portion of the outstanding put bonds will be tendered. At that time, a repricing committee will propose adjusting the rate on the put bonds so that the tendered bonds can be remarketed.

Floating fixed rate bonds (FFRBs)   Long-term floating rate financing with the option of fixing the rate under more favorable market conditions can be obtained without the expense of refunding through FFRBs. An FFRB is issued for a maturity of 30 years to 40 years. During the floating rate period, which can extend to the entire term of the bond, the interest rate floats relative to a predetermined index.

Bonds with warrants (warrants)   When a "warrant" is sold with a bond, the purchaser of the bond is entitled to buy an additional bond of the same coupon rate at any time within a one-year period. The investor is most likely to exercise the option if interest rates on alternative investments go down.

Leasing: using vs. owning
Leasing is another financing alternative available to municipalities. Leasing is equivalent to borrowing; one borrows physical assets instead of cash to acquire the assets. Lease payments typically are a fixed obligation, just like principal and interest payments on bonds.

A lease is a contract through which an owner of property conveys the right to use it to another party. The decision to lease, from the perspective of the lessee (the party to a lease agreement who is obligated to pay the rentals is entitled to use the property) is based on whether it costs less to borrow the money to buy the property or to acquire the use of the property by leasing it. Other considerations, which typically enter into the lease or own decision, include the following:

1. Risk of obsolescence of the asset
2. Intended period of use of the asset
3. Avoidance of restrictions accompanying debt financing
4. Preservation of debt capacity for other needs.

In a tax-oriented lease, the potential use of the investment tax credit (ITC) and depreciation is transferred from the user of the property (the lessee) to the owner (the lessor) in return for lower rental payments. Under the appropriate conditions, leasing can offer advantages to both the public and private sectors in that the private sector is able to use tax benefits, and the public sector pays less for needed property. There are numerous types of leases, including:

Operating lease   An agreement between the lessee and the lessor for rental of property for a specified period of time. The lessor would probably take certain tax benefits and be responsible for maintenance in return for a payment of a periodic fee.

Financing lease   In this type of arrangement, the lessee negotiates a purchase with a supplier of property and simultaneously arranges for a bank or leasing company to buy the property. The lessee then rents the property from the bank or leasing company and is obligated to make periodic payments.

Sale/leaseback   The owner of an existing facility or asset sells it to a financing entity and enters into a lease for use of the property. Because the new owner realizes certain tax benefits, the sale/leaseback approach may result in savings to the user, compared to traditional financing approaches. The usage fee covers the financing cost of the purchase asset.

Leveraged lease   A combination of debt and equity is used to construct a new facility or to obtain ownership of an asset. The equity contributor obtains the tax benefits of ownership and finances the bulk of the project employing tax-exempt bonds or other debt instruments. Leverage comes from using a small percentage of equity, usually about 20 percent, to acquire the tax benefits on the larger value of the asset.

Leveraged leasing became a particularly attractive option for partnerships formed by municipalities and private sector firms as a result of certain exceptions contained in the Tax and Fiscal Responsibility Act of 1982 (TEFRA).

Potential users of financing techniques that combine leasing and tax benefits should be wary of pending legislation, which, if passed, may impose limitations upon the use of these techniques.

Privatization

A financing and service delivery alternative that combines many of the advantages of the approaches described above is privatization. The privatization concept is based on public/private partnerships. The key is that both sides gain, but neither benefits at the expense of the other. The private sector gets a business opportunity, enhanced by the use of tax benefits. The public sector gets a needed service at a lower cost than otherwise possible and, if desired, eventual ownership of the facility that provides the service.

Certain types of projects can be constructed by the private sector more efficiently and at a lower cost than if the identical project is constructed by the public sector. This is because the private sector does not have to abide by the bureaucratic procedures and procurement regulations of federal, state and local funded projects, and through operational efficiencies realized through economies of scale.

The private sector, pursuing a legitimate "service contract" with a local government unit, is also eligible for tax benefits not available to tax-exempt municipalities. The benefits include ACRS depreciation, tax credits and the deductability of interest payments on the debt used in the project financing. When private sector construction and operational savings are combined with available tax benefits, the lower project costs which result can be shared with the local community in the form of lower user fees, while providing a fair return on the investment to the private sector.

While many local government officials are still frowning over the cutbacks in federal grants and state support for capital intensive infrastructure projects, some see a brighter future. Advisors to public officials are formulating creative and innovative financing approaches. Public officials and their advisors are becoming familiar with these alternative approaches, learning where and when the different concepts make sense. Equally important, they are discovering how to blend the concepts together to provide the most cost-effective form of service delivery to the public.

PART 4

Creative Purchasing Techniques

Life Cycle Costing

League of California Cities

Life cycle costing is a purchasing technique used to determine the *total* lifetime cost of purchasing and operating an item. Specifically, it examines and incorporates hidden costs of an item, such as energy consumption. Often, when comparing two similar items, one initially may appear less expensive. However, because that item may be less energy efficient than the other, it uses more energy over its lifetime and thus costs more to operate. Therefore, only looking at the initial sales price may be misleading. The item with the greater purchase price may be cheaper to operate, and thus less expensive in the long run.

Life cycle costing can be used in two ways. First, it can be used to evaluate competing bids by breaking out operating and energy costs. Calculating the lifetime or life cycle costs for different bids will identify the most cost effective purchase. Second, life cycle costing can be used to set performance standards when preparing a bid specification. Energy efficiency standards can be required in the specifications, along with other requirements, ensuring that the city purchases the item that will be cheapest to operate during its lifetime.

This article identifies the types of items which may be evaluated and compared for energy efficiency and cost. It provides a method to break down each item's distinctive costs, frequency of replacement, and projected energy costs for the item's lifetime. It includes the types of formulas and sample worksheets that can be used to easily identify the least-cost items.

Reprinted from *A Guide to Life Cycle Costing: A Purchasing Technique That Saves Money*, prepared by the Energy Resources Management Assistance Program of the League of California Cities, 1984.

When to use life cycle costing

Most of the purchases made by cities are done through a bid process. The initial price of those items purchased in great quantity or entailing a large cost are often taken at their face value, without looking at the long-range costs involved. With just a little more time taken to calculate these costs, a city purchasing agent can determine long-term hidden costs. Life cycle costing can be used to evaluate two competing bids, or to set performance standards in preparing bid specifications.

This technique may be used for any energy consuming item, unless the purchasing agent is limited by other technical requirements.

Figure 1 shows how life cycle costing can be used to compare two different 15 horsepower electric motors.

What may seem to be the less expensive motor from Vendor A will actually cost more to run during its lifetime than the motor offered from Vendor B. By only examining each motor's initial bid, one might conclude "If we buy Motor A we will save $300." However, Motor A uses 18.64 kilowatts/hour, while Motor B uses 13.98 kilowatts/hour. We find that Motor A will actually cost $5,592 more than Motor B over their lifetimes. Thus, spending $300 more initially for Motor B is cost effective.

Ideally, life cycle costing techniques can be used for *all* energy consuming purchases. If this is not possible or practical, cities may wish to prioritize items based on frequency of replacement *and* energy consumption. For example, a swimming pool pump is replaced infrequently. However, because it is a large electricity consumer, using a life cycle cost analysis for its replacement can be extremely effective, and should be a high priority, Similarly, frequently re-

Life cycle cost	Motor from Vendor A	Motor from Vendor B
Bid cost	$600	$900
Duty cycle	1,000 hrs/yr	1,000 hrs/yr
Life	15 years	15 years
Efficiency rating	60%	80%
Energy consumption (kilowatts/hour)	18.64	13.98
Energy cost (kwh consumed × $.08/kwh × 15,000 hours)	$22,368	$16,776
Life cycle cost (bid cost + energy cost)	$22,968	$17,676
Life cycle cost difference ($22,968-$17,676)=$5,292		

Figure 1. Example of life cycle cost analysis.

placed items, such as lights, are candidates for life cycle cost techniques.

There is no limit to the many items to which life cycle costing can be applied. For example, swimming pools and wastewater treatment plants all use some type of motor and pump. Boilers and heating, ventilation and air conditioning systems vary in their efficient use of energy. Lighting systems for city buildings and streets are frequently upgraded to more energy efficient lamps and ballast systems, as are park and tennis court lights. Life cycle costing can also be used to buy the most fuel efficient city vehicles.

Just as Figure 1 illustrates how life cycle costing can be used to evaluate the lifetime costs of a moderately expensive item, it can also be used for very inexpensive items. One city found, for example, that although the 34 watt "Super Saver" fluorescent tubes cost 34¢ more than the standard 40 watt tubes, they save about $1.17 in annual energy costs. When one considers that most cities have hundreds, if not thousands, of fluorescent lights, the savings can multiply to become significant.

Some city facilities use items that require certain technical specifications. For example, an engineer who is responsible for an air conditioning unit may require equipment that meets narrow specifications in terms of cooling capacity. Since an air conditioner's cooling capacity is measured in BTUs (British thermal units), a purchasing agent may want, for example, an air conditioner that can cool a building containing 100,000 square feet at a certain BTU level. Once that capacity is determined, the purchasing agent can write the bid specifications to require a minimum energy efficiency (a performance standard). Or, the agent may state that the energy efficiency must be specified in the bid, and then evaluate the bids based upon level of energy efficiency. This enables the purchasing agent to select the item which meets both the technical standards and the lowest operating costs within those specifications. Specifying technical performance standards and energy efficiency may limit the brands of models of an item offered. However, performance and energy requirements are still ensured. In some cases it may be necessary to "trade-off" energy efficiency performance standards for other performance standards, should special technical specifications be severely limiting.

How to do a life cycle cost analysis

Two cost categories must *always* be determined and included when evaluating a bid or when preparing a bid specification. These are:

1. *Acquisition costs*—includes the purchase price, sales tax, transportation and installation

---

The basic life cycle cost formula is:

Energy consumed × cost of energy × duty cycle × life
= lifetime energy cost

Lifetime energy cost + acquisition cost = basic life cycle cost

Where:

Energy consumed = energy units (kilowatts, therms)

Cost of energy = dollars per energy unit (cents per kilowatt, therm)

Duty cycle = number of hours the item operates in one year (i.e., if a natural gas boiler runs on the average of 10 hours per day, 100 days per year, the duty cycle is 1,000 hours per year)

Life = length of time until item needs replacement (i.e., air conditioners generally have a life of ten years, assuming a duty cycle of 1,000 hours per year).

Thus, the formula used for a natural gas boiler would appear:

(# of therms/hour) × (¢/therm) × (# hours) × (# years)
= energy $$

(energy $$) + (purchase $$) = basic life cycle cost

The eight additional cost items may also be included if desired.

---

2. *Operating costs*—includes the energy consumed in operating the product.

These core costs may be all the purchasing agent wishes to use in the analysis. However, eight additional costs can be examined to present a more comprehensive picture of the expenditures in an item's lifetime. Their inclusion, when applicable in each analysis, will help the purchasing agent identify the "true cost" of ownership. The additional life cycle cost categories are:

3. *Maintenance costs*—includes both routine and preventive maintenance
4. *Failure costs*—includes down time, rental costs and production losses
5. *Training costs*—training personnel to use equipment (tuition, time away from job, lodging, meals, transportation)
6. *Consumable supply costs*—incurred through the use or operation of an item
7. *Storage costs*—for the item itself or its repair parts
8. *Labor costs*—for operation of an item (wages/benefits, labor to replace items)
9. *Secondary costs*—to dispose of by-products of a commodity.

By-products, such as waste heat, may be utilized to reduce energy costs, thus creating a savings

10. *Cost of money*—includes the interest paid for loans or the interest which could have been made had the money been invested elsewhere.

Payback period

When one uses life cycle costing techniques, one frequently can justify purchasing the more expensive item by indicating its lifetime cost savings *and* the time it takes to recapture the additional initial expense—the payback period. Calculating a payback period is common practice in city management. If one considers the two similar motors in Figure 1, the payback period for the additional $300 for Motor B is under one year. That is, the more expensive item pays for itself, and the city begins saving money, after the motor pays itself back through reduced energy consumption.

It is up to individual cities to determine whether various payback periods and lifetime energy cost savings are appropriate to their individual needs. It may be appropriate to reexamine policies that require accepting the lowest bid for a job or product and begin to incorporate the use of life cycle costing wherever possible.

Preparing a bid using life cycle costing

Life cycle costing becomes invaluable once the purchasing agent is ready to prepare a bid. Setting bid specifications is an attempt to inform the supplier what the minimum needs are. Energy consumption, as included in the specifications, is a standard of quality because it defines a minimum performance level. For example, a bid specification may state that an air conditioner must have a minimum energy efficiency ratio. By establishing minimum performance standards, such as miles per gallon or kilowatts per hour, those vendors who do not meet that criterion are noncompliant.

There are several pitfalls of including energy efficiency in bid specifications. First, setting minimum performance standards unrealistically high may result in a bid that is too restrictive to enable bidders to reply. Second, setting performance levels too high may result in a product that does potentially save money, but results in an acquisition cost that is much higher and thus, not cost effective.

The sample bid in Figure 2 illustrates how energy consumption standards can be incorporated into a bid specification. If a particular brand comes close to the type of item needed, as indicated in the example, it may be helpful to potential bidders to reference that brand. This assists the bid reviewer to narrow the field of products that will meet the purchaser's specific needs.

STATE OF CALIFORNIA
DEPARTMENT OF GENERAL SERVICES
OFFICE OF PROCUREMENT

INVITATION FOR BID AND BID
THIS IS NOT AN ORDER
OSOP-83 (REV. 6/81)

| DATE MAILED | AGENCY | PURCHASE ESTIMATE NUMBER | PAGE OF |
| MONTH DAY YEAR | BILLING CODE | | |

IMPORTANT: Read attached General Provisions carefully before bidding, especially Section 7 regarding taxes. Retain one copy for your files.

NOTICE TO ALL BIDDERS: Section 14835 et seq. of the California Government Code requires that a 5% preference be given to bidders who qualify as a small business. The rules and regulations of this law, including the definition of a small business for procurements made by the Office of Procurement, are contained in Title 2, California Administrative Code, Section 1896, et seq. A copy of the regulations is available upon request. Bidders desiring to claim preference as a small business must so indicate on each bid, as follows:

TO BE FILLED IN BY BIDDER

Cash discount ___ % will be allowed for payment in ___ days. Cash discount of less than 20 days will be considered net.

P.O. DESTINATION UNLESS BIDDER STATES OTHERWISE

THIS BID MUST BE DELIVERED TO THE OFFICE OF PROCUREMENT BEFORE 2:00 P.M. OF THE DUE DATE.

BID NO.:   DUE DATE:

This address must show thru window

State Office of Procurement
1823 14th Street
P.O. Box 1612
Sacramento, CA 95807

1. Are you claiming preference as a small business
    ☐ YES   ☐ NO
    If yes, complete the following:

2. ☐ Non-manufacturer   3. Aggregate receipts for last three years
    ☐ Manufacturer

| FOR STATE USE ONLY | DELIVERY DATE REQUIRED | DELIVERY ADDRESS | | FOR FURTHER INFORMATION CONTACT |

| P.E. LINE PG. NO. NO. | QUANTITY | UNIT | STOCK ITEM NUMBER | DESCRIPTION—BRAND NAME AND MODEL | UNIT PRICE | EXTENSION |

BIDDERS NOTE IN ACCORDANCE WITH GENERAL PROVISIONS 1 (C)

All Bids submitted including Telegraphic Bids must indicate unit prices for each separate line item quoted and totals. Bids submitted which indicate lot total price only and do not indicate unit prices shall be considered non-responsive and the bid shall be rejected. IN THE EVENT OF DISCREPANCY BETWEEN UNIT PRICE AND EXTENSION OR TOTAL PRICE, UNIT PRICE SHALL PREVAIL.

DO NOT RETURN "NO BIDS". Failure to quote three consecutive Bids may result in removal from Bid List by *written notification* for that commodity group.

TO CLAIM SMALL BUSINESS PREFERENCE YOUR FIRM MUST BE APPROVED BY THE SMALL & MINORITY PROCUREMENT BUSINESS ASSISTANCE DIVISION. QUESTIONS REGARDING SMALL BUSINESS PREFERENCE APPROVAL SHOULD BE DIRECTED TO THAT OFFICE AT (916) 322-5060. THE SMALL BUSINESS PREFERENCE IS FOR CALIFORNIA BASED SMALL BUSINESSES ONLY.

| 01 | 1 | 24 | EA | 4110-034-0809-7 | REFRIGERATOR, Household type, frostless, minimum 13.5 cu.ft. total refrigerator volume, approx. 10.8 cu. ft. fresh food section, approx. 3.5 cu. ft. freezer section, 2 reversible doors, fresh food section shall have a minimum of 3 adjustable shelves, equipped with rollers. | | |

Maximum Consumption of 6.5 KWH/24 hours

Reference Brand: Sears #60441 or #61441.

Proposed Brand: _____

Model No.: _____

Delivery charge if applicable _____

Ship To: Atascadero State Hospital
          Atascadero, CA

The undersigned offers and agrees if this bid be accepted within 30 calendar days from the date of opening, to furnish all of the items upon which prices are quoted, at the prices set opposite each item, delivered at the designated point(s) by the method of delivery and within the time specified above and subject to the attached General Provisions. Small business claimants also attest, under penalty of perjury, that the small business claim made above is true and correct.

PLEASE COMPLETE THE FOLLOWING

NAME AND TITLE (TYPE OR PRINT)	FIRM
SIGNATURE	STREET ADDRESS
TELEPHONE NUMBER	CITY	STATE	ZIP CODE

Figure 2. Sample bid.

When preparing a bid specification it is important to inform the vendor that the award will be based upon life cycle costing, among other criteria. This can be done in a variety of ways, including a bidders note. The note can be worded differently to reflect how seriously energy efficiency will be considered in the overall bid. An example of a bidders note is shown here, with alternative verbs included in parentheses to illustrate the different tones possible:

Commodity	Useful life	Duty cycle	Energy cost constant[1]	Applicable standards
Air conditioners	10 years	1,000 hours/ year 10 hours/ day 100 days/ year		8.2 energy efficiency ratio (EER) for 200 v and over 8.3 under 200 v with heat pumps, 8.7 for all others
Air conditioners (central)	10,000 hours	10 hours/ day 100 days/ year		8.0 EER water cooled 8.0 EER air conditioner (seasonal energy efficiency ratio)
Electric motors	5 years (5,000 hours)	4 hours/ day 250 days/ year	$.0325 watts/life	
Heat pumps	12 years	1500 hours/ year (heating) 900 hours/ year (cooling)		2.5 A.C.O.P. (average coefficient of performance) 7.5 EER (cooling)
Fluorescent lighting fixtures	20 years (36,000 hours)	36,000 hours/life of tubes	$2.34 watts/ life	
Tumblers (steam)	10 years	2,000 hours/ year 8 hours/ day 250 days/ year		
Police vehicles	2 years 90,000 miles			Gasoline $1.32/gallon Interest rate 10.78% Discount factor 1.718 Fuel consumption adjustment factor 1.83 Fuel standard = 14 mpg

Figure 3. Life cycle cost index.

This bid may (will) be awarded on the basis of bid price plus energy usage and cost based on life cycle costing. All bidders, including those quoting on the reference brand, may (shall) complete and return the attached energy/life cycle cost form and submit with the bid the requested manufacturers' technical data sheet. Failure to comply with this requirement may (will) result in the bid being rejected as incomplete or nonresponsive.

Commodity	Useful life	Duty cycle	Energy cost constant[1]	Applicable standards
Ice making (automatic)	1,750 days (250 × 7 years)	24 hours/ day 250 days/ year	$.0017/lb.	Hot water cost = $.004/ gallon Steam = $.05/lb. Water =$.000261/gallon
Tumblers (gas)	20,000 hours (10 years)	2,000 hours/ year 8 hours/ day 250 days/ year		
Refrigerator- freezers	15 years	18 hours/ day 365 days/ year	$0.975 year/ kwh	Energy consumption (EC) standard w/anti-sweat 487 kwh + (55 kwh × volume)
Centrifugal liquid chillers	10 years	5 hours/ day 250 days/ year		3.8 C.O.P. (min.)
Microfiche readers	5,000 hours	1,000 hours/ year (5 years) 4 hours/ day 150 days/ year	$.0325 watt/ life	Consumption breakdown 150 watts (90 watt lamp and 60 watt fan)
Traffic signal lamps	8,000 hours		$0.52 watt/ life	

Figure 3. Continued.

Examples of typical energy consuming commodities are presented below to indicate how energy standards can be included in bid specifications. (See also Figures 3 and 4.)

Vehicles A minimum specification of miles per gallon has the potential of increasing fleet mileage average and reducing energy consumption. Comparison listings are available from the Environmental Protection Agency. Life cycle costing is a viable approach here.

Refrigerator/freezer combinations Specification of maximum kilowatt use per month has the potential of reducing electrical energy use. Comparison listings are available from the California Energy Commission and the Association of Home Appliance Manufacturers (AHAM).

Commodity	Useful life	Duty cycle	Energy cost constant[1]	Applicable standards
Tires, passenger (tubeless)				Bias = 80 specification minimum Bias belted = 100 specification minimum Radial = 160 specification minimum
1983 fleet vehicles	7 years 100,000 miles			Gasoline = 1.39 per gallon Interest rate = 12.07% Discount factor = 4.5536
Reciprocating chillers	19.320 hours/life (15 years)	1288 hours/ year 15 years		
Electric typewriters	7 years (medium) 10 years (heavy)	4 hours/ day 150 days/ year 7 hours/ day 250 days/ year		Consumption standard = 40 watts
Fluorescent ballast (electronic)	60,000 hours		$3.90 watt/ life	
Duplicators (offset)	1,250 days		$0.0813 watt/life	
Transformers (general application)	44,000 hours (5 years)	24 hours/ day 365 days/ year		

1. Energy cost constant=(energy rate) × (life). Energy rates vary according to utility service area and time.

Figure 3. Continued.

Air conditioners   Specifying a minimum energy efficiency ratio (EER) will ensure the purchase of the most energy efficient air conditioner. EER values are available from the California Energy Commission and AHAM.

Heat pumps   Minimum specification of EER and coefficient of performance (COP) has the potential of reducing energy consumption by heat pumps. EER and COP values are available from the California Energy Commission and the AHAM.

Pilot lights   Commodities with pilot lights are consumers of natural gas. A specification to substitute an intermittent ignition device

<u>COST ANALYSIS</u>

75 WATT INCANDESCENT LAMP VS. 18 WATT FLUORESCENT

1. IDENTIFY   (_____)

	Fluorescent	Incandescent
Lamp _____	$10.00 _____	$.15 _____
_____	_____	_____
_____	_____	_____

2. COMPARE   (_____)

Watts ____	18 watts ____	75 watts ____
_____	_____	_____
_____	_____	_____

3. FORMULAS

    a. Life Cycle Cost (LCC) = Energy Cost + Lamp Cost + Maintenance.

    b. Energy Cost = (watts ÷ 1000) x (cost/kwh) x (life).

    c. Lamp Cost = (hours life) ÷ (lamp life) x (cost per lamp).

4. CALCULATIONS

                              Fluorescent   Incandescent

    a. Energy Cost = $_____ $_____

       (_____W) x ($_____/kwh) x   (_____Life)   (_____W)x($_____/kwh)x(_____life)

      1000   1000

    b. Lamp Cost = $_____ $_____

       (7500 hr) ÷ (7500 life) x($10.00 lamp)   (___hr) ÷ (750 life)x($___lamp)

    c. Maintenance Cost = $_____ $_____

5. LIFE CYCLE COST = 4.a + 4.b + 4.c

    Energy Cost

    Lamp Cost   _____   _____

    Maintenance Cost   _____   _____

                  LCC $_____   LCC $_____

6. LCC SAVINGS

    (_____Fluorescent) -   (_____Incandescent) = $_____ Savings

Figure 4. Life cycle cost analysis worksheets. These sample worksheets contain space to identify the individual costs contained in a product's lifetime. The first two are set up to assist in the comparison of the same products from two different vendors. The third enables the purchasing agent to compare products with both the core costs (energy consumed and purchase cost) and the additional costs of maintenance and fixtures. These worksheets have been developed by and are available from the California State Department of General Services, Office of Procurement. Additional worksheets are available for other items from that office.

COST ANALYSIS

5 HORSEPOWER ELECTRIC MOTORS
5000 Hour Life and .08 $/Kilowatt Hour

1.   VENDOR A.

a. Initial Cost = $_____

b. Watts Consumption = 745.7 watts x 5 HP ÷ _____efficiency = _____watts/hour

c. Energy Cost = _____watts x .000080 $/watt x 5000 hours life = $_____

d. LCC Cost = $_____ initial cost + $_____ energy = $_____

2.   VENDOR B.

a. Initial Cost = $_____

b. Watts Consumption = 745.7 watts x 5 HP ÷ _____efficiency = _____watts/hour

c. Energy Cost = _____watts x .000080 $/watt x 5000 hours life= $_____

d. LCC Cost = $_____ initial cost + $_____ energy = $_____

COST COMPARISON

	VENDOR A	VENDOR B	DIFFERENCE
Initial Cost	_____	_____	_____
Energy Cost	_____	_____	_____
LCC Cost	_____	_____	_____

Figure 4. Continued.

for a pilot light will eliminate the wasted energy consumption. Furnaces, ovens, water heaters, and gas ranges are common items using pilot lights.

Insulation Although insulation does not consume energy, it is used to conserve energy. A specification to increase insulation in a building or to set minimum insulation standards for a building or

<u>COST ANALYSIS</u>

<u>22000 BTU Air Conditioners</u>

	Vendor A	Vendor B
1. Identify		
a. Initial Cost	_____	_____
b. BTU Output	_____	_____
c. Energy Cost	.078 kwh	.078 kwh

2. Compare

   a. Energy Efficiency Rating (EER)   _____   _____

   b. Watts Input   _____   _____

   c. Operation Hours/Life   _____   _____

3. Formula

   a. Life Cycle Cost = Energy Cost + Unit Purchase Cost

   b. Watts Input   = BTU ÷ EER

   c. Energy Cost   = (watts ÷ 1000) x ($ kwh) x (Life)

4. Calculations

   a. Watts Input $\frac{BTU}{EER}$ = _____ $\frac{BTU}{EER}$ = _____

   b. Energy Cost $\frac{\_\_\_\_}{1000}$ x .078 kwh x _____ life $\frac{\_\_\_\_}{1000}$ x .078 kwh x ____Life

                           = _____   = _____

5. Life Cycle Cost   Energy Cost_____   Energy Cost_____

                      Purchase Cost_____   Purchase Cost_____

                      LCC $_____   LCC $_____

Figure 4. Continued.

heating/cooling unit has the potential of saving energy and adds to the life of the heating/cooling unit.

Hot water heaters Setting a maximum loss rate and a minimum recovery efficiency has the potential of saving natural gas or electricity. The California Energy Commission has set minimum performance standard levels for water heaters.

Refrigerated water fountains A specification to establish a minimum water temperature setting for water cooling prior to delivery has the potential for saving energy, since it ensures that the water will not be excessively cold.

Motors Efficiency and power factor are the major concern for motors. Some manufacturers are offering high-energy-efficient motors, but at this time there are not industry standards or comparison standards. The high-efficiency motors will save energy and may be cost effective.

Gas space heaters The California Energy Commission established regulations effective June 22, 1979. Appropriate specifications can be incorporated into the bid specs.

Life Cycle Analysis: A Management Tool

T. Ashby Newby

Much is being written and said today about life cycle cost, guaranteed maintenance, total cost purchasing, or whatever you want to call it—versus initial acquisition price. Naturally, in business, the amount of profit is determined by the total cost of a system during its entire life. This includes all costs associated with the system during the period of operation. It becomes a management tool for decisions on purchasing capital equipment.

Probably governmental units do not use this approach as much as they should, simply because of the type of organization involved, or specifically due to the fact that complete records are not kept or readily made available to the purchasing department. Specifications are used to offset many factors which affect overall costs.

Tires

Let's take a look at the cost of automobile tires. The price is known when the tires are installed, but you don't know actual cost until you replace them. When you ascertain the number of miles accumulated and figure the cost per mile, it is only then that it can be determined whether you made a good buy. If the initial cost was $25 or $65 per tire—which accumulated the most miles at the least cost?

We have used total cost purchasing for tires for some years now. Our department formerly purchased tires by specifying what is called a manufacturer's "first-line" tire. This was generally understood to be the same quality tire that comes on a new automobile. At least it carried the same name. Each manufacturer has several levels of tires, but there is nothing as yet to indicate the quality, only price. A premium tire simply means a premium price. A third-

Reprinted with permission from the September 1983 issue of *Public Works*.

level tire of one manufacturer may well outlast the premium tire of another. In fact, tests reported last year by the National Institute of Governmental Purchasing indicated this to be true.

A few years ago, the lack of criteria to indicate the quality of tires disturbed me, so I had our tire buyer and a representative of our Research Council make a detailed study of tire-buying practices. This was done, with all major manufacturers taking part.

As a result, a plan was devised. Since 1966, we have purchased the majority of our tires, particularly for cars and trucks, on a guaranteed mileage basis. Off-the-road and odd sized tires are excluded. The Highway Department has literally saved thousands of dollars through this method of purchase. Briefly, our principle is as follows:

1. Tires furnished must be manufacturer's designed first-line tire or better, with skid-resistant tread design acceptable to the Highway Department.
2. Bidder will guarantee the average mileage for each size tire with a minimum guarantee of 20,000 miles for each automobile tire and 40,000 miles for truck tires.
3. Bidder must quote a gross price for each size tire with a guarantee to buy back the scrapped carcass at a specified price. The difference between the two prices is the net price for each size tire.
4. The net price divided by guaranteed mileage will then equal the guaranteed cost per mile.
5. The period of record keeping runs for five years, with final settlement made at the expiration of this period.
6. Speedometer readings are entered on a card when a tire goes on and comes off a vehicle. These data are fed into the computer and total mileage computed on each tire.

Other examples

There are many other items which we purchase that are not awarded on the basis of initial price alone, but are associated with other cost-related factors. A few of these are concrete pipe, traffic paint, various chemicals, snow plow blades and cleaning materials.

Many industries, due to profit motivation, keep more detailed cost records than probably is done by governmental agencies; therefore, they can readily identify life cycle cost elements. For example, in the purchasing of a piece of capital outlay equipment, say a generator or shop equipment of some nature, consideration is given to all costs involving acquisition, operation and maintenance. These replacement cost factors might include acquisition, operation, and maintenance.

Acquisition   Initial cost, including delivery; installation cost; removal cost, when declared surplus; value of surplus equipment; and any other costs associated with acquisition.

Operation   Direct and indirect labor costs; power costs; taxes, insurance; space cost; scrap and waste material; cost of other tools associated with operation; cost of other supplies and expendable items; other fuel costs; and loss of production due to down-time.

Maintenance   Labor costs for repairs and preventive maintenance; lubrication costs; cleaning and painting; cost of repair parts and spare parts inventory; and cost of tools for maintenance.

Some of the more critical cost elements used by one industry to compute the basis for an award for production equipment are: acquisition cost; initial engineering; installation cost; manning; mean time to repair; mean time between repairs; preventive maintenance cycle; preventive maintenance down-time; time between overhaul; cost to overhaul; parts cost per year; and input power.

Guaranteed maintenance and buy-back

Another method of arriving at life cycle cost involves a bid with guaranteed maintenance and buy-back of the equipment at the end of its useful life. The city of Chicago reportedly first used this method successfully in the purchase of refuse trucks, and more recently, for other equipment.

Refuse trucks are units that require considerable maintenance. John Ward, the former purchasing agent for the city of Chicago, said that the manufacturer could perform the repairs on this equipment cheaper than could city employees. This may be true in Chicago; in Virginia and many other states and cities, I do not believe this would be the case. However, once again, all costs would have to be analyzed to arrive at proper conclusions.

After hearing and reading that several cities and counties had purchased items of road and maintenance equipment on the guaranteed maintenance basis, the Highway Department decided to take a look at this approach. Advocates of the guaranteed maintenance method said that low bid buying resulted in the loss of tax dollars because it only considered one cost feature—the initial price. They stated that initial price procurement did not place a dollar value on such factors as machine availability, operating costs and resale value.

Other advantages of the total cost plan would be to:

Eliminate the guesswork from budgeting. No longer would an operating department have to guess at the operating cost of equipment during the year. The cost of operation would be stated in advance by terms of the contract.

Reduce the amount of time equipment is down for repairs and not available for work.

Establish the total cost over the life of the equipment.

Some of the apparent disadvantages of total cost purchasing might be to:

Require detailed record keeping for review by the supplier.

Cause interference by the supplier in regard to maintenance practices. It is not always possible or practical to follow an operating manual to an exact degree.

Cause some suppliers to use political pressure to have the user keep the equipment at the end of the contract where there is an option to purchase.

Force the user, at the end of the contract, to perform unnecessary repairs to get the equipment into good shape. If the user refused, a violation of the contract might be claimed.

Force some small suppliers out of business if all purchases are made on a total cost basis. Such dealers simply may be unable to obligate their firms to a guaranteed parts cost and repurchase plan over a period of five years.

A study made

In any event, we decided to make a study of the method. Our research had a two-fold purpose—to determine historical cost for the life of equipment currently in use by the department and to ascertain if the guaranteed total cost plan was more economical than our present method of purchasing. In other words, we were going to bid one method against the other, not just accept bids on the guaranteed cost plan.

Our Equipment Division had detailed records from which we could compile historical data and compute present costs. This took considerable research, so we confined our study to one item of equipment—the motor grader.

Meetings were held with all suppliers of graders, to get comments and suggestions and to be certain that they were in accord with our method of approach. After several meetings with the suppliers and with the preliminary data researched, we reached the following conclusions:

1. Initial price, repair parts costs, delivery time and resale value were elements to be considered in the acquisition of graders.
2. An interest factor would have to be applied to compensate for differences in initial cost.
3. Under present utilization practices, graders used by the department are replaced at the end of ten years.

The resale value of various graders was substantially different—in some cases by as much as $5,000. While it was believed that the higher resale value should be allowed to offset higher initial bid prices, it should be recognized that there is a monetary factor to a delayed period before resale prices are received.

Considerations

If, for example, the state purchased one grader for $20,000 and received $10,000 at the end of ten years, and purchased another grader for $10,000 and received nothing at the end of ten years, it would appear that because the state is making a net profit of $10,000 in each case the offers are equal. This is not a fact, since for the first grader the state would be forgoing the use of $10,000 for a period of ten years.

We would actually be sacrificing $4,800 based on 4 percent compound interest for ten years. In other words, for the $20,000 to be an equal offer, the resale value would have to be $14,800.

Naturally, if we were to receive alternate bids, it was going to be necessary to project our past experience into the future. In other words, evaluation would have to be based on total cost per hour and the award made on that basis. With the possibilities of variance in the initial prices of the equipment under the guaranteed total cost plan, it was necessary to include interest as a criterion for proper evaluation. The rate was established at 4 percent compound interest, and was computed for both the guaranteed total cost method and the initial cost method.

Using this system, bids were requested on 15 heavy-duty motor graders. Prospective suppliers were furnished a formula showing how each bid would be computed in determining the net cost per hour. The figures for our comparative analysis of two proposals are contained in Table 1. It should be noted that we have based the analysis of the initial cost proposal on the ten-year period, which represents our average usage pattern, but have analyzed the total cost bid for a five-year period. In Virginia, we are told, the supplier cannot obtain a bond covering items of this nature for a period in excess of five years. Also, suppliers indicated that it would be difficult to sell a motor grader more than five years old, since that is the optimum age for resale value. We saw no reason to change the ten-year replacement program, which has proved best for us, for the initial cost bid.

The analysis

In the table, we have listed initial prices for both methods. These represent the total payments to be made by the purchaser upon delivery of the equipment. They are $26,448 and $14,591 for total guaranteed cost and initial price bids respectively.

Next, we have added interest to be charged—based on 5 and 10

Total guaranteed cost		Initial price bid	
Initial price	$26,448.00	Initial price	$14,591.00
Compound interest		Compound interest	
4 percent, 5 years	5,712.77	4 percent, 10 years	7,003.68
Guaranteed maximum		Estimated parts	
parts cost	700.00	cost	3,556.00
Total initial price	$32,860.77	Total initial cost	$25,150.68
Guaranteed repurchase		Estimated resale	
price (5 years)	19,042.00	value (10 years)	1,313.19
Net bid price	$13,818.77	Net total cost	$23,837.49
Hours used (5 years)	6,350	Hours used (10 years)	12,700
Net cost per hour	$ 2.1761	Net cost per hour	$ 1.8770

Table 1. Comparative analysis of alternate proposals.

years of ownership, respectively—amounting to $5,712.77 and $7,003.68.

Then, we have added the parts costs to both proposals. For the total guaranteed cost bid, it is a certification from the supplier that parts cost will not exceed a stated sum—in this case, $700. We stipulated that the prices of the parts could not exceed the published list prices. For the initial cost bid, we projected our historical data. We used the average hourly parts cost, as computed, and multiplied it by 12,700 hours, a figure of our choice. This estimated parts cost amounted to $3,556.

At this point, the total initial prices have been determined to be $32,860.77 for the total cost bid and $25,150.68 for the initial price bid.

Next, we come to the repurchase price, which was viewed with different opinions. In our specifications, we required that the equipment be repurchased after five years and left no possibility of a negotiated purchase at the end of the contract period. Some firms wanted to negotiate the repurchase. For the initial price bid, we included the estimated retail value at the end of ten years. This figure was based on sales of similar equipment as surplus. The two figures—$19,042.00 for buy-back after five years and $1,313.19 for salvage value at the end of ten years—were compatible with Forke Brothers Equipment Auctions, which is nationally known and publishes an annual resume of sales of heavy equipment.

Applying the recoverable amounts to our analysis, we arrived at a net price of $13,818.77 for the total cost bid and a net total cost of $23,837.49 for the initial price bid.

While these totals appear to favor the total guaranteed cost proposal, it must be remembered that the periods of ownership involved are different. Thus, when the net costs per hour of use were calculated, the total cost bid was measured against 6,350 hours of use while the alternate bid was measured against 12,700 hours. As a result, the net costs per hour were determined to be $2.1761 (total cost bid) and $1.8770 (initial cost bid). These are the figures we are really interested in—to provide the basis of awarding the sales contract to the method that provides us with the least overall cost per hour of use. It is apparent that it is cheaper for us to purchase equipment under the initial price bid.

If the two bids were compared without applying the interest consideration, the total cost bid would be $1.28 per hour, as compared with an initial price bid of $1.33 per hour. Without considering interest, we would have made the award to the total guaranteed cost proposal. However, in fairness to the taxpayer, you cannot ignore the interest factor. The same minimum specifications were used under both methods, and our records indicated that either piece of equipment was capable of meeting our needs and would be acceptable. However, one grader was priced approximately $12,000 higher than the other. Had we forgone the interest consideration, we would have immediately paid out for the 15 graders approximately $180,000 of state funds that could have been used for other highway purposes. The supplier would have had the opportunity to invest the $180,000 and received far more than a 4 percent return.

Suppose we had advertised for total guaranteed cost only. The low bid on the initial price and historical cost experience was $1.8770 per hour, while the lowest guaranteed cost was $2.1761 per hour. For one grader operating 12,700 hours, the cost difference would have been $3,798; and for 15 graders the differences would have been $56,970. Thus one method must be compared against another to determine which offers the lowest actual total cost.

It is my opinion that if guaranteed maintenance does prove cheaper, this system can probably work better in a city or county than in a statewide organization. I say this because there may be several suppliers in or near larger metropolitan areas, but the number of suppliers to serve promptly all of the rural areas in which we operate is limited.

The city of Chicago no longer requires buy-back of equipment, only guaranteed maintenance. Their award is based on the original cost plus the cost of maintenance for the pre-determined life of the equipment, with the maintenance cost paid on a monthly basis.

Chicago cites these savings on the guaranteed maintenance plan:

1. Down-time is reduced considerably; their contract provides a penalty for slow maintenance.
2. Parts inventory is reduced, as is parts obsolescence. Less storage space is required.

3.   Overhead is reduced, since fewer workers are required in the mechanical forces.

To enter into an agreement for guaranteed maintenance, some suggested requirements to be included in the contract would be:

Make specifications broad enough to include all suppliers of quality equipment.

Spell out penalties for down-time, for failing to furnish back-up units, and other necessary requirements.

Outline clearly methods of payment, escalation clauses and other important considerations.

Be sure that specifications outline the responsibilities of both supplier and agency, including responsibilities for damages due to fire, theft, malicious mischief, collisions and acts of God; payments for fuel, lubrication and equipment washing; and authority to cause the removal of an unqualified or reckless operator.

If life cycle cost, guaranteed maintenance or any similar plan is under consideration, it is desirable to ask for alternate bids, taking into consideration past historical costs of operation. This is the best way to determine if a savings can actually be made. The best way to serve the public is to "get more value for the tax dollar."

Value Management: Applications in the Public Sector

Public Technology, Inc.

Value management applications

Increasingly, because of inflation, statutory bond limits, decreased revenue bases, and voter reluctance to increase taxes, cost savings of great magnitude have become mandatory for state and local governments. The current and specific emphasis on cost savings varies among jurisdictions—from reducing initial procurement costs or cutting an operating budget area, to achieving long-term cost reductions in energy consumption. The need, however, for saving time, money, energy, and other resources is one felt by every government jurisdiction.

Value management (VM) is a proven management tool used extensively in private industry and in several federal agencies that was developed specifically to identify ways to save time, money, or other resources without sacrificing necessary performance or service levels. The term *value management* is used here as a broad conceptual description for a range of studies for cost reduction which may have different orientations. Thus *value engineering, value analysis, value control,* and *value improvement* each come under the general heading of *value management* and may be used interchangeably. Consideration of long-term costs usually occurs as part of these studies. VM uses an interdisciplinary study team comprising in-house personnel and outside consultants. The study team follows a standard and rigorous methodology to meet target savings goals, often 10 percent to 15 percent of present costs.

VM techniques have been applied to many areas as described

Reprinted with permission from *Value Management: Applications in the Public Sector* (Washington, D.C.: Public Technology, Inc., n.d.), sponsored by the Public Buildings Service, U.S. General Services Administration, under contract GS-OOB-02104.

later. Cost reduction in construction—often to bring a project back within the budget—has been the most frequent application in government. Many subjects, however, can be studied efficiently with VM. Industry has used the approach to cut materials and manufacturing costs for existing products. VM studies in government applications have ranged from cutting costs and improving service in interoffice mail routing to long-range budget evaluation and review. Energy conservation through life cycle cost (LCC) considerations is a major application receiving much current attention. Several states have adopted LCC legislation. The VM approach is often used in conjunction with other management techniques such as systems analysis, design-to-cost, work simplification, cost reduction, standardization, and management by objectives.

The performance record of VM has been consistently good in a wide range of applications. Value management studies frequently produce a return on investment of 8 to 1 or better. In 1974, the Public Buildings Service saved more than $10 million with a return of nearly 13 to 1 for every dollar spent on VM.

Besides the large cost saving potential of VM, there is another reason why local and state government decision-makers should be aware of the approach. There appears to be a definite trend for federal grant agencies to impose mandatory VM study requirements on construction projects. The Environmental Protection Agency is making VM studies a mandatory requirement for wastewater treatment facility grant projects over $10 million. Inquiries by PTI indicate that other federal agencies, such as the Federal Highway Ad-

---

VM applications

Construction
Energy conservation retrofitting
Large-order procurements
Budget review
Improving delivery of public services
Department reorganization studies
Manpower reduction
Federal or state VM requirements

VM goals

Generate change and promote innovation
Stretch financial, manpower, and material resources
Simplify methods, procedures, and practices by saving
    time, money, and energy
Eliminate outmoded requirements
Update standards, criteria, tolerances, and objectives
Solve problems creatively and economically

ministration, are likely to include VM requirements in the near future.

Defining value management

VM is a standardized and rigorous method for studying a given set of functions in order to develop more economical, cost-effective, or resource-conserving alternative ways to perform the required functions. Simple cost reduction almost always involves a drop in performance requirements: VM does not.

Existing solution   Value management is used to reduce costs generated or expected to result from a planned course of action, a design, or by an existing system, product, procedure, or organization. It can be used to review budget baselines, designs for systems and facilities, or existing hardware or procedures. A VM study usually results in "before" and "after" cost and performance data. The "before" component may be planned or actual achievements.

Definable functions   VM is a quantitative review technique that centers on studying the costs for performing functions. For it to be effective, functions must be clearly defined. In addition, performance requirements and costs must be largely quantifiable. Attempting to apply VM to an organization, system, etc., where this cannot be done will rarely be successful.

In a VM study, functions are separated and defined. Separating the functions and differentiating between needs and desires often yields one of the great benefits of a VM study. This procedure can sometimes uncover things that are being done that fill no significant function. Eliminating the function entirely can obviously represent a large cost saving.

Performance requirements for functions are defined and critiqued. VM studies frequently bring management attention to performance requirements that are unnecessarily stringent or perhaps too lax. Management must then decide if these performance requirements are valid. Esthetic appeal, for example, is a valid performance requirement—but not for something that is hidden from view.

Costs may be of several basic types including capital outlay, manpower, use of vital materials, and time. They may be initial or life-cycle costs. The decision on which kinds of costs are to receive the highest reduction priority is made by top management before the VM study begins or after alternatives are identified. For example, if a local government jurisdiction is faced with an increased demand for a particular service and also has a hiring freeze, the decision-maker is likely to single out man-hours per service as the most important focus for cost reduction. Generally, unless specific direction is provided by management, the value study will concentrate on reducing initial dollar costs and identifying life-cycle dollar savings that can be realized within a reasonable pay back period.

Cost-saving goals   Before the value study begins, management must establish reasonable cost-saving goals. The reason for determining a goal figure before the study begins is to help define the proper resources to be devoted to performing the value study. It is, of course, impossible to know the extent of cost reduction that can be achieved before the fact, but a 15 percent actual cost reduction is an approximate rule of thumb based on experience. Targeting an investment in VM for a 10 to 1 return is another rule of thumb that may be used.

Limited study focus   Another characteristic of a VM study is its concentration only on specific areas of the overall study problem— in particular, areas where costs are concentrated. A value study of a building design, for example, might concentrate on only 20 percent to 40 percent of the elements of the overall design. Because a value study is usually conducted as an intense effort over a short time, it gets best results by paying special attention to areas where costs are highest.

Team approach   Almost always a value study is conducted as a team effort. The team(s) should include a diverse group of people, each an expert in one or more major aspects of the problem. A few generalists may be included. Individuals who must finally implement study recommendations should definitely be included on the team(s). The key person, of course, is the team leader who must bring considerable VM experience to the study as well as an objective viewpoint. The more VM experience the team leader has, the better the VM results are likely to be. He at least should have previously participated in three to four VM studies. For most local governments conducting VM studies, the team leader will be an outside consultant brought in to conduct the study. Experience in VM is desirable for other team members, but not a necessity.

Generally, the VM team will not include the individuals who designed or now operate and administer the design, system, product, or procedure under study. In a VM study of a facility design, for example, the architect/engineer who created the original design usually will not be part of the VM team reviewing the design. He will, however, be consulted during the value study for information. The original designer will be asked by management to comment on the VM recommendations. If he rejects the recommendations, he will be asked why changes proposed by the VM study group should not be implemented. In the case of a building design, the original

---

Systematic approach: the job plan

Information phase: Gather data—cost, criteria, specifications, and concepts.

Functional phase: Determine all functions; evaluate worth; separate needs from desires.

Creative phase: Use creative thinking; generate other means to satisfy the function.

Judicial phase: Evaluate and judge each idea for merit.

Development phase: Select the best idea and develop it in detail; determine its cost effectiveness and test if necessary.

Presentation phase: Transmit the idea to management on its capability to meet functional requirements and its life-cycle cost benefits.

Implementation phase: Incorporate the approved change.

Follow-up phase: Report costs and savings; see if the change is working as planned.

---

architect still signs the changed drawings and must therefore give a final approval of all changes.

Job plan   A VM study is the formal application of a standardized methodology, called the job plan, to the subject at hand. The basic job plan was developed based on extensive experience with VM studies in many diverse applications. Real benefits in following the job plan are that study time is saved that would otherwise be devoted to developing a methodology for the study and that control steps are provided for the VM process.

Standard methodology   After the study team is formed, and perhaps divided into subgroups, all available relevant data on the subject are assembled. The team then defines the study subject in terms of the functions which it performs and the subfunctions performed within it. Costs and worth figures are then assigned to each function. The original function is then carefully considered from numerous points of view and alternative methods for performing the function are conceived and evaluated. Evaluation is based on having a low cost-to-worth ratio (see Figure 1). From this process a set of recommended ways to accomplish the basic function, complete with impact prediction, will be developed.

VM study team recommendations are then presented to management. Frequently, management will not implement all study team recommendations. Depending on the caliber of people on the study, their inventiveness, and on the study subject itself, VM study recommendations may have great or little appeal to management. Frequently about half of the recommendations are implemented.

Item, system or operation	Basic function	Cost	Functional comparative	Worth of comparative	Value index
Tie clip	Hold tie	$ 2.50/EA	Paper clip	$ .01/EA	250
Ball point pen	Make marks	$ .98/EA	Nail	$ .01/EA	98
Door latch set	Retain door	$ 8.00/EA	Magnet	$ .50/EA	16
Wax floors	Protect surface	$ .10/SF	Kraft paper	$ .02/SF	5
Window	Provide ventilation	$50.00/EA	Hole & damper	$5.00/EA	10

Figure 1. Function-cost-worth-value index illustrations.

Because of inflexible constraints such as budgets, implementation of even excellent recommendations may have to be delayed. These matters being noted, most VM studies lead to implemented savings that far exceed study costs.

Value management program types

Several options exist for setting the basic organization of a value management program. These basic options are described below, but note should first be made of two points: (1) There is no need to utilize only one of these forms of VM programs since they work well together, and (2) selection of any basic program type will have its own cost, time, risk, staffing, and training ramifications for the VM user.

Value service clause   The most frequent application of value management in state and local government involves use of value service clauses in architect/engineer (A/E) and construction manager (CM) contracts. Basically the value service clause requires the designer to perform certain value studies for the owner on a professional services basis for a fixed negotiated (or quoted) fee. Certain items of the designer's VM activity may be covered under overhead or may be reimbursable.

The value service clause is an extension of the regular services of an A/E for an owner in that it requires the A/E to perform additional studies, hold special meetings, and produce reports not otherwise covered by contract requirements, and it involves using additional staff personnel not directly connected with the design of the facility. Use of personnel trained and experienced in VM is usually made a contract requirement.

Several levels of VM service clause activity are possible. The Public Buildings Service of the General Services Administration (GSA), for example, includes VM service clauses in most A/E professional service contracts for the design of buildings, extensions, alterations, repair, and improvement contracts. See accompanying

---

Value management service clauses

For A/E contracts possible requirements are:

A/E is invited, not required, to suggest design criteria changes.
GSA may perform VM review for A/E.
A/E performs a design criteria review.
A/E hosts an executive seminar.
A/E performs two task-team reviews.
A/E prepares cost-worth model.
A/E reviews and incorporates changes.
A/E provides post-construction review of construction contractor VM changes.

For CM contracts the general requirements are:

CM performs a design criteria review.
CM hosts a VM workshop.
CM performs task-team design reviews.
A/E participates in CM task-team design review.
A/E attends workshop hosted by CM and participates in VM study selections.
CM provides post-construction review of construction contractor VM changes.

---

box for the types of services a consultant could conduct for GSA depending on the project size.

When the construction management approach is being used on a project, the construction management firm provides the necessary value studies of the A/E designs. VM studies by construction managers have proven to be especially worthwhile because of the extensive and current construction materials and labor cost knowledge of a good construction manager.

A separate VM fee should be in either the A/E or CM contract. The VM provisions should spell out the VM level of experience needed and the fee. If no VM is done, no VM fee is paid. The project A/E should be reimbursed for work necessary to incorporate VM study recommendations in the design.

In-house program   A typical in-house value management program involves a series of VM studies on a variety of topics selected by management. A full-time experienced VM program manager could be responsible for assisting in selecting study subjects and assembling teams for each study from in-house staff and possibly outside individuals. In local government, knowledgeable citizens could also provide valuable input in many study areas. The program manager, besides leading the various studies, would also keep program records and encourage implementation of study results. While desirable in many ways, an in-house program requires substantial financial commitment from management to cover the program manager's salary and overhead and other costs involved in the VM studies. Because of this substantial commitment, most first-time users of VM in state and local government are likely to use one or more of the other VM program options before considering a formal in-house program.

Value specialist as consultant   Contracting with a professional value specialist enables an agency or local jurisdiction to bring in an expert to conduct a specific VM study of short duration. Use of a VM consultant can also be employed as an alternative to an A/E value service clause on a facility design project. An outside value specialist can also help to plan an in-house program, operate it, and train others to take over the program.

The best method of identifying competent VM specialists is to make inquiries to the professional societies whose members practice VM. In 1959, the Society of American Value Engineers (although most members are not engineers) was incorporated. Today, there are 40 chapters and SAVE affiliates in 20 countries. SAVE has an extensive program for accrediting certified value specialists (CVS). Both GSA and SAVE keep current lists of value professionals, both CVS and non-CVS, and may be asked to provide referrals.

VM incentive clauses   VM incentive clauses are used in large procurement contracts. While the incentive clauses do not mandate that any value study be conducted, they provide substantial financial incentives for a contractor to propose cost-saving contract changes and therefore to conduct VM studies independently. Value incentive clauses pertain to vendors already under contract to the purchaser. The incentive clause offers the contractor a stated percentage of any net dollar savings (initial and/or life-cycle cost) generated through a contractor-suggested contract change approved by the purchaser. The percent of net savings returned to the contractor is frequently as high as 50 percent but may be more or less as established at the option of the purchasing agency.

VM incentive clauses offer the purchasing agency a means to encourage and take advantage of value studies by contractors at little financial risk. First, the purchasing agency is under no obligation to accept contract change proposals that are submitted. Second, because the purchaser's only significant cost is the staff expense for reviewing the value change proposals, there is only an insignificant financial commitment for the purchaser. Finally, because the value incentive award pertains to only a specific procurement contractor, the purchasing agency can use this knowledge to change its specifications for all subsequent procurements and thereby gain the full measure of savings after any royalty-sharing period has passed.

Value management users

Value management studies and programs are widespread in private industry and in federal agencies. State and local government application, however, appears to be in its infancy, although many successful uses have occurred.

Private sector   Value management studies evolved during World War II when materials and labor shortages forced industry to develop many substitutes for traditional materials and parts. Development of the basic techniques for a value study is usually credited to Lawrence Miles while working at General Electric Company. Since this beginning, many companies have experimented with VM projects and programs and a large number have established formal programs as a result.

In industry most VM attention is directed toward studying existing products. One industry source notes that 20 percent to 60 percent cost reductions have in some instances been experienced when value management was first applied to an existing product. Construction has been receiving increased attention as a VM application in the private sector, but presently this still represents less than 1 percent of the private sector construction.

Many corporations have regular value management programs in continuous operation. Others use VM studies only at specific times for specific circumstances. The experience of Schwinn Bicycle Company in establishing a value analysis program in 1975 is indicative of industry experiences. Sixty of Schwinn's personnel were selected to participate in this ongoing program. Included were industrial engineers, manufacturing supervisors, middle-line managers, foremen, design and manufacturing engineers, representatives of finance, and others. Schwinn study teams identified over $1 million in potential savings. To date, projects for realizing over $300,000 of

---

Representative private users

General Electric	Pratt and Whitney
Caterpillar Tractor	American Telephone and
Black and Decker	Telegraph
Joy Manufacturing	Lockheed
Schwinn Bicycle	Sylvania
Mack Truck	Radio Corporation of America
Philco-Ford	General Dynamics
Hughes Aircraft Company	Magnavox
Collins Radio	

the projected annual savings have been implemented at Schwinn. This is substantially in excess of the approximately $45,000 spent for the VM study.

Federal government   Since the mid-1960s, VM use has become widespread in federal agencies, especially for facilities construction. Value studies and value incentives are increasingly used in other procurements and services as well. Use of VM requirements for federally assisted construction is of great current interest.

Value management (or value engineering) programs developed independently within several federal agencies such as the Naval Facilities Engineering Command in the early 1960s. Large-scale federal use of VM was given a boost by hearings on value engineering conducted by the Senate Public Works Committee in 1967 and 1973. More recently, the General Accounting Office (GAO) issued a report entitled *Need for Increased Use of Value Engineering: A Proven Technique in Federal Construction.* A GAO study on the potential of value studies for wastewater treatment facilities encouraged the Environmental Protection Agency to publish mandatory VM requirements in the *Federal Register* for wastewater treatment facility grant projects of $10 million and above.

Federal agency users

Bureau of Reclamation—VM incentive provisions in all construction contracts over $200,000.

Corps of Engineers—30 full-time value engineering managers, 3,000 VM trained personnel (FY 1974 savings—$55 million).

Department of Health, Education, and Welfare—Value analysis has been a portion of HEW cost avoidance program and has been responsible for over $230 million in cost avoidance in both federal and federally assisted construction during the past six years.

Federal Highway Administration—Starting value workshop training program for federal and state highway personnel. Most savings are in operations and maintenance areas.

General Services Administration—Started program in 1970. VM provisions now used in major design, construction, and supply procurement contracts. Reported $10 million in savings in 1974 with a return on investment of $12.85 for every dollar spent.

National Aeronautics and Space Administration—A limited program in the facilities area started in 1968 has resulted in 10 to 1 return. Studies are conducted by consultants. Potential savings identified were $1.7 million in 1975.

Veterans Administration—Agency has both in-house and value incentive clause programs. Incentive clauses are used in all construction contracts of $500,000 and above. In two and one half years, government savings from incentive clause use have been more than $390,000.

The EPA decision resulted from a number of detailed studies, each of which reported substantial savings. For example, one typical $4.1 million sewage treatment facility was value studied in a series of 40-hour training workshops. The original facility designer accepted design changes that represented a reduction of 25 percent in construction costs and lower operations and maintenance costs.

State and local government construction   Increasingly state and local governments are becoming users of value management. Several jurisdictions have utilized VM in one form or another for five or more years with good results. However, although VM use in state and municipal government has often been spectacular, there are still relatively few jurisdictions that are serious and continual VM users.

Success in VM studies in state and local government often has not been achieved without difficulty. A prime concern voiced by several users involves the impact of VM recommendations on in-house staff. In particular, the individuals affected by a VM study should be made aware that the study seeks to provide assistance and suggestions and is not intended as criticism. Top management commitment of both time and budget is essential to overcome resistance to innovation and to achieve implementation.

Most VM application by states or localities has been in the construction area—from sewers and schools to sewage treatment plants and a football stadium. Typically VM studies were utilized because construction budget estimates for a project were skyrocketing. For example, after the new Detroit Lions Stadium in Pontiac, Michigan, was first designed, construction bids came in much too high. A construction manager was brought on the project and used a VM team to bring costs down. The project, which had promised to be a disaster, was finally completed on time and within budget.

A similar application of VM occurred with a sewage treatment plant in Plainville, Connecticut. Although final cost figures are not yet in, the original $7.5 million construction cost estimate was reduced by $1.4 million through a VM study. Also, $212,000 in estimated annual operating expenses was cut from the original estimated operation and maintenance budget of $533,000. Because the town received federal aid for construction but must support all operating costs itself, the projected savings of nearly half of the annual operating expenses was most welcome.

In another construction application, a new facility for the Medical University of South Carolina was estimated at being 22 percent over budget. A value consultant involved in the job reports that a three-day value study in cooperation with the project architect succeeded in reducing costs 28 percent without reducing vital requirements in the facility.

In Montgomery County, Maryland, a proposed medical pathological waste incinerator design received a VM study. Approximately $400,000 was cut from the initial construction cost estimate of $2.7 million. Further, an estimated $700,000 in 20-year life-cycle cost savings were developed in part because of a study recommendation for changing fuels. The cost for this study was approximately $20,000.

The Chantilly High School in Fairfax, Virginia, again demonstrates the use of value management for a construction crisis. In 1972 the school had been designed and construction bids came in at $8.4 million, which was unacceptably high. A value specialist was brought in under contract to the county to aid in redesign. This VM study brought construction costs down to $7.4 million, saving about $1 million. Also, construction bid acceptance was based on life-cycle cost considerations that substantially lowered long-term ownership costs. Besides saving both initial and long-term costs, county officials believe they received a better building than was first proposed. Fairfax County has used VM subsequently on several new elementary schools.

State and local government: other applications   Although construction examples such as those above represent the most frequent VM applications in local and state government, there are numerous examples where VM has been applied equally well in quite different contexts. The Commonwealth of Pennsylvania, in particular, has used value studies successfully in a variety of areas. Partial centralization of printing operations recommended by a value study produced approximately $2 million annually in tangible savings in a $13 million annual budget. Printing machinery productivity was increased nearly 300 percent—from 8 percent to 23 percent of manufacturer's rated capacity. A value study on highways found that labor rates had risen so that is was less expensive to plow new fallen snow than to erect the usual snow fences. Institution of day-by-day patient case monitoring in state hospitals as a result of a Pennsylvania value study has led to over $40 million in savings in less than two years. A value study of school space utilization led to cancellation of over $100 million in planned expansion programs.

Pennsylvania is not the only jurisdiction to use VM in areas other than construction. In Minnesota, a value study significantly reduced the costs of putting stripes on highways. In Florida, better sensing indicators improved sewage treatment, and all costs were recovered in a year. In the District of Columbia, a value study performed for free by the local chapter of the Society of American Value Engineers saved $200,000 in a single police radio procurement contract. In Royal Oak, Michigan, another SAVE-sponsored study used citizen participation and resulted in recommendations for decreasing congestion in the high school and for improving communications between the school and parents.

The Value in Value Engineering

Robert A. Feger

Today, very few owners sit down at the inception of a building program with a blank checkbook—if they ever did. With today's tight money and uncertain economy, the office building developer/owner must make some tough decisions and encourage creative teamwork by the architect and contractor to produce a quality building within the budget and schedule.

Unfortunately, too many owners face any unpleasant economic facts when working drawings are completed and the job is bid. But when cuts have to be made at this stage, the redesign can be costly and the delays significant. There is a remedy, however, that gives the owner more effective—and earlier—control over project costs and schedule. It is called value engineering.

What is it?

Value engineering is *not* just cost-cutting. It involves analyzing a project design from the construction viewpoint with the goal of balancing performance and quality against initial and life cycle costs. The objective is to optimize quality, time, and cost.

By bringing in a qualified construction manager/general contractor at the beginning of the design phase, the owner can analyze costs at the stage where he can exercise the most control over them. Value engineering gives the owner, the architect, and the contractor the information on which to base sound decisions. For a small, upfront investment of time and money, the owner can realize significant savings—without sacrificing the quality or design integrity of the building.

The key to success is to start early in the project. Typically,

Reprinted from *Mortgage Banking*, May 1982, published by the Mortgage Bankers Association of America.

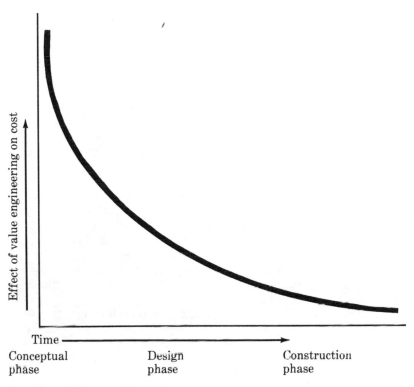

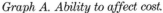

Graph A. Ability to affect cost.

value engineering is conducted at several stages of the project, beginning after the functional planning phase when schematics have been prepared. Value engineering is often conducted again during the design phase, and what are called value management studies are conducted during the construction phase. The important fact for the owner to recognize is that potential savings are greatest in the early stages, and decline as the project progresses (see Graph A).

Steps to follow

Depending upon the owner's needs and the complexity of the project, value engineering efforts range from informal suggestions to a formal, organized process. Normally, value engineering incorporates the following steps:

1. The information stage, in which the construction manager/ general contractor's estimating group identifies the high-cost or "problem" areas of the project, based upon a study of the schematics.

2. The brainstorming phase is the creative aspect of the value
    engineering process, during which the estimators and often
    the entire building team take a "second look" at the specifica-
    tions and try to determine what alternate systems or prod-
    ucts or construction methods could perform the required
    function at a lower cost.
        Sometimes this may involve a comparison of several
    structural systems or skin types. Often, it goes beyond sys-
    tems and products to look at construction methods that
    might be employed, bidding techniques that might save
    money, purchasing procedures, administrative systems and
    processes, scheduling, and life cycle costs such as mainte-
    nance and energy utilization.
3. The recommendation phase allows the entire building team to
    evaluate the value engineering results. The value engineering
    team has identified what it believes are viable alternatives
    that will either enhance the quality, lower initial or life cycle
    costs, or shorten the construction schedule. It is up to the ar-
    chitect and the owner to accept or reject the alternatives—or
    to modify them either to suit the owner's needs or enhance
    the architect's design.
        At Kitchell, we view the value engineering reports only
    as recommendations. Often we do no more than lay out the
    facts and costs. What value engineering does is to give the
    owner as well as the other team members the information
    and perspective needed to weigh alternatives.
4. During the implementation phase, the building team takes
    the recommendations that are accepted by owner and archi-
    tect, and works them into the final design and construction
    schedule.

How the value engineering effort can meet the needs of owners
with different priorities and interests can be illustrated by some
Kitchell projects on which value engineering was successfully applied.

A successful application

One example of the successful use of value engineering is the Camelback Executive Park, built in Phoenix during tight market conditions in 1977 and 1978. An intensive value engineering effort for the
developer/owner not only shaved $475,000 off the original $4.75 million budget but, by reducing corridor space by 25 percent, boosted
the owner's gross-to-net ratio to 90 percent.

Initially, the architect had been given as part of the criteria
that each floor have two office bays off a central corridor. When the
value engineering team took a second look at the result, they came
back to the owner and asked whether that central corridor was a

1. Move mechanical building to north side of the
   parking structure $18,000
2. Change chilled water distribution from loops
   on all 3 floors to a loop on 2nd floor and feed up
   and down for the 3rd and 1st floors   9,700
3. Change one elevator from a duplex to simplex   16,800
4. Substitute lump sum contract for mechanical in lieu of GMP   10,000
5. Furi roof in lieu of rigid insulation and built-up
   Owens Corning Fiberglas composite of Fiberglas and urethane   22,600
6. Use precast concrete frame   94,500
7. Decrease building height 1′ 0″ (4″/floor)   5,200
8. Delete stair towers and bridges (incorporated in shell)   53,000
9. Cut 25% of corridors (which added leasable square footage)   10,800

These savings plus others resulted in total savings of $474,800

Figure 1. Camelback Executive Park value engineering highlights.

necessity. Wasn't he planning to lease full floors? As a result, the
project team was able to eliminate some central corridors, placing
the elevators at the end of each building—thus providing the owner
significantly more leasable square footage without increasing the
building size.

The comprehensive value engineering effort identified several
other areas in which substantial cost-savings could be made that
did not weaken the quality or design of the building (see Figure 1).
In all, 32 alternatives were implemented for a savings of close to
$475,000, with no delay in schedule.

More examples

Developers often demand the most from value engineering, because
they must maintain a tight rein on costs to keep rentals competitive,
while still offering as attractive and prestigious a structure as possible. Both goals were achieved by Douglas Development Company
in their Irvine, California, Crocker Bank Tower project, thanks to a
cooperative team approach by architects William L. Peirera Associates and David A. Klages & Associates; Douglas Development; and
Kitchell.

Extensive value engineering was conducted on each area of the
project to keep it within the budget without sacrificing any element
of the unusual and energy-efficient design. Detailed studies of materials and construction techniques for stressed metal skin, metal
panels, manufactured composite panels, cement based panels, and
plaster systems resulted in the selection of a high-quality plaster
application on metal lath and structure. The lath-and-plaster was
not only the lowest in cost by $140,000, but offered the most flexible
application for the building's unusual configuration.

Value engineering was also used to compare structural systems
and exterior wall systems for the Southwest Forest Industries na-

tional headquarters building in Phoenix. The value engineering analysis on the structure compared a structural steel frame, a prestressed, precast concrete structure and a combination of precast concrete and structural steel. The structural steel frame used for the building proved to be $103,000 less than the prestressed, precast concrete structure and $117,000 less than the combination structure.

The three exterior wall systems studied were a precast concrete exterior with interior finish; a synthetic plaster called Dryvit; and a light weight, aluminum-faced composite panel material called Alucobond. Although the Alucobond was not the least expensive in initial cost, it was chosen because of its aesthetically pleasing, "high-tech" look and low maintenance.

Some owners don't want value engineering, despite its well documented results. Some are not willing to spend the small initial investment that the review entails. Experts estimate that a comprehensive value engineering effort will cost from 0.1 percent to 0.5 percent of the project costs and will take several weeks to a month. Savings realized from the effort range from 10 percent to much more. Savings of 100 percent are not uncommon.

The other drawback for some owners is the time they must devote to the effort. Once again the savings may justify the involvement by the owner, but the process can be painful. The nature of the process requires that some hard decisions be made.

What to look for

How can the owner who wants thorough value engineering make sure that he will get it? First, consider value engineering capabilities when you select a construction manager/general contractor. Is he willing to listen to your needs? Does he offer a strong technical staff of estimators and schedulers? Does he have prior examples of value engineering studies that yielded good results for the clients? Check the references and success stories.

Second, select one person in your organization who can represent you on the project team. This person must be able to make decisions or obtain decisions quickly and be willing to get involved.

Third, if you are serious about value engineering, you may want to write into the contract with your architect and construction manager/general contractor the specified stages at which you want value engineering studies conducted—usually after schematics are completed, during design/development stage, and, finally, when working drawings are completed.

Basically, value engineering is value seeking, an effort that involves the entire building team—the owner, the architect and the construction manager/general contractor—in getting the most building for the least cost. It isn't easy, but most owners who have used it find the results well worth the effort.

For Further Reference

Part 1: Techniques for Financial Evaluation and Policy Making

Bahl, Roy. "The Fiscal Health of State and Local Governments: 1982 and Beyond." *Public Budgeting and Finance*, winter 1982, pp. 5-21.

Bradbury, Katharine L. "Fiscal Distress in Large U.S. Cities." *New England Economic Review*, November/December 1982, pp. 33-43.

_____ . "Structural Fiscal Distress in Cities—Causes and Consequences." *New England Economic Review*, January/February 1983, pp. 32-39.

Brown, Richard E.; Williams, Meredith C.; and Gallagher, Thomas P. *Auditing Performance in Government: Concepts and Cases.* New York: Ronald Press/John Wiley and Sons, 1982.

Cabnet, Bernard. "Performance Auditing in Metropolitan Dade County, Florida." *Governmental Finance*, November 1976, pp. 44-48.

Carren, Paul M. *Performance Auditing: The Sunnyvale Experience.* Management Information Service Reports, vol. 9, no. 10, Washington, D.C.: International City Management Association, October 1977.

Coli, Ed. "Sunnyvale's Performance Audit and Budget System." *Governmental Finance*, December 1980, pp. 9-13.

Corcell, Francis A. "A Checklist Approach to Operational Auditing." *The Practical Accountant*, August 1983, pp. 73-76.

Final Report: An Evaluation of the Financial Trend Monitoring System. Washington, D.C.: International City Management Association, 1981.

Fountain, James R., and Lockridge, Robert. "Implementation and Management of a Performance Auditing System." *Governmental Finance*, November 1976, pp. 12-21.

Godick, Neil B. "Operational Auditing: What It Does and How It Works." *The Practical Accountant*, July/August 1979, pp. 67-70.

Godsey, W. Maureen. *Financial Jeopardy! Policies and Practices That Can Affect Financial Health.* Washington, D.C.: International City Management Association, 1980.

_____ . *Tools for Making Financial Decisions.* Washington, D.C.: International City Management Association, 1980.

Groves, Sanford M. *Evaluating Financial Condition.* Washington, D.C.: International City Management Association, 1980.

_____ . *Financial Trend Monitoring System.* Washington, D.C.: International City Management Association, 1980.

Hand, Richard S. "Neighborhood Indicators: The New Dimension in Urban Fiscal Management." *Governmental Finance*, June 1980, pp. 15–18.

Hara, Lloyd F. "Performance Auditing: Where Do We Begin?" *Governmental Finance*, November 1976, pp. 6–10.

Herbert, Leo. *Auditing the Performance of Management*. Belmont, Calif.: Lifetime Learning Publications/ Wadsworth, 1979.

Jadallah, Salih M. "A Generalized System for Performance Auditing in the Public Sector." *The Government Accountants Journal*, spring 1982, pp. 1–9, and summer 1982, pp. 1–7.

Kaiel, Michael. "Performance Auditing in Portland, Oregon." *Governmental Finance*, November 1976, pp. 38–43.

Matzer, John, Jr. "Financial Policies Payoff." *Public Management*, April 1980, pp. 6–7.

McLain, Lewis F., Jr. "How Strategic Planning Can Help Put Budgeting in Perspective." *Governmental Finance*, June 1981, pp. 35–40.

"Measuring Governmental Fiscal Condition." *Governmental Finance*, June 1980, pp. 24–27.

Meddaugh, E. James. "How to Perform an Operational Audit." *The Practical Accountant*, December 1979, pp. 63–68.

Oatman, Donald. "Diagnosing and Curing Financial Management Problems," *Public Management*, June 1979, pp. 18–19.

O'Keefe, Herbert A. *Performance Audits in Local Governments—Benefits, Problems, and Challenges*. Management Information Service Reports, vol. 8, Washington, D.C.: International City Management Association, April 1976.

Petersen, John. "Simplification and Standardization of State and Local Government Fiscal Indicators." *National Tax Journal* 30, no. 3, pp. 299–311.

Rosenberg, Philip, and Stallings, C. Wayne. *Is Your City Heading for Financial Difficulty?: A Guidebook for Small Cities and Other Governmental Units*. Chicago: Municipal Finance Officers Association, 1978.

Scheps, Philip B., and Schechter, A.

Lawrence. "Financial Policy Considerations under Conditions of Rapid Growth." *Governmental Finance*, December 1983, pp. 39–46.

Seidel, Karen. "Indicators of City Fiscal Stress: An Analysis of Oregon Data." *Resources in Review*, November 1983, pp. 6–10.

Tierney, Cornelius E. "Behavioral Aspects of Performance Auditing: Creating a Productive Environment." *Governmental Finance*, November 1976, pp. 22–27.

Weinberg, Mark. "The Urban Fiscal Crisis: Impact on Budgeting and Financial Planning Practices of Urban America." *The Journal of Urban Affairs* 6, no. 1 (winter 1984): 39–52.

Woodward, M. June. "Scientific Approaches to Performance Measurement in the Audit Process." *Governmental Finance*, November 1976, pp. 30–36.

Part 2: Revenue Management and Forecasting Techniques

Anderson, Ralph. *Revenue and Expenditure Forecasting Guidebook*. Sacramento: League of California Cities, 1981.

Bahl, Roy, and Schroeder, Larry. *Forecasting Local Government Budgets*. Syracuse: The Maxwell School of Citizenship and Public Affairs, 1979.

_____."The Role of Multi-Year Forecasting in the Annual Budgeting Process for Local Governments." *Public Budgeting and Finance*, spring 1984, pp. 4–13.

Bahl, Roy; Schroeder, Larry; and Montrone, William. *Forecasting Municipal Revenues and Expenditures*. Management Information Service Reports, vol. 11, no. 10, Washington, D.C.: International City Management Association, October 1979.

Bahl, Roy, and Montrone, William. *Forecasting Municipal Revenues and Expenditures: A Primer and Handbook*. Boston: Coalition of Northeast Municipalities, 1980.

Black, Fischer. "The Trouble with Econometric Models," *Financial*

Analysts Journal, March/April 1982, pp. 29–37.

Burchell, Robert W., and Listokin, David. *Fiscal Impact Handbook*. New Brunswick, N.J.: Center for Urban Policy and Research, 1978.

Butler, Daron K. "Revenue Forecasting and Management." *Public Management*, June 1979, pp. 10–11.

Caplan, Larry, and Lefenfield, Robert M. *Fiscal Analysis Guidebook*. Baltimore: Regional Planning Council, 1979.

Chang, Semoon. "Forecasting Revenues to Municipal Government: The Case of Mobile, Alabama." *Governmental Finance*, February 1976, pp. 16–20.

————. "Municipal Revenue Forecasting." *Growth and Change*, October 1979, pp. 38–46.

Cramer, Robert M. "Local Government Expenditure Forecasting." *Governmental Finance*, November 1978, pp. 3–9.

Crow, Robert Thomas. "Forecasting Demystified." *Public Power*, May–June 1980, pp. 34–39.

David, Irwin T. "Evaluating Municipal Revenue Sources." *Governmental Finance*, February 1976, pp. 6–14.

Dutton, William H.; Kraemer, Kenneth L.; and Hollis, Martha S. "Fiscal Impact Models and the Policy-Making Process: Theory and Practice." *The Urban Interest*, fall 1980, pp. 66–74.

Gardner, Henry L. "Getting the Most from the Taxes Already in Place." *Western City*, March 1983, pp. 6 ff.

Glisson, Patrick C., and Holley, Stephen H. "Developing Local Government User Charges: Technical and Policy Considerations." *Governmental Finance*, March 1982, pp. 3–7.

Henderson, Harvey H. "Revenue Forecasting in a Working Perspective." *Governmental Finance*, November 1978, pp. 11–15.

Multi-Year Revenue and Expenditure Forecasting—Report of National Workshops. Washington, D.C.: Public Technology, Inc., 1980.

Multi-Year Revenue and Expenditure Forecasting—The State-of-the-Practice in Large Urban Jurisdictions. Washington, D.C.: Public Technology, Inc., 1979.

Petersen, John E. *State and Local Fiscal Forecasting*. Washington D.C.: Government Finance Research Center, 1979.

Schoenfield, Stanley. "Generating Revenues Beyond Taxation." *Peat Marwick Management Focus*, May–June 1982, pp. 16–18.

Schroeder, Larry. "Local Government Multi-Year Budgetary Forecasting: Some Administrative and Political Issues." *Public Administration Review*, March/April 1982, pp. 121–26.

"User Fees in the Public Sector." *Midwest Monitor* 9, no. 2 (March/April 1983).

Zorn, C. Kurt. "Issues and Problems in Econometric Forecasting: Guidance for Local Revenue Forecasters." *Public Budgeting and Finance*, autumn 1982, pp. 100–110.

Part 3: Infrastructure Programming and Financing Techniques

Aronson, J. Richard, and Schwartz, Eli. *Capital Budgeting for Local Governments*. Management Information Service Reports, vol. 14, no. 1, Washington, D.C.: International City Management Association, January 1982.

Building Prosperity: Financing Public Infrastructure for Economic Development. Washington, D.C.: Government Finance Research Center, 1983.

Choate, Pat, and Walter, Susan. *America in Ruins: Beyond the Public Works Pork Barrel*. Washington, D.C.: Council of State Planning Agencies, 1981.

CONSAD Research Corporation. *A Study of Public Works Investments in the United States*. Washington, D.C.: U.S. Department of Commerce, 1980.

Dossani, Nazir G., and Steger, Wilbur A. "Trends in U.S. Public Works Investment: Report on a New Study." *National Tax Journal* 23, no. 2, pp. 123–48.

Fitzgerald, John C. "When Cities Have to Think Short-Term." *Western City*, December 1982, pp. 6–12.

Glenn, Gary O., and Lanspery, Paul A. "Capital Improvement Costs, Delays Can Be Controlled." *American City & County*, October 1983, pp. 44–46.

Hatry, Harry. "Maintaining Capital Facilities." *The Bureaucrat*, winter 1981–82, pp. 54–55.

——. *Maintaining the Existing Infrastructure: Overview of Current Issues in Local Government Planning.* Washington, D.C.: U.S. Department of Housing and Urban Development, Office of Policy Development and Research, 1982.

Hatry, Harry P.; Millar, Annie P.; and Evans, James H. *Capital Investment Priority-Setting for Local Governments.* Washington, D.C.: The Urban Institute, 1982.

Hatry, Harry P., and Steinthal, Bruce. *Working Paper: Selecting Capital Facility Maintenance Strategies.* Washington, D.C.: The Urban Institute, 1983.

Hirten, John E. "Who Is Managing the Rebuilding of Our Infrastructure?" *Public Works*, May 1984, pp. 78–80, 116.

"Infrastructure Financing: A Tale of Two Cities." *Urban Land*, December 1983, pp. 25–27.

Johnson, J. Chester. "Current Financial Condition and Capital Financing Options for State and Local Governments." *Governmental Finance*, September 1982, pp. 51–55.

Local Capital Improvements and Development Management Literature Synthesis. Chicago: The American Society of Planning Officials, 1977.

Matson, Morris. "Capital Budgeting-Fiscal and Physical Planning." *Governmental Finance*, August 1976, pp. 42–48, 58.

Matzer, John, Jr., ed. *Capital Financing Strategies for Local Governments.* Washington, D.C.: International City Management Association, 1983.

Mercer, J. L. *Programming and Controlling Capital Improvements.* Management Information Service Reports, vol. 4, no. LS-2, Washington, D.C.: International City Management Association, February 1972.

Meyer, Robert A. "CPM Scheduling in Public Works." *Public Works*, January 1983, pp. 44–46.

Pepper, Richard S. "Step Up Productivity on Your Next Building Project." *Public Works*, April 1984, pp. 60–61.

"Recommended Approaches to Financing Infrastructure to Serve New Development." *Urban Land*, February 1984, pp. 16–18.

Renewing Our Infrastructure: Workable Ways to Build and Maintain Public Facilities. Berkeley, Calif.: Association of Bay Area Governments, 1983.

"Tax Exempt Bonds: A Vital Financing Tool." *American City & County*, June 1984, pp. 42–44.

Vogt, A. John. *Capital Improvement Programming: A Handbook for Local Government Officials.* Chapel Hill: Institute of Government, University of North Carolina, 1977.

Wacht, Richard F. *A New Approach to Capital Budgeting for City and County Governments.* Atlanta: College of Business Administration, Georgia State University, 1980.

Wiggins, C. Don. "A Case Study in Governmental Capital Budgeting." *Governmental Finance*, June 1980, pp. 19–22.

Part 4: Creative Purchasing Techniques

Batdorf, Leland, and Vora, Jay A. "Use of Analytical Techniques in Purchasing." *Journal of Purchasing and Materials Management*, spring 1983, pp. 25–29.

Brown, Robert J., and Yanuck, Rudolph R. *Life Cycle Costing.* Atlanta: Fairmont Press, 1980.

Coe, Charles K. "Life Cycle Costing by State Governments." *Public Administration Review*, September–October 1981, pp. 564–68.

Dowst, Somerby, and Kolbe, Robert. "VA 75." *Purchasing*, 17 June 1975, pp. 1–16.

Dull, C. Bernerd, and Udell, James F. "Value Engineering for Public Works." *Public Works*, November 1976, pp. 50–52.

Esterbrooks, Robert C. "The Right Machine—Available When Needed—At the Lowest Total Cost." *Public Works*, August 1973, pp. 80–81.

Garber, Gregory L., and Whitley, Robert D. "Purchasing Energy-Efficient Equipment through Competitive Bidding." *Public Works*, October 1981, pp. 50–52.

Gecome, Richard M., et al. *Energy Efficient Purchasing for Local Governments*. Athens: Institute of Government, University of Georgia, 1980.

Harris, Harlan. "Life Cycle Cost Used by County with 1,300 Machines." *Public Works*, February 1984, pp. 42–43.

"Help Vendors Board the VA Bandwagon." *Purchasing*, 29 May 1980, pp. 94–98.

Kiser, G. E., and Rink, David. "Use of the Products Life Cycle Concept in Development of Purchasing Strategies." *Journal of Purchasing and Materials Management*, summer 1980, pp. 12–17.

"Life Cycle Costing Saves Money for Albuquerque." *Public Works*, June 1984, p. 100.

Loya, Felix. "Total Cost Purchasing Saves City Dollars, Simplifies Budgeting." *The American City*, January 1973, pp. 59–60.

O'Connor, John F. "The Real Story: What's Wrong with Value Analysis." *Purchasing*, March 31, 1983, p. 37.

Pruett, James M., and Hotard, Daniel G. "The Value of Value Analysis." *Industrial Management*, vol. 26, no. 2 (March–April 1984): 29–32.

Raedels, Alan R. "Measuring the Productivity of Materials Management." *Journal of Purchasing and Materials Management*, summer 1983, pp. 12–18.

Raia, Ernest. "Getting the Most Out of Value Analysis." *Purchasing*, March 1983, p. 35.

"Total Cost Bidding: One County's Guarantee for the Taxpayer." *Public Works*, March 1982, pp. 58.

"Value Analysis 1984: A Status Report," *Purchasing*, 29 March 1984, pp. 79–97.

Value Management: A GSA Handbook. Washington, D.C.: General Services Administration, 1972.

Weiss, W. H. "Value Analysis." *Supervision*, March 1983, pp. 6–8.

Zemansky, Stanley D. "Life Cycle Cost Procurement." *Costing Government Services: A Guide for Decision Making*, Washington, D.C.: Government Finance Research Center, 1984, pp. 115–39.

Practical Management Series

**Practical Financial Management:
New Techniques for Local Government**

Text type
Century Expanded

Composition
Unicorn Graphics
Washington, D.C.

Printing and binding
R. R. Donnelley & Sons Company
Harrisonburg, Virginia

Cover design
Rebecca Geanaros